D0941801

This latest excursion takes Miss Kimbrough and her companions to Athens, around the Greek mainland, to Chios and other famous Aegean islands, to Yugoslavia, to Paris and London, with a highly unusual voyage on the Thames.

And, either by accident or design, wherever Miss Kimbrough and her party went they found abundant hospitality as well as curiosities, surprises, mishaps and amusing adventures—like that which kept Miss Kimbrough in the Yugoslavian customs for hours. Then, too, there were exciting, bizarre and moving sights and impressions—such as Miss Kimbrough's first view of the Acropolis—which she shares so vividly with her readers.

In *Water, Water Everywhere*, as in her previous books, Miss Kimbrough has managed to include along the way a great deal of information any traveler—armchair or otherwise—will want to know about the fascinating places she has visited.

Written with the same wit and lightness of spirit for which the author is famous, *Water, Water Everywhere* is one of the liveliest and most varied and entertaining of Miss Kimbrough's books.

WATER, WATER EVERYWHERE

Books by Emily Kimbrough

OUR HEARTS WERE YOUNG AND GAY
(*with Cornelia Otis Skinner*)

WE FOLLOWED OUR HEARTS TO HOLLYWOOD

HOW DEAR TO MY HEART

IT GIVES ME GREAT PLEASURE . . .

THE INNOCENTS FROM INDIANA

THROUGH CHARLEY'S DOOR

FORTY PLUS AND FANCY FREE

SO NEAR AND YET SO FAR

WATER, WATER EVERYWHERE

WATER, WATER EVERYWHERE

BY

Emily Kimbrough

DRAWINGS BY MIRCEA VASILIU

HARPER & BROTHERS PUBLISHERS NEW YORK

Printed in the United States of America

FIRST EDITION

K-F

Library of Congress catalog card number: 56-8755

FOR

CHARLOTTE WILES KIMBROUGH

1876—1924

Acknowledgment with love to
Eleanor Donnelley Erdman,
dear friend and traveling companion,
irrepressible and indefatigable notetaker

WATER, WATER EVERYWHERE

Chapter One

HALFWAY up a rope ladder I thought of Leo Ganter. The ladder was swaying on the side of a little Yugoslavian ship in the harbor of Piraeus, but the Lord only knows where Leo Ganter was. I hadn't seen him for forty years, but at that time I had given him a very false steer. Swaying on the ladder I realized my mistake.

In Muncie, Indiana, he and I had had our fortunes told one hot afternoon by a gypsy. She had set up a tent on the outskirts of the fairgrounds while the county fair was in progress. I had pointed out her establishment to my parents as we went through the gate to visit the fair. Mother's comment had been all gypsies were dirty, the place probably reeking with germs, and fortunetelling superstitious nonsense.

It was my custom to arrange my daily program according to the laws of my parents, but I gave a generous interpretation to the words of these Solons. A refusal of permission for some project I planned, the refusal accompanied by ". . . and I mean this, Emily," I accepted as binding. Anything less, I took as a justifiable loophole if I were called up to an accounting before my mother and the hairbrush. Therefore, I interpreted my mother's pronouncement on the gypsy as permission to visit her. The only real obstacles were my lack of money and a card pinned to the flap of her tent that stated, together with her supernatural powers, the admission price, twenty-five cents. I was, however, an optimistic child about most things, particularly money. There seemed to me always to be a way of obtaining it when needed. I never took it from anyone's purse, or person, but any other means of acquisition I felt worthy of my best efforts, and I exercised them whenever opportunity was presented to me.

The opportunity presented that afternoon was Leo Ganter. We had encountered him and his parents on our promenade around the fairgrounds. He was a contemporary and friend of mine. The families were also friends and so when they engaged in conversation it was easy to take him to one side for a private interview. I chose a spot under the cake and pie counter for our talk. I told him in simple terms, because at times I had found him slow to catch on and accept a proposed program of mine, if he did not give me twenty-five cents I would tell his mother he had taken off his shoes and socks and gone wading with me in the gutter after a heavy rain of the week before, though she had expressly told him to do no such thing.

It was a great surprise to me to learn years later that in some circles this manner of obtaining money is called blackmail.

Leo had a quarter. I was not surprised. He always seemed to have money, a fact I had pointed out to my parents more than once. Since he was not very bright by my standards of intelligence, he showed it to me immediately and then demurred about handing it over because, he said, it was all he had. He got no pity from me. I reminded him, as I had been forced to remind him on other occasions, that for my previous birthday he had promised me a pony, and had arrived at my party with a book instead, and the poor excuse that his father had not seen his way clear to purchasing a pony for a neighbor's child. Furthermore, and I had reminded him of this, too, the book itself had been *Captain January*, a book with a very sad ending that had melted me into a bawling pulp of misery. For this I also held Leo responsible.

That day, under the pie and cake counter, Leo had been out of hand due to the proximity of our parents. He said if I told on him my mother would hear me, and I would "get it" for being a tattletale. It had seemed expedient to me, therefore, to compromise, a process with which I was not familiar. I had suggested we have a joint fortunetelling for the price of one. This business deal had been accomplished with some difficulty from the gypsy, and a little confusion for Leo and me. She had delivered her reading rapidly and with no indication to which one of us her separate pronouncements applied. Outside her tent when the reading was finished, we had sorted them out and I had ceded to Leo her prediction of travel—"On many waters, on many boats." I had asserted positively, "You're going to join the navy."

On the first of June, in 1955, I remembered the gypsy of forty-odd years ago in the fairgrounds of Muncie, Indiana. Here I was, at this moment of remembrance, climbing a ladder, eyes shut, clammy fingers imbedded in the rope of the rungs, while friends and oarsmen from a bobbing boat below pushed, sailors hanging over the rail above endeavored to pull, and everybody shouted. Me, with roots and a childhood in Indiana, that had gone no farther astream than a wade in the gutter after a heavy rain. Obviously the gypsy's prophecy had been for me, but this was not the time nor the place to correct that mistake. I gave up the idea of clarifying Leo's life, and, with fore and aft assistance, boarded the little boat.

For me the prospect, if not the actual planning of the trip, had begun even before I had visited the gypsy on that hot afternoon. If a love that was really passionate, and a devotion that was certainly lifelong, together with a not inconsiderable knowledge of the subject are qualifications, then Mother was a scholar of Greek. She had taught me the Greek alphabet before I learned English letters. Her theory was, and I commend it, that to a child all letters have strange and bewildering shapes; therefore, Greek characters would present only their inherent difficulties, not the additional ones incurred by a familiarity with the English. My primer was excerpts of Homeric Greek compiled by her. Her bedtime stories to me were of "Jason," "Hercules," and other heroes. By the time I got around to reading for myself "The Sleeping Beauty," I classified Prince Charming as one of the most sickening sissies I had ever encountered.

When we moved to Chicago I went to Miss Faulkner's School and under her brilliant tutelage began a more orthodox course in Greek than Mother had provided.

I had continued Greek in college. My textbooks were not the editions the other students used. I brought with me the volumes that had been Mother's at the Girls' Classical School in Indianapolis. This was, I think, the only sentimental request she ever made of me. It was her compensation, she said, for not having been allowed to go to college, her parents feeling it might make her independent, therefore, unwomanly She had never gone to Greece either; although as far back as those days when, with tongue protruding from the corner of my mouth and sweating hand in a strangled grip around the pencil it held, I had endeavored to form my alphas and betas, her favorite make-believe had always begun, "One day, when you and I are in Greece . . ."

In 1955, Mother had been gone for thirty-one years, without ever having been to Greece, and I had forgotten, to my shame, almost all the Greek I had ever learned. Nevertheless, to see Greece was an obligation I felt had been laid upon me.

Because I was born in Indiana and at a time when a trip to the seashore took two full days and a little over, almost anywhere seems to me, even now, to be "a fer piece." Not that people from Muncie didn't travel. We ourselves went to Atlantic City and Cornwall-on-Hudson. Not many of us went to Paris or London, but a considerable number visited the Holy Land, and at least two people I knew for a fact went to Africa to visit the missionary from our Presbyterian Church. Atlantic City and Africa seemed to me equally remote.

The passing years have not brought a perceptible improvement in my knowledge of geography. If my IQ were based, God forbid, on my knowledge of that subject, I would pass my days in the sheltering arms of an institution. I have normal vision for my age, but my ability to visualize is almost nil. Sounds cut the paths of association in my memory. Therefore, when I look at a map, and I used to look at one frequently in a desperate effort not to remain so deeply submerged under the normal, I see the map, of course: boundaries, rivers, mountains. But when I have closed the atlas and attempt to visualize what I have been studying, I conjure up practically nothing at all except a blur of color, and the sight of the places whose names ring tantalizingly in my ear, as unrelated as they were before I opened the book. Therefore, since I am incapable of finding out for myself how to get almost anywhere from wherever I happen to be, I accept eagerly and humbly what anyone tells me.

"You must come to Greece," Gina Bachauer said, the first time I met her. "It is very simple to do."

Madame Bachauer, as a pianist, is acknowledged one of the great artists of the world, but she possesses also those qualities that make for greatness as a human being; a warmth of heart, a generosity of spirit so ample it envelops her friends like a luxuriant cloak, and with these gentlenesses, an arrogance that snubs to extinction any obstacle that dares intrude itself upon a course she has set. I had met her and her husband only an hour before at a music party given by mutual friends. Somehow, Madame Bachauer, her gay, sensitive, delightful husband, Alex Sherman, and I, by some inner communication, had withdrawn from other guests. Pre-empting a corner we had begun a conversation and a friendship that brought forth Gina's unequivocal statement that I must come to Greece, and she had added, "We will find for you a boat." I felt confident she would and recognized, too, on the instant, her use of the pronoun was neither editorial nor royal. It was Olympian.

Last winter I went instead with friends to the Cajun country in Louisiana.* At Grand Isle, Darn, one of the friends, said to me, "Let's take another trip. Have you any ideas?"

Immediately, though I had not thought of it in the meantime, I answered, "Yes. Greece."

Sophy, overhearing, had joined up for the expedition instantly. Kat said she and her husband were going to England, she couldn't possibly change that plan; Kat comes from Boston. Ellen, who had been to Greece only recently with her husband, assured us as she had so many times it was the most wonderful trip they had ever taken, and volunteered to show us their maps as soon as we returned to New York. I shuddered at this suggestion, though I knew the matter was bound to come up.

Sophy and Darn, who had been my friends for many years, thanked Ellen, assured her they could hardly wait to trace with her the route she had taken, and urged her in the same breath to leave me out of it.

We came home in time for Thanksgiving. Eager to share the pleasure we had had, I began at once a book about the Louisiana trip, while Darn and Sophy looked at maps, read books about Greece, and Darn engaged a Berlitz professor for the study of the language.

I took along on a lecture tour my manuscript of the Louisiana journey and, working on it one day in my hotel bedroom in a small Midwestern town, realized that Luz, though one of the companions of the Louisiana trip, had not been with us the day we had talked about Greece. I remember now how I pushed to one side the pages on which I was writing, took out a piece of the hotel stationery and wrote her in Little Rock, where she lives. Her answer arrived at my house even before I had returned home.

"Yes, yes, yes," she wrote. "Just tell me when we start and any other little details."

* *So Near and Yet So Far.*

The details were not so easy to come by, although my friends, if not my honesty, would force me to admit I had very little to do with them. Sophy, by self-appointment, is the executive, and Darn, by her own insistence, Sophy's deputy. They looked at maps of course, but since Darn lives in Pasadena and Sophy in New York, the ideas each derived from her isolated viewing involved a heavy correspondence. Darn generously invited me into a little of their planning by writing to ask my opinion of what clothes we should take. Because in my answering letter I told her it was imperative we take long white gloves and blue jeans, she replied crisply she would not trouble me further.

On the trip I asked my companions many a time *where* we would be were it not for my learning about kid gloves, blue jeans, and a hundred other aids and necessities from Kakia Livanos. The first time I asked this, Sophy answered with the suggestion that since I was almost always uncertain of *where* I was, I should phrase my question differently. After that they reiterated devoutly their gratitude to Kakia and brushed aside my contribution.

Kakia Livanos, her sister, Maria, and her husband George, were my friends by way of Gina and Alex. They are Greek, but Kakia and George live in New York, Maria in London.

During the winter of our planning, Maria arrived in New York. With Kakia and George, she came to my house for tea. I had thought Gina's enveloping generosity and hospitality, her own particular attributes. I learned they are not entirely peculiar to her. They are indigenous to the Greeks.

That winter afternoon at tea in my apartment, my Greek guests requested paper and pencils all around. While they set down memoranda to themselves of the people to whom they would write about our coming, they dictated to me oddments of helpful information.

I wrote page upon page at top speed in my notebook: places to see and things to take. Interspersed throughout, the reiteration—"Must visit Chios."

It was not until our guests were leaving that I learned the invitation behind this reiteration. It was tossed out during the flurry of departure in the manner of what I believe in the theater is known as a "throw-away line." I caught and held it fast.

"Our house in Chios is open" is the way the line was tossed by the Livanoses. "You will take it for as long as you want. Everything will be ready."

Everything was ready for us on the *Queen Frederica* as well. Sophy reported after her first visit to the Home Lines offices, a month before our sailing, she had had a delightful conversation with Captain Vespa. Captain Vespa was business head of the line, the title "Captain" designated his rank; he did not operate a vessel of his firm. He had told Sophy the Livanoses had already informed him of our proposed trip. Together, Captain Vespa and Sophy had studied the plan of the ship and selected staterooms so charming that Captain Vespa had shaken hands with her in a spontaneous outburst of enthusiasm. Sophy reported to Darn, Luz and me this interview. She said nothing about a second meeting until we were on board the *Frederica* and within an hour of sailing, on the 21st of April. *Then* she told us five days before she had paid a return call on Captain Vespa, though in the month's interim the memory of the first visit had been kept green by telephone and correspondence.

The recent call had been solely for the purpose of gathering up the tickets and paying for them. Captain Vespa had greeted her as an old friend, and in this capacity had chided her playfully over betraying such American efficiency that she must come so far in advance for the little tickets, since we were not going until *May 21*. Why did she not, rather, let him call her, say about ten days before our date of sailing? They would have a pleasant chat, perhaps a little tea, and then he would have the tickets for her. This conversation had taken place five days before we had every reason to believe we were sailing.

It is not by charm alone, nor entirely due to her own insistence on the office, that Sophy is reappointed the executive of any expedition that includes people who know her. She can become fractious when I dawdle over buying postcards, restive if the day's program does not permit her a brisk walk in the fresh air. But present her with a crisis, and she becomes Sophy the Serene, at the same time, the General, ready at a moment to shift her point of attack, but never willing to surrender; a combination, in fact, of Alexander the Great and Florence Nightingale. She had exercised these talents; therefore, we were on the ship. She had dissuaded Captain Vespa from threats of self-annihilation and then held his attention firmly to the ship's diagram for the sailing on April 21, and a complete readjustment of cabin space.

We were still in speechless shock from this news, when two gentlemen entered our cabin. As they crossed the threshold one of them knocked on the door behind him. "May we come in?" he inquired.

"Come in, Captain Vespa," Sophy said. He kissed her hand. She introduced him to Luz, Darn and me. He kissed our hands. Our group of four travelers had been augmented by friends and family come to see us off. He bowed to them inclusively. His companion was not identified.

Captain Vespa went into our bathroom, closed the door behind him. The companion waited on our side of the closed door, his head bent a little in a listening attitude. The rest of us waited, too, and we made a considerable group of listeners. We endeavored to make conversation but we were distracted by the sound of the toilet flushing. Captain Vespa came out of the bathroom immediately, closing the door behind him. With an imperious nod to the other gentleman to do the same, he placed his ear against the closed door. The other gentleman promptly rested his head close to Captain Vespa's. Captain Vespa put his finger to his lips, rolling his eyes in our direction.

When there was no further sound from within the bathroom, Captain Vespa spoke. "Just testing," he said, opened the door again and disappeared from our sight. We heard the toilet flushed. He was instantly back in view again, door closed, associate summoned. Both heads again pressed against it. Captain Vespa is thorough in his investigation. He repeated his test some four or five times. When he had satisfied himself, he allowed the mechanism to rest. Leaving Mr. Anonymous still at the door, he came over to the rest of us. His voice was low, his tone confidential.

"I have listened to sound of rushing water," he said.

It had seemed to all of us that was what he had been doing.

"I have heard it in this room."

He waited for our corroboration. We nodded.

"Therefore," he continued, "it is not good for four ladies in two staterooms with one bath, too much noise. So," triumph raised his voice, "I am adding for you another stateroom down the corridor, with bath. It is not a good stateroom like this one, but for

Vasiliu

the circumstances . . ." he shrugged his shoulders and extended his hands, palms up.

We thanked him hurriedly, each talking above the other. This saved us from further elaboration on his part. He kissed hands all around, wishing us a happy and undisturbed voyage. From the bathroom door his associate bowed to each of us, and followed his leader from the stateroom.

I allowed them time to move on, presumably to other errands of mercy, and then left our quarters in search of a telephone; the one in our cabin had not as yet been connected. I found one in service just inside the promenade deck, not an ideal setting for intimate conversation, with porters, stewards, passengers, guests milling about and noisily obstructing one another. Nevertheless, I called Kakia Livanos at her apartment, shouted to her we were aboard, about to sail in delightful quarters, and that already we had received the most extraordinary service. I did not elaborate this. I repeated several times how grateful we were; we had never had such service as this in our lives. As I hung up the receiver I said to myself, "That's the God's truth."

Returning to our quarters, I brought word that in the social center from which I'd just come, gongs were banging and requests shouted for all visitors to go ashore.

Our guests took the hint; I have been told frequently that subtlety is not one of my gifts. They left. We went with them as far as the deck.

I challenge anyone's enjoyment of being surrounded by family and friends to be greater than mine, but I do not like these folk to linger when I am about to leave the country. Their presence makes me want to give up the whole trip and go back home with them. I am convinced at this moment of separation that, of all the foolish ideas I have ever entertained, this is the most idiotic: deliberately to remove myself from my dear ones. My stomach quivers with each possibility that rushes through my mind of catastrophe to them or to me.

Unquestionably there is a destiny, and it shapes my ends by seeing to it that I am one of the last passengers on a ship to receive my luggage in my stateroom. Long after every other passenger has emptied each bag and stowed it empty out of sight, I am awaiting my first piece of luggage. I do not know how this is brought about but I am sure why it happens. It is to prevent my leaving the ship.

As we left our cabin, we had some difficulty stepping over and around the rapidly accumulating mound of baggage deposited in the center of the room, but not a single piece of it bore my initials.

I stood at the rail with the other travelers and waved to my dear group on the dock, the most charming, attractive people to be found anywhere. With the exception of my own coterie, the individuals pressing their stomachs against the rail on either side of me the length of the ship I considered at that moment a heterogeneous assemblage of spooks. I wish people who come to see you off would have the wit to leave, once they have quit the ship. The dullards invariably crowd to the rail of the dock, waving and shouting messages you cannot hear. Though reason assures you they are inanities like "Don't forget to write," the disturbance of your emotions convinces you they are urgencies that must be communicated. This increases your misery.

I saw the gangplank raised and lowered again to pick up a late arrival whom we watched run the length of the pier. I thought for a minute if I ran as fast as he I might pass him on the gangplank and be safe on the dock. It was only a thought.

The straggler was gathered up, the gangplank lifted once more. The *Queen Frederica* eased away, the figures on the dock diminished in size, the waving arms and handkerchiefs blurred together. Come what may, we were on our way to Greece.

Chapter Two

WE SAILED at eleven-thirty in the morning, the day was clear, the water winked impudently in the sunlight. The temperature and a breeze required for one's comfort no more than a suit and a fur. By the time we were into the river channel and nosed toward the sea I found it difficult to believe that less than half an hour earlier I had wanted to knock to one side a late arrival, and return to the dock. Walking once around the deck for a quick survey of my new surroundings, the breeze lifting my hair, my fur, and my skirt a little, as I took deep breaths to attract the first whiff of salt in the air, I thought ruefully of my inability to break the pattern of my leaving home. Each departure—and I could not be classified as a homebody as I travel frequently—follows a well-worn path in my emotion: the anticipation of the trip, my mounting excitement as the time for leaving approaches; at the moment of leave-taking this anguish so sharp as to make me enraged at all those who have the effrontery to wish me a happy trip. Instantly the departure has been accomplished my immediate return to anticipation, deep pleasure and happy abandonment of all those to whom I had so recently clung. No fool like a sentimental old one, I decided morosely and went to my cabin.

The four of us were in two cabins as Captain Vespa had earlier pointed out in some detail. Actually, it was a suite of two sizable rooms. The first one entered from the corridor had an adjoining bath as Captain Vespa had also demonstrated. The second room was separated from the one off the corridor by French doors. Along the wall facing these doors, a row of windows gave on the sea. This was actually the sitting room of the suite, but two beds were let down from a wall. For the rest, the room was comfortably furnished with a couch, tables, chairs. At the moment of my arrival very little of this was visible. What occupied the center of the first room and blocked access to, even sight of, the one beyond, was a mound of luggage and a slightly lesser heap of packages.

My companions were supervising a steward, who on his knees was opening or trying to open a crate large enough to house a three-year-old child or a fairly sizable dog. Of the two, I devoutly hoped it was the latter. But when the protecting excelsior was removed, making a third pile to impede even entering the suite, the steward removed from the crate and set on the floor a replica of the Venus de Milo. Cards tied around her neck with elaborate pink bows carried affectionate greetings to Darn from jokester friends in California and added messages such as "Take me back where I came from," and "Carry this coal to Newcastle." As a joke it was not easy to explain to the steward, who was Greek. He protested with vehement pantomime and spare vocabulary we would find many beautiful statues in his country. Darn, for whom the possibility of offending someone is a source of acute distress, was goaded by her anxiety into trying to make the little man believe this was so treasured a possession she could not leave it behind. With some difficulty she lifted and clasped affectionately to her bosom the cold white object. Our little steward, eying her dubiously, gathered up as much of the excelsior as he could encompass with his arms, and left.

Darn was still holding her present and demanding to know if any of the rest of us had a better idea when two stewardesses joined me at the doorway. They regarded Darn and her souvenir with politeness that lasted only a minute. Each catching the eye of the other, they burst into a fit of the giggles, heightened by the gesture each made in trying to restrain her chortling by clamping her hand over her mouth. Darn, with dignity, set Venus down on the floor and again and with careful articulation pronounced a few words. I surmised they were in Greek but the stewardesses were not so enlightened. The words from Darn had a sobering effect but produced no other results than the abrupt cessation of the giggles. I thought it highly possible that as Greeks they had not been able to understand Darn's use of the language. In French, I asked if they were from Greece. Darn glared at me but I could see she was nervously apprehensive of their answer.

"No, madame," one of them answered. "I am Spanish." She indicated her companion. "Yolande is Italian."

Darn revealed a sense of relief by a loftiness toward me. "That was certainly a silly question to ask," she told me. "You evidently didn't know I was speaking Greek to them. If they had been Greek we would have had an interesting conversation." She noticed her Venus again, glowered at it, and added, "I might have explained this joke."

"Shall I explain it in French?" Sophy suggested. "I happen to speak superbly."

The matter was settled by the stewardesses themselves, who worked their way into the room, a feat I had not been able to accomplish, gathered up the rest of the excelsior, together with boxes that had held flowers, wrappings that had contained books, smiled tolerantly at Darn, ingratiatingly at the rest of us, and left the room with sufficiently cleared space for me to enter and join my friends in the hurly-burly of unpacking. We paused long enough to draw lots for the apportioning of rooms. Darn and Luz drew the outer one on the sea, Sophy and I the one with the bath. We agreed to confine our residence to these adjoining rooms in spite of Captain Vespa's concern; it was cozier. Sophy was not so sympathetic with the coziness as she was antagonistic to the extra cabin because it was inside and therefore would not provide fresh air.

Luz and I became friends at boarding school and went through college together. This is as specific as I care to be about the passage of time, but in all those years I have never known her to be truculent. She is always the diplomat. Therefore, as sometimes happens with diplomats, nobody asked her which she would prefer. It was settled among the other three that the extra cabin would be alloted to leftovers, the pile of empty luggage, extra clothes not in daily use, hanging space for the daily wash, and Darn's Venus.

At the mention of daily wash Luz remembered she had a present for each of us. She distributed four boxes. Inside was a piece of cord that taken from the box was less than a foot in length. It was thick and made of plaited rubber with a loop at either end. Luz explained and demonstrated that stretched out it would extend at least the length of a bathtub. With the loop attached to whatever was convenient at either end, the plaiting could be spread apart by the fingers and a garment inserted. It would then clamp down and hold secure a line of wash. We agreed it was one of the most ingenious inventions we had seen, and it turned out to be thoroughly successful for everybody but me. The others said it was because I didn't give it a fair trial. I grant I am not handy with gadgets. I also maintain they invariably turn against me. The one time I tried this one, a loop slipped off the hook on the door to which I had attached it just as I had hung up my wash, and springing back to its original size, caught me on the side of the head and very nearly knocked me unconscious. I recommend it enthusiastically for other travelers.

The gong for lunch interrupted our unpacking. Sophy and I discovered we had been assigned to the Captain's table, Luz and Darn to one adjoining. This was not at all as we had wanted it and we had taken the trouble, immediately on boarding the ship, to request of the head steward a table for four. We reminded him of this at the door to the dining room, as he checked us in and gave us our seatings. He was apologetic and promised to correct the error. Jostled as he was by other passengers requesting their seating, we could not harass him further and glumly went our separate ways.

The Captain did not come to lunch. We had not expected he would on the first day, but perhaps because at that table one is acutely aware of its host and equally of his absence, the rest of us were absurdly shy and uncommunicative. We could hear spirited conversation going on at the adjoining table, though not the conversation itself. Sophy and I were the only women at ours, and the four men with whom we lunched were discouragingly indifferent to us. At the end of the meal one of them rose to his feet. He was the most attractive of the four in appearance, and had sat next to Sophy. She had seen to that.

He bowed and announced, "My name is Panaiotopoulos. You will excuse?" and left.

Resuming our unpacking after lunch we reported our dismal meal including the announcement, except for the name, that marked its close.

"I can't tell you who he is," I said. "I doubt I'll ever be able to. I never heard so many syllables gathered together in one word. If this is a sample of Greek names, with all those Greek friends the Livanoses said they were writing to, I am socially on the rocks as of now."

Sophy is not so easily defeated. She said at once she was going to ask him to write it down. "If I see it," she boasted, "I know I can learn it."

Luz and Darn had had a livelier time than we. I pointed out to them that would not have been difficult and was not proof, in my opinion, they were socially more adept than we. I was envious when they described their table companions, particularly one who had turned out to be the owner of a Greek restaurant not very far from where Darn lives in Pasadena. He had invited her to visit his establishment at home and she had accepted enthusiastically. He had also been helpful about explaining differences between the social customs of America and Greece. In Greece one must be more formal he had cautioned them, and demonstrated as illustration that in Greece, when using a toothpick at the table, one must shield the operation with a cupped hand.

We had finished our unpacking and were stowing the empty bags in the extra room when we were called to lifeboat drill by whistle blasts and banging gongs. I was relieved to find my friends took the drill as literally as I take it. They are, perhaps, more docile by nature than I. It has been pointed out to me I am not always amenable to rules, but I am the very spirit of co-operation, on shipboard, about anything that concerns my getting safely across the ocean. I do not subscribe to the regimentation of having my deck chair in a line with other passengers on the promenade deck; I prefer the privacy and open air of the upper deck. When the games mistress, or the hostess, whatever her title, invites participants in the jolly sports activities, I am on the run in the opposite direction. But the captain of a ship will never find a more willing and eager helper than I. If he would only ask me I should be happy, in time of fog, to spend a wakeful night on the bridge as assistant to the lookout. In me he has always, from embarkation to debarkation, a vigilant passenger anticipating at all times a shipwreck or a mutiny.

Our life jackets were bright orange and of such a cut as to raise our arms a little and stretch our necks into an elevation and rigidity of chin that gave us an elephantine hauteur. The meeting place assigned to us was the lounge. The officer in charge of our lifeboat checked off our names, and we sat down in a corner, gathering together four straight chairs, the only kind that would accommodate our inflexible posture.

Conversation among the four of us seldom lags, and that afternoon we enjoyed a recapitulation of the day, from the time of our assemblage on the ship to the present moment. We were discomfited to discover the present moment of the life drill had passed us by. The drill was over, the other passengers had dispersed. Some of them, returning to the lounge for tea, brought us uncomfortably up to date by their audible conjectures that we were novices at sea and had been intimidated by the drill into thinking life jackets must be worn for the duration of the trip. Only the enforced set of our heads lent dignity to our embarrassed exit from the room.

Back in our cabins we were not in the mood for further conversation and by mutual and almost silent consent took a nap.

Sophy lifted us physically and emotionally, at six, by the simple statement she had brought out her shoebag. When Sophy travels, her shoebag serves a double purpose. It carries shoes, but tucked into the toes and encircled by the sling heels of these are bottles of drinks for the group. Since we are individualists in taste as well as in temperament, she bears a heavy load, though not uncomplainingly. To be that beast of burden, we have frequently pointed out, is her own choice, and we give her complaints no ear. Praise and gratitude but no sympathy is our motto. Previous travels together have sifted us down to a fairly set pattern, no part of it more firmly set than our drinking habits. They are mild in quantity but strong in the manner of their taking. We do not like bars nor cocktail lounges; nor do we like drinks sent from either of those sources. They are both expensive and, we consider, inferior. We like the intimacy and informality provided by our own surroundings, and we vastly prefer Sophy and her shoebag to any other bartender as a source of supply.

We were on our feet instantly at Sophy's call. We bathed, and again the extra room proving helpful, dressed in record time. By a quarter to seven we were in comfortable armchairs around the table in Luz's and Darn's bed-sitting room. A steward had brought us ice and Sophy was contentedly dispensing a Martini to Darn, Bourbon to Luz, white wine and soda to me, and a tall, cold Scotch and soda for herself.

Dinner that night was a considerably brighter occasion than luncheon had been, at least for Sophy and me. Darn and Luz insisted loyally that, while the tone of their new environment was somewhat different from the one they had quitted, the sprightliness was no greater. They had been moved to the Captain's table and he was present as a charming host.

Our number was also increased by Mr. and Mrs. Papadakis. Mrs. Papadakis was shy but strikingly beautiful. She spoke very little English but her bridegroom spoke a great deal of it. He had married, he told us, Miss Greece of 1954, and went on to inform us of his other accomplishments. He was indeed doubling in brass and leading the bloodhounds. In addition to conducting his wife on a visit to her homeland, he was in charge of a body of patriots assembled from various parts of the United States for a pilgrimage to Sparta and bound together by their common ancestry. Mr. Papadakis slapped his chest for emphasis. "We are all Spartans. Very strong, very manly." He was also an American, he told us with equal emphasis, and we corroborated his assertion that it would be difficult to find a more splendid combination. He told us, too, his pilgrims, the Laconians, would be greeted at every stopping point by official receptions. Before the meal was finished, he had invited my friends and me with warm cordiality to become members of his band. It would be a privileged way of seeing Greece not available to the average tourist. We did not doubt this, and we told him so, adding that our own plans could not be abandoned.

Somehow, during this recital, and it established his social competence, the Captain managed to introduce the other guests at his table. One, an Italian, told us at a later meal, when Mr. Papadakis was lunching in tourist class with his pilgrims, he was in his government's service in charge of immigrants from Italy to the United States and other countries. I think he was returning for a fresh batch. One of the officers of the ship was also with us, but I have forgotten his name. For the second time Sophy and I heard the name Mr. Panaiotopoulos. As the Captain pronounced it we indicated to our friends by lifted eyebrow the hopelessness of acquiring, for our own pronunciation, such a gathering of letters. We were able to grasp and understand that Mr. P. was a representative of the Home Line, that he had to do with public relations; that this was a supervisory trip such as he made from time to time, and that he spoke English very well.

The Captain's name was Constantine Condoyannis, though certainly I could not have repeated it at first hearing. On a Greek ship the title of its commanding officer is Master, not Captain. He was one of the most delightful men, we agreed in the privacy of our cabins, any of us had met in many a day. We were none of us surprised to find later he had been an admiral in the Royal Greek Navy. He was retired when he was asked to captain the *Queen Frederica* to give special prestige to the first passenger ship under a Greek flag, and had agreed because, he said, the land had become dull. He gave more than prestige, we found. As an administrator he exacted and achieved a high standard of excellence in food, service and conduct of personnel. As an individual he conveyed a charm, cultivation and sophistication of background and wide travel that made him both a skillful host and a delightful companion. He introduced us that first night not only to one another, but to some Greek dishes and Greek wine.

We discovered both a Greek and a French cuisine were provided. We experimented a little with the Greek, interpolating with French, just to be on the safe side. We need not have been so cautious. The Greek dishes we considered delicious. Darn experimented, too, with her recently acquired modern Greek vocabulary. Her pronunciation of it caused Mr. Panaiotopoulos to wince visibly. The Captain, either through wider experience in social aplomb, or more frequent exposure over the years in his naval career to hardship, received the impact from Darn with equanimity.

Mr. Panaiotopoulos spoke with the voice of a man in pain. "Please," he begged, "do not pound the words. The Greek language is for flowing, not hammering."

Darn tended to be somewhat subdued during the remainder of the evening, but as she was climbing into bed announced loudly, though the topic had not hitherto been introduced, "Well, anyway, when I asked for goat cheese in Greek, that's what I got, and none of the rest of you had any."

I would have liked to tell her, only to clarify once and for all my position in the matter, that I not only had not eaten goat's cheese at dinner, but that I hoped not to eat it at any time during the entire summer. I had a feeling, however, this was not the moment to add that information to her store of knowledge. I remembered that earlier in the day she had told me she had learned only one sentence in Greek, and that was entirely for my benefit. At the start of her lessons she had explained to her teacher time did not permit her to study verb forms and sentence constructions. She would concentrate only on vocabulary with one exception. She wished to be able to say whenever a meal was ordered, "My friend is unable to eat anything with onions or garlic in it." I therefore permitted her to go to sleep unchallenged about the goat cheese.

The ship's newspaper came on our breakfast tray. I found one item more interesting than all the other news because it increased my satisfaction in the way the ship was run. It read, "A staff of sixty-eight men in the Engineering Department works around the clock in three shifts to see that the ship continues in a forward direction."

The day was so bright as to require dark glasses on the uncovered top deck where we settled early. The air was warmer, too, than it had been the day before. I pointed this out as proof of the assertion in the newspaper that the ship was continuing in a forward direction.

Sophy is a chronic deck pacer. She sets herself a specific number of laps each day. Furthermore, sluggards such as I, who count twice around ample exertion for one day, must listen to her exultant computation of laps into miles. Luz accompanied Sophy, but, as I pointed out on the way down to lunch, a very significant difference in their characters was evidenced by the fact that Luz did not count aloud. Luz's answer surprised me. "I never get to finish a sentence anyway," she said. "You all talk so much faster than I do. I wouldn't even get to count beyond 'three.' "

Lunch was a lively meal, though the Master was not with us; neither was the one-time Miss Greece of 1954, now Mrs. Papadakis. Her bridegroom explained she was not feeling well. Darn has the curiosity of a scientist or of a child of four, and the outspokenness of the latter. She instantly inquired solicitously of Mr. Papadakis, "Could your wife be . . . ?"

I have not been Darn's friend since we were eleven years old without knowing something of her traits, and I forestalled her. "Seasick?" I threw in loud and fast.

Since the sea that morning was as placid as the water in the finger-bowls on our table, my diagnosis seemed unlikely but Mr. Papadakis endorsed it eagerly.

"She is exactly seasick. Very, very seasick."

I saw my friends nodding and smiling at one another and frowned at them. I told them later they had acted like members of a mid-wives association.

Vasiliu

I endeavored to distract Mr. Papadakis from observing their head wagglings by asking what in his opinion were the differences between Greek and American girls. Having lived most of his life in America he must know some American girls, I said, but he had married a Greek. A puppy is no more responsive to a biscuit dangled invitingly before him than Mr. Papadakis, I had surmised correctly, to a tidbit that promised a taste of oratory. He seized the tidbit and savored it with gusto.

"Now that is something," he assured me, "I like very much to talk about, because there is big difference. American girls and women," he included politely, "are very, very nice. I like them." With a smile and slight bow he bestowed his accolade on each of us. "But," his eyes flashed as he began his declamation, "they like to be friends. That is not natural, it is not in the nature of women to be friends." He disposed of friendship among women quickly. "All women, Greeks, Americans, everybody, they are suspicious of one another, envious, jealous. Two girls see a man. They are friends since children. Each wants the man, of course. Poof goes the friendship! You will see." He favored us with a round of benevolent smiles. "But perhaps you will not meet any men."

"Nonsense," Sophy interjected tartly. "Of course we'll meet men, but—"

Mr. Papadakis overrode her blandly. "You will see," he repeated. "It is not that way when men are friends." He thumped his chest to identify the embodiment of manhood. "Men are friends with each other because they fight together. Women do not fight together. That is what makes friendship. And now," he had no page to turn but he conveyed visibly the impression he had reached the heart of his speech, "American women with men. There is the friendship again, and that is the most unnatural of all. A woman cannot be friend with a man. Greeks know that. Americans should learn it. When a man meets a girl either he is indifferent or he is not. If he is indifferent there is nothing. If he is not indifferent that is not friendship. My wife will be polite to all my friends, and I have many friends. Greek girls are very polite. That is how they are brought up. She will dance with my friends, but she will not be friend to my friends. Oh, no. I lock the door to that."

The ship's engineer had come to the table during this peroration, and indicated to the waiter his order by pointing to the items he wished from the menu. As Mr. Papadakis paused for dramatic effect, the engineer made a memorable contribution. "I know women all over the world," he explained modestly. "They all write me six letters. Number one, she tells the weather. Two she tells what she has been cooking and what she can cook for me. Number three she writes what clothes she has and what I can bring her. Number four she tells people she has seen, maybe I do not even know them. Five she tells where she goes. Six she tells me she loves me. . . . Friendship, whatever you call it, is all the same. She writes six letters."

Darn said later she considered lunch had been very instructive.

After that day the Master presided over both lunch and dinner, and conversation spread over a wide range of topics. Friendship was not again included among them.

Each night the Master introduced a new wine and Sophy, the sommelier of our group, wrote down the name and its quality. She was the first to cluck her tongue appreciatively over *retsina*, the resinated wine that is peculiar to Greece. The rest of us found it very peculiar indeed to our taste, and were a little annoyed at Sophy for liking it.

I identified the reason for our pique by saying in the privacy of our cabin but in the hearing of the others, "You're just making character with the Master."

Sophy's answer was, "Remember what Papadakis said about friendship among women?"

I have found over long years of friendship that Sophy's moment of expressing her thought is frequently ill-timed and not always endearing to those who otherwise hold her in deep affection. I counted it not well-timed either for Luz to choose that moment to observe dreamily, looking off into space, "Mr. Panaiotopoulos has asked me to call him 'Panny.' "

We had mastered his name and I considered that an accomplishment, if not equivalent to the scaling of Mt. Everest, at least to the ascent of the Matterhorn. Success had come by way of Sophy's suggestion that the name be written down. On the afternoon we gave a small cocktail party in our suite, we had paced the floor, each carrying a slip of paper on which "Panaiotopoulos" was written. We had tested one another by pausing unexpectedly and pointing a finger dramatically at another member of the group with a peremptory, "Say the name aloud without looking." Half an hour of this concentrated mouthing, and when the guests arrived, Panaiotopoulos was trippingly on our tongues.

It took longer to adjust the taste of resinated wine to my palate, but when I had acceded to Sophy's suggestion to drink it with a sweet, I found I liked it. Sophy was so pleased by this surrender, counting it absurdly a personal triumph of her own, she insisted that all the wine for dinner that night be her treat.

Sophy's place at the table was beside the Master. When at the beginning of the meal a waiter set before him a folded piece of paper, Sophy reiterated her determination to usurp for once his prerogative as host. With playful charm, she wrested the paper from the Captain's hand as he picked it up, over the Captain's firm protests, which she misinterpreted. She was discomfited on opening what she thought was the wine chit to find she had intercepted an important radio message the Captain had ordered brought him immediately on its anticipated arrival.

Chapter Three

THE days settled down to a soothing monotony of pattern and, particularly soothing to me, a uniformity of sunny weather. The sea continued calm and Mrs. Papadakis' appearance at meals continued to be erratic, causing my companions to wag their heads to one another appreciatively each time Mr. Papakadis reported the indisposition of his bride "due to seasickness."

Every morning Sophy circled the upper deck calling out each lap as she passed our secluded row of chairs where Darn and I lay stretched out lazily and read or dozed in the sun. Luz walked with Sophy but did not count, at least not out loud. After lunch Darn and I went to our cabins, read and napped. Sophy and Luz returned to the upper deck, possibly for further exercise, more probably for a nap. After our naps Darn and I walked the deck but did not comment on it, and presently it was six o'clock, when the steward would appear with a pail of ice and glasses, and Sophy would open her shoebag. Each afternoon, sometime between naps and dinner, Sophy and I would play a rousing game of Scrabble in which Luz occasionally joined. Darn chose this time for a private session of laundry and hairsetting in the extra room.

I had bought shortly before our departure a traveling set of Scrabble. It was distinguished as a traveling set because the container was a leather case with a handle by which it could be carried. Sophy was patient, for perhaps two days of the voyage, over my pointing out the special merits of this set. Then she told me she considered it unnecessary for me to preface each session of play by a walking demonstration around the cabin of how it could be carried. A month later in Yugoslavia I was to wish I had dropped it overboard, but on the *Frederica* it punctuated happily the interval between a nap and the shoebag hour.

Two days running Darn won the ship's pool. These were the only times we visited the bar, at our insistence and Darn's forfeit.

The morning of the twenty-eighth of April we breakfasted for the first time in the dining room, and were the earliest arrivals there. The Captain had told us the night before we would see Tangier early in the forenoon, and shortly thereafter reach Gibraltar. We gave his time schedule a generous interpretation in our eagerness to have a first glimpse of land and were on our top deck, ours because we had appropriated it, shortly after seven. The sun had not yet dispersed the early-morning mist and Tangier first came to us a gray mass, like a cloud bank on the horizon.

Luz had brought on the trip an excellent pair of field glasses. She was the only one of us that morning who had very little use of them. We were aware of this only when Sophy, who had held them to her face so long I was inquiring if she were thinking of making them a permanent substitute for her glasses, lowered them and, ignoring me, asked Luz if she would care to use them. Luz characteristically answered she didn't want them, insisting she was busy fixing her camera for taking pictures. Sophy generously allowed me to take them.

A rolling countryside of green fields emerged, a soft landscape, to my considerable surprise. I had imagined it would be rocky, barren, forbidding. Certainly I did not convey to my associates my surprise. I am on the alert not to attract attention to my geographic misconceptions. I attracted their attention, instead, to a traffic rush in the sea all around us. The phenomenon was not the boats themselves, though I think I had never seen so many kinds of craft assembled, but in the manner of their appearance. Only a moment ago, or so it had seemed to me, the sea had been as empty to our view as it had been during the seven days of our crossing. But while I was engrossed in bringing the land of Morocco into my vision, some Cadmus must have been at work, I thought (I'd been reading Greek mythology for seven days), and brought a rush of sea craft to the surface of the Straits of Gibraltar. Planes were flying overhead, fishing craft below thumbed an impertinent bow at us as they whisked out of the way of our stately progress. In their midst, a clown troupe of porpoises made a sudden appearance. Farther off three or four freighters glided close to one another in a line. They were like old ladies, withdrawn from such cavortings as surrounded us, and like old ladies revealing disapproval that disturbs the digestion, by erratic belches of smoke from their funnels.

As if on a cue we four involuntarily moved off to separate points of the compass, each calling back to the others reports of the sights within her vista. Darn was the one who sighted a string of rowboats unmistakably coming toward us, and from the height at which we stood looking like the humping progress of an outsized inchworm. I was vaguely aware the ship was moving slowly, but I was too preoccupied with the bustle below and around us to note it sufficiently, even to wonder why, until Luz called out, her soft southern voice sharpened by excitement, "We've stopped. There's Gibraltar!"

By God's mercy, and the way ships are constructed, I did not fall down into the Mediterranean. The railing on which I was leaning, like the rails on all ships, was of a height to prevent falling without climbing first. But I was so astonished by the news she sent and the sight I saw that I was only contained on board by the fencing.

We realized later it was not bright of us to have overlooked Gibraltar and seen instead a thread of rowboats, considering their relative size, but the vivacity of the scene on the water and the kaleidoscopic way in which it shifted had evidently closed in our range of focus to a pinpoint of concentration. We had not, therefore, looked above the water line. I am not so surprised when places turn out to be unlike my notion of them as I am surprised and delighted when they are revealed exactly as I had imagined they would be. Not an aspect of Gilbraltar contradicted my anticipation of that formidable landmark.

We did not "put in" at Gibraltar, if that is the proper expression for bringing a ship to a pier. We anchored at some distance off shore. From that moment on I scarcely gave Gibraltar itself more than an occasional and cursory glance. Nothing about it changed. Each time I looked at the scene below, however, the aspect of it had changed and every aspect pleased, sight, sound and smell. The inchworm of little boats came close, broke out of line and clustered, clamoring, around the knees of the ship. Each one was occupied by three, four, sometimes more, men; slim with dark skin and eyes, a bandanna around each head, and from every throat such shouting as to dim the sound even from the planes overhead. In each little boat one man stayed at the oars holding the position that had been fought for when the line had broken up. The other occupants stood. I do not know how they stood, with waves bouncing and turning the boat beneath them, but I did not see one man shift his position, nor give so much recognition of the violent motion beneath him as a sway of his body. Their hands and arms up to the shoulder were draped with merchandise they urged us, deafeningly, to buy: scarves, appallingly garish to wear, but glorious highlights against the dark skin of their vendors; dreadful necklaces and bracelets of beads and imitation pearls, picturesque at a distance, flashing in the sunlight.

I do not know how the vendors balanced on their feet, nor do I understand how, with their arms loaded with merchandise, they were able to throw up as high as the cabins and promenade deck of our ship a heavy cord, aimed so true a passenger at his stateroom window or the rail of the deck could catch it easily. The passengers did catch them. This established a pully arrangement. Up the line would be sent with speed from the dancing boat below a covered basket and, in it, vivid and varied junk for selection and purchase.

I would have bought something just for the fun of receiving and returning a basket, but happily I was above their range, so my luggage was not increased by any of those souvenirs. With a restraint for which I commended myself because I am, usually, a pushover for anything offered for sale picturesquely, I only watched and took pictures.

The noise did not diminish. I think it would have been impossible for any lungs to increase the volume these produced. The words bellowed were in English, of a sort. "Beautiful souvenir. One dollar. One dollar. You buy?"

A tender shoved its way through, jostling the little boats to either side. The men standing in them paid not the slightest attention. The oarsmen maneuvered other positions skillfully and without diminishing, much less ceasing, their yelling. Passengers bound for Spain were taken off our ship onto the tender, and an automobile was transferred. The tender moved away. From the violence of the exhaust I think it must have had a powerful engine. I could scarcely hear any sound from it. Another tender elbowed the little boats out of the way once more; they had closed in immediately our passengers had left. This time people came aboard bound for Italy and Greece.

When the last of these had left the tender and the tender itself departed, I felt the *Queen Frederica* shiver a little, as if someone had walked over her grave. She was alive again, functioning, moving. The oarsmen below rowed their boats out of our way, the shouting continued, the words changed. What had been offered before at only a dollar now was urged in a rapid diminuendo through seventy-five, fifty, twenty-five, to ten cents. Abruptly the tumult stopped. We were out of basket reach. Nothing more could be sold however far the voices carried. Economically, therefore, they shut off, in unison and so abruptly it could have been a chorus watching a conductor's baton. Through Luz's glasses I saw the men slip off the gaudy merchandise they had not sold, sit down in the boats, pick up their oars. Presently they were only dark spots on the blue sea.

At lunch we were introduced by the Captain to two new guests added to our table, His Excellency Señor Sebastian de Romero Radigales and the Señora. They had come on board at Gibraltar and we learned they were on a visit to Greece, Mme. de Romero's homeland, where His Excellency had been Spanish Ambassador for many years.

In my experience nothing more inexorably reduces an American to the cultural status of a hillbilly than his proximity to a foreigner who moves easily from his own to a number of other languages in one conversation. His Excellency's English was faltering, but understandable. He spoke French with ease. We shared that language though my French limped. I sat in silent exasperation at myself while both he and Mme. de Romero moved into Italian with the government immigration official, interspersed occasionally with Mme. de Romero's rush into Greek with Mr. Panaiotopoulos or the Captain, followed each time by an apology to us, in English, that her eagerness to hear news of her dear country and mutual friends there had allowed her to abandon, momentarily, other languages. I expressed to His Excellency my envious admiration of Mme. de Romero's versatile tongue. He endorsed my admiration with charming pride, adding she had come to Spain as his bride and learned the language so quickly and so well that, in a short time, she could have been mistaken for a Spaniard by birth, and that she also spoke German, French and Italian easily. But he, he shrugged his shoulders and shook his head apologetically, had never learned Greek as she had learned Spanish, nor, with a quick smile, "As you have see, madame, your English; but you speak French too."

I counted this no more than evidence that I was talking to a skillful and experienced diplomat. Immediately after lunch I lay down in my cabin determined that instead of napping that day I would memorize at least one page of modern Greek vocabulary from a little book provided to all passengers. I slept for three hours and waking remembered that before dropping off I had taught myself that the Greek for "yes" sounds like "no," because it is "*né*" and the word for "no" sounds like "okay" by the pronunciation of the letter "h," though the word is written "*ohi*." This, the accomplishment of a Greek major at college, and the child who had prattled the Greek alphabet at her mother's knee.

As I was reviewing mournfully my years of Greek amnesia, Sophy came in briskly, her cheeks pink, her eyes sparkling, hair windblown. She recited the number of laps she had counted off, and what had I been doing in the three hours since lunch? She then observed she found me surly and prescribed champagne for dinner. This would be provided by Darn, who quite properly, Sophy said, had reported to her as sommelier a note from the wine steward. The note read that by cabled order from friends at home champagne for her had been put on board at Gibraltar. I endorsed the prescription.

Sophy spent the morning of the twenty-ninth arranging, by wireless messages, for a car to meet us in Naples and drive us out to Pompeii. This involved conferences with Mr. Panaiotopoulos about where to send the message, conversation with the wireless operator over the sending and insuring of an answer. It made a happy morning for her, she told the table at lunch, marred only by Darn's and my insistence on giving her suggestions. Luz deplored the loss of their morning walk together. That absence, I asserted, was what had made the morning a particularly pleasurable one for me. Urged by our executive not to harry her with any more suggestions, I had withdrawn to my chair on our deck, and neither my book nor my view to sea had been blotted out by the shadow of Sophy on her morning gallop, hallooing the numbered rounds as she passed.

The arrival at the table of the de Romeros put an end to this exchange of friendly barbs. In deference to His Excellency's difficulties with our language we spoke French for the remainder of the meal, and French is acknowledged a polite language.

Saturday, the thirtieth, was sunny and warm, though we were up and on our deck before the mists had been entirely burned away. It was all the more dramatic then to see Vesuvius unveiled by the sun, and we were very close to tears when we were told by a passing sailor we had misspent our emotions. Pointing a finger at the lovely image on our horizon, he said, "Is island. Ischia."

We went immediately down to breakfast and had no further dealings with whatever land may have been offered for our inspection. However, we did not miss the Bay of Naples. When we came up on deck again that glorious panorama surrounded us, hills, city and blue sea. We were in the very center of it; the ship was edging toward the dock. In the immediate foreground we saw a large structure, evidently the administration building of the port. It was obviously of recent construction and modern austere design, but what caught our fancy as well as our attention was the sight of jaunty lace curtains, fluttering in the breeze at every window in the upper stories, and gay potted plants that lined the balcony along the second floor; a charming contrast to the severity of their surroundings.

I have never understood why a platoon of officials is required to authorize debarkation. If the idea behind such numbers is that many hands make light work and expedite the departure of passengers, it is an erroneous conception. The many hands always get in the way of one another. Passports are dealt out from one pair to the next, round the circle again, frequently back to the wrong owner, so that the melee among the officials within the circle spreads to the periphery of passengers.

We four came down the gangplank at very long last; hot, because the place chosen for the rite is always the most airtight room on the ship; disheveled, because there is always considerable jockeying necessary for a place in line and even more jostling in order to maintain it. The car Sophy had ordered was waiting for us. We had some difficulty in identifying it and its driver. A crowd of chauffeurs surrounded us on the dock, each urging his vehicle. The only advantage in ordering our motor in advance by wireless was that it had provided for Sophy a morning's diversion from the daily routine of shipboard. It was entirely due to Luz that we located our driver at all. None of us realized she had so sharp an ear, but it picked out from the chorus of voices around us the sound of Sophy's name or something like it, traced the sound to its source and extracted our chauffeur.

He was a good driver as Italian drivers go, though in my opinion they all go like maniacs. I have been told by friends, who have studied the matter, that the Italian's method of driving is an expression of an innate and endearing quality: a childlike curiosity that prompts him when approaching an intersection, for example, to press down on the accelerator in order to see more quickly what might be coming from either direction. Our driver possessed this quality and evinced it at each corner, but in between drove fairly slowly. He had to, because we had landed on the day of the great motorcycle races. I do not know what races, but we were informed by expansive gestures, both hands off the wheel, the race was so large it covered all the highways and we would have to travel to Pompeii by back streets.

Even on these our progress was slow, thank Heaven, because of vehicles and pedestrians, though neither group paid what I would have called attention to the other; bumpers nudging pedestrians, and pedestrians paying them not so much heed as a glance over the shoulder. We saw steep crooked streets, too narrow for a car to travel, houses, apartments, piled one on top of another on hills; flowers and children everywhere, all of them beautiful.

Outside the entrance to Pompeii we changed our shoes in the car. This was Darn's idea, and I pause in my chronicle to laud it, underline it, and ring it with stars. I cannot give her full credit for the shoes themselves. It was Sophy's suggestion, I think, that we include in our equipment "topsiders," the brand of tennis footwear that boasts rubber soles with an extra firm grip. "I have a feeling," she had written to the others, "that ruins have to be climbed to, and among. I recommend topsiders." Luz, Sophy and I bought them. Darn did not.

Darn has a tendency to improve on basic inventions and she had exercised it, this time by having rubber soles attached to a pair of oxford wedgies she owned. Her assumption had been that the wedgies would fit more snugly than tennis shoes, and so give her added support. They supported her, but with the addition of the extra rubber soles as if she were on stilts. There are hotels dotted about the mainland of Greece and the Aegean Islands in which today a chambermaid is the possessor of a pair of canvas shoes with rubber soles, purchased optimistically by Darn in one town, and discarded in the next. She did not find a pair that was right, but of all of them the wedgies were the least stabilizing when climbing.

The rest of us, not so imaginative as she, had bought off-the-shelf models and found them thoroughly satisfactory. Nevertheless, Darn was the one who suggested carrying them along and provided a receptacle. We had hooted at the sight of it when in the midst of unpacking on the first day out she had displayed it and explained its purpose. I have seldom seen a more dismal-looking object. Olive drab, it certainly was, the material a nylon mesh. Its only virtue was that from a small, flat square, that could be tucked easily into a handbag, it unfolded into a deep, capacious carrier with handle on either side, providing not only room but strength enough to carry four pairs of shoes. The primary reason for carrying and not wearing them was vanity. There is something incongruous, conspicuous and certainly unstylish about the sight of a pair of sneakers, white or baby blue, and in sizes six to eight or nine, twinkling beneath a sober suit or traveling dress, particularly when the face above the costume is middle-aged. When the moment comes for climbing or trudging, however, style is no object.

Pompeii is a fascinating trudge, extending over sixty-five acres. We did not cover all the acreage. What we did see we tried to discover for ourselves without benefit of guide. That was not sensible. After turning down several who stood at the entrance gate offering their services, we tried to orient ourselves from the maps and plans we had purchased. By "we" I mean, of course, Darn, Luz and Sophy. I did not waste money on a map, and they had no success with theirs. Accordingly, after some quarter of an hour or so of wandering, we encountered another guide and gave in to him. From then on the excursion was thoroughly rewarding and absorbing.

The guides, we discovered, are in the employ of the government. They are well-informed, speak several languages. This one spoke English well. My friends discovered within the first fifteen minutes the maps and guidebooks they had purchased were thoroughly inadequate. They had bought them from vendors who had swarmed around our cars as we drove up to the gate. On our way out we saw and purchased books published under the auspices of the government, and for sale inside the entrance. These are the ones to use.

Of course there was not time to see all we would have liked, but we liked deeply all we saw: the House of the Vettii, those two rich merchants who built handsomely and encouraged gaiety in the interior decorating, by way of panels and friezes. Examining these, I realized once more I was experiencing a pleasant surprise brought about by my own intellectual deficiency. I evidently do not absorb what I have been taught. Slides shown on the screen, when we studied Pompeii in the eighth grade at Miss Faulkner's, were seldom in color; still, how could I have been surprised to find on those same friezes actually before me in Pompeii, Pompeian red? There were other colors too, of course, though not all the colors remain, nor all the walls, but as a friend of my grandmother's used to say, "A gracious plenty." The little statues and the fountain are still in the garden and roses were blooming there.

I thought as we left, and I had an absurd impulse to tiptoe, "This is the city and this was the palace of the Sleeping Beauty."

We walked along the streets, pausing at very nearly every doorway, measuring with our arms wide the circumference of great casks standing in the oil merchants' shops. We visited the baths—the cold room, the warm or tepidarium, and the hot or caldarium—and were shown by the guide how the heating of these was accomplished by a circulation of warm air under the raised floor and in the space between double walls. Each time we paused or turned back for a closer inspection of something we might have passed, the guide would urge us, "Ladies, ladies, may I speak? The time is short. To see the most beautiful part we must hurry."

We were seeing the most beautiful part, I thought. I could not discover that any point to which he urged us was more interesting than the one he had persuaded us to quit.

We came back to the ship by way of the highway, the Auto Strada. There were bright red poppies in the fields on either side and along the edge of the road. When I think of an Italian countryside I see always scarlet poppies, white bullocks in the field, and swallows circling overhead. We saw them all that day. From the highway, too, we had a superb view of Vesuvius.

Our driver responded to my heartfelt plea to drive very, very *andante*. Nothing at Pompeii surprised me more than his co-operation. When I close my eyes and think of Italy I do *not* see cars driving *andante* past poppies and bullocks. I see lunatics racing among the hill towns, giving notice of their approach on a winding mountain road by a wild tattoo on their horns, after they have rounded a bend and are face to face with me at full tilt. The drive back to Naples from Pompeii is the one I shall try to substitute for the others in my memory.

Even driving reasonably we would have reached the ship in a third of the time it had taken us to drive out, because we were on the highway; but on the busiest street in Naples, the Corso Humberto, at the most crowded hour and day of the week, five o'clock on Saturday afternoon, we had a blowout. What a crowd we had, too, gathered within two minutes, possibly less! Two policemen were required to clear enough space for us to leave the car and for the chauffeur to fix the tire. We took some of the crowd with us, though not by invitation, as we strolled up and down the street looking in shop windows.

Sophy, who is mechanically minded and proud of it, had offered to help the chauffeur change the tire. When the chauffeur and those nearest us in the crowd understood by her pantomime what she was suggesting, I doubt they could have been more startled had she volunteered to give them a strip-tease entertainment. That was when and why we decided to leave the car, and concentrate her attention, as well as our own, on the shop windows. Close onto fifty people, I think, gave us the news that the car was ready and escorted us back and into our vehicle. We drove off among spirited hand-waving and a few cheers.

We were on board again in good time for the shoebag, and enough over, in fact, to allow Darn to retire to the extra cabin to wash her white gloves. I have known Darn since we were eleven years old and I roomed with her in college. Therefore, I have seen her not wearing white gloves. But I do not remember seeing her outdoors without them except on the hockey field or in a swimming pool, and certainly I have never seen gloves that remain so white as hers. My conviction is she carries extra pairs in secret pockets and changes when no one is looking, but I have not as yet over the years been able to verify this suspicion. It came the nearest to being confirmed that afternoon, when, going to summon her because the ice had come, I found she had washed six pairs.

That night at dinner, the Captain asked if we would like to see Stromboli, but told us only after we had declared emphatically our eagerness for the sight we would come within view at three in the morning. We were too far into our eagerness by that time to back out of it, but Luz did say, strategically, she was afraid none of us had an alarm clock. It was a good try on her part, but unsuccessful. The Captain would have us telephoned from the bridge.

That night going to bed, we told one another the Captain was not a man to forget. The telephone rang at a quarter to three. My bed was the nearest to it so I answered. I had come too suddenly to the surface from too deep a sleep, however, to grasp the meaning of the message that came to me, in the English employed. What I heard and interpreted was, "Do you enjoy the night on the ship?"

I said I did and even managed to include, "Thank you for asking." When I had hung up, I said aloud into the darkness, "Of all the idiotic things to ask a passenger at this hour."

The others had been awakened by the telephone to a higher stratum of comprehension than mine. They were already scrambling out of bed; Sophy had turned on the lights. They got into top coats and bedroom slippers, and told me impatiently as I sat blinking in my bed the call had been the promised alert for Stromboli. Nothing like the sound of "Stromboli" had come to me over the wire, but I left my bed and, fumbling my way into coat and slippers, followed the others on deck.

It was a beautiful night, clear of fog and starry above. We had been watchers of the sky and horizon for ten minutes or more, first on one side of the ship, then the other, taking turns at Luz's glasses, when Sophy asked in a small voice, "What are we looking for?"

"Stromboli!" we told her in unison, trailing off our incredulity with, "What on earth did you think?" and "What do you suppose brought us out in the cold at this hour?"

I doubt that I shall see Sophy so subdued again as she was in our midst on that cold 3 A.M. "I know it's Stromboli," she told us apologetically, "I just don't know what it is."

I shall put a garland of roses around this moment in my memory book, this one moment in my life, three A.M. on Sunday, May the first, nineteen hundred and fifty-five, when I was able to give a piece of geographic information, and I gave it. "Stromboli," I said, "is a volcano." Let others talk of what India is east of, and what Trans-Jordan comes between, or bring a forefinger to a dot on a map like a flying dart to the bull's eye. Once upon a night in the Mediterranean, I said, "Stromboli is a volcano."

Not long after that beautiful moment we saw a small, steady light at the rim of the horizon. We saw it almost simultaneously; we had not returned to our separate posts after my remarkable announcement. We watched it for some minutes, silently, in wonder that we should be seeing such a sight at such an hour. Luckily we did not turn our backs simultaneously to return to our cabins. Luz was still watching, as the others, murmuring about bed and the before-dawn chill, were moving toward the door to the warm inside. She said, sharp and high, "Look! Oh Heavens, look!"

The tone of her voice caused the three of us to turn on our heels and see, boiling up into the sky, a mass of blinding red, and around its rim of color, black, tumbling clouds. I have seen floods and a tornado. I never saw a cyclone, nor a waterspout, nor an avalanche, but of all the tempestuous things in nature I have witnessed, I never looked at anything so terrifying, so awful, and so beautiful in its wildness and brilliance as Stromboli's eruption.

We stayed on deck half an hour after the last glow had died away, and in that time saw two lesser eruptions, neither of them comparable to the giant. I do not know what the light was we had first identified as the great volcano; we had difficulty even finding again such a pusillanimous twinkle when the fireworks had ceased. Probably it was a lighthouse on or near the island itself.

We went to bed for an hour, but we were up again a little after five and on our top deck, because we were passing through the Straits of Messina. "Idiotic," I said to myself, because I was close to tears. I walked away from the others and told myself again as I leaned over the rail how ridiculous this emotion was. Nevertheless it was disturbing to my equanimity to be actually, physically, moving between Scylla and Charybdis so many years after a little girl had first heard the story read by her mother. "On the other part are two rocks, whereof the one reaches with sharp peak to the wide heaven, and a dark cloud encompasses it; this never streams away, and there is no clear air about the peak neither in summer nor in harvest tide. No mortal man may scale it or set foot thereon, not though he had twenty hands and feet. For the rock is smooth, and sheer, as it were polished. And in the midst of the cliff is a dim cave turned to Erebus, toward the place of darkness, whereby ye shall even steer your hollow ship, noble Odysseus. Not with an arrow from a bow might a man in his strength reach from his hollow ship in that deep cave. And therein dwelleth Scylla, yelping terribly . . . a dreadful monster is she, nor would any look on her gladly, not if it were a god that met her. . . .

"But that other cliff, Odysseus, thou shalt note, lying lower, hard by the first: thou couldest send an arrow across. And thereon is a great fig-tree growing in fullest leaf, and beneath it mighty Charybdis sucks down black water; for thrice a day she spouts it forth, and thrice a day she sucks it down in terrible wise. Never mayest thou be there when she sucks the water, for none might save thee then from thy bane, not even the Earthshaker! But take heed and swiftly drawing nigh to Scylla's rock drive the ship past, since of a truth it is far better to mourn six of thy company in the ship, than all in the selfsame hour."

We were moving through this dark and fearsome place on a gentle spring morning with the sun just risen and soft over the horizon.

I turned to rejoin my friends and saw a sailor come out on our deck carrying a wreath of flowers. I watched him incredulously, because I thought he was going to toss it on the water, a propitiatory offering to the gods to see us safely through the straits, and that we were not only in the physical world of Odysseus but in the pattern of his times. The sailor did not take the wreath, however, to the ship's rail. He climbed a ladder up a mast, and watching him I wondered confusedly if greater importance would be given by throwing the offering from a height. When I saw him attach the wreath to the mast, and climb down the ladder again, I knew what this was and laughed aloud with pleasure that I had witnessed a holdover from an old pagan rite, not one to avert the dangers from Scylla and Charybdis, but to celebrate the arrival of spring. This was the first of May and he had hung a May Day wreath.

Chapter Four

WE DOCKED at Messina at half past six, but our group did not leave the ship immediately. We stood at the rail engrossed in watching the meeting between a group of passengers with their relatives and friends on the dock. What caught our attention was the sight of the men kissing one another, each man kissing every other man, and not one of the women kissing anybody, man or woman. There were children of all ages down to babies in arms, all of them except the infants dressed in deep black.

Mrs. Fidao, the hostess on the *Queen Frederica*, a delightful person who had become our friend, joined us as we were watching. We questioned her about the people on shore. She was curiously reluctant at first to answer, and a little evasive. Finally, smiling at our persistence, she told us the arrivals were bringing back for burial a very old lady, the matriarch of all the people we were watching on the dock. She had died in New York, where she had lived for nearly fifty years, but before her death had begged to be returned to her homeland. Mrs. Fidao's reluctance to tell us this, she admitted on further questioning, was because of an old superstition that it was unlucky to travel on a ship that carried death. Another thread, I thought, weaving into the old pagan pattern, that made Scylla and Charybdis living monsters of terror; that paid homage to spring with flowered garland and put a taboo on the acknowledgment of death in a ship's cargo.

Mrs. Fidao went ashore with us. Messina has no piers. The ships that dock there sidle up to the quay that is in itself a widening of the main street. It was curious to step directly from the *Queen* into a thoroughfare with some traffic going by, though it was only seven o'clock, and a Sunday morning. A cluster of horse-drawn carriages was only a few yards away from the gangplank. The drivers of these urged us to ride about the town and up to the monastery on the top of the hill overlooking it, from which we would have a magnificent view. We indicated we preferred to walk. Mrs. Fidao led the way because she knew the town.

For a time we headed a considerable procession. Some of the drivers, disgruntled by our decision and perhaps hopeful we might change our minds, brought their carriages in stately single file behind us and called out to us from time to time a hopeful and inquiring "Hello?" When discouraged they had finally turned back and the clop of the horses' hoofs on the cobblestones was gone, the place was still, and we lowered our voices hastily from the pitch that had been necessary over the "Hellos" and the horses. In such quiet the church bells startled us. Mrs. Fidao had brought us to the church square, hurrying us a little so that at a quarter past seven we might see the mechanical gilded figures from the tower, much like the ones in Venice, move out from niches in the tower and strike a massive gong while the church bells pealed.

Very little of the city is old, though the cathedral was begun in the early eleventh century. The town was almost completely destroyed by the dreadful earthquake of 1908. Its record of tenacity would be difficult for any community to equal. It fell to the Carthaginians in 397 B.C., freed itself and rebuilt the city. Octavian's troops took it. It shook itself free. The Saracens overwhelmed it, and later the Normans. The plague and cholera, a century apart, each wiped out the greater part of its inhabitants. The people of Messina do not take kindly to being eradicated, in fact they do not admit it: they rebuild. If the town on May Day looked to me a little shiny new, even a little smug, under the circumstances I count this not only pardonable but estimable.

We were very nearly left in Messina. Mrs. Fidao had deserted us at the church: she must get back to the ship she had told us. We had continued our leisurely exploration, made a circle of the town and had come to the quay alongside the *Queen* when one of us happened to catch sight of Mrs. Fidao on deck. She seemed to be waving directly at us and in rather an excited fashion for so calm a person as we had found her to be. Next, we saw her dispatch a sailor down the gangplank. He came on the run to us and indicated by pantomime we should follow him at the same gait. We did, apologizing our way through the crowd gathered to watch the ship, and felt a little foolish, we said to one another, as we jog-trotted in single file behind our leader.

Mrs. Fidao was waiting at the top of the gangplank. We asked what had happened. Nothing, she said, except that the boat should have left half an hour earlier. A mistake, fortunate for us, had been made over the baggage of an American couple among our passengers who had reached their destination here at Messina. They were going to take a motor trip through Sicily and had brought their station wagon with them from New York, also their dog. The dog had traveled with them in quarters close to theirs, the car had not. The car that had been swung out from the bowels of the ship and deposited at their feet, was not their station wagon. Therefore, it had to be returned and exchanged for the proper one. This had occasioned a half-hour delay. Had Mrs. Fidao not happened to accompany us, no one would have known we had got up and gone ashore. There had been no such foolishness as landing cards for Messina. She also had happened to spot us in the crowd, innocently and interestedly watching the transfer of automobiles. Obviously we had misunderstood the hour for departure.

The other three were deeply mortified and apologized to the Captain at lunch. I saw no reason to feel chagrined. It seemed to me thoroughly understandable that we should be somewhat off in our timekeeping when the day had begun for us with the eruption of Stromboli at three. I was perplexed to find it was still Sunday.

The Captain asked us to be his guests that evening at the last-night gala. It would be held in the tourists' lounge, he told us. I think none of our group will forget the occasion, even if we had not participated in one of the native dances which, to our considerable astonishment, we did at the end of the program.

The Master and his officers led us from the dining room with some ceremony to the cabin-class salon. Along a passageway we asked if we might pause a moment at the open doorway of a cabin to speak to Mrs. Fidao and watch her adjusting and putting the final touches to Greek costumes on a group of young women crowded into the small room.

When we had moved on I asked the Captain if a supply of costumes was kept on the ship for such occasions as this. He said they did have a few but that the majority of them had been brought by their wearers. He went on to say probably none of the young women who had brought them had been to Greece before. He happened to know that on this crossing most of the Greek passengers were members of Mr. Papadakis' or another pilgrimage, whose leader we had not met. Because these were traveling under special auspices he knew their personnel more intimately than he would have known about individual passengers. Therefore, he was sure of what he was saying: that the younger members of the two groups were American born. Among Greeks, however, the national feeling was so strong every one of these, he was sure, knew the old Greek dances and songs far better than their relatives whom they would meet for the first time in Greece, and who had never left their homeland. The costumes were family treasures, brought out and worn in America on Greek national holidays, and every Greek child, wherever born or brought up, learned his native language, was made to use it, and never allowed to forget it. This was carried on faithfully, no matter how many generations lived in a foreign land.

"A Greek is always Greek," he said. "That is why when the Turks leave our land after five hundred years of occupation, we are not Turkish, we are Greek, as if the Turks came just the day before." Greek had not been allowed to be taught in the schools during that occupation, he said, but parents had taught the children at home, quietly, and they had spoke it at home, very quietly. He shrugged his shoulders and smiled apologetically. "Greeks are Greeks," he concluded.

Shortly after our arrival the program began with a few words of welcome from the Captain. He was followed by a Greek priest who evidently made a stirring address, because he was frequently interrupted by bursts of enthusiastic applause. We nudged Darn at each one of the interruptions during the early part of the speech, but at each prodding she only shook her head.

Finally, she whispered, "Well, he hasn't mentioned food or railway tickets or hotel rooms or weather."

We did not query Darn again.

In spite of the austerity of his long black robe, stiff, high cap, and hedge of beard that concealed the lower part of his face, the youthfulness of the speaker emerged in the tone and vitality of his voice and the motions of his slight figure. I had seen him first shortly after we had boarded the ship and pointed him out to my companions, commenting on the similarity between his hairdo and mine. I do not remember having seen before a priest of the Greek Orthodox Church, and therefore had been surprised to notice his hair was long and gathered up in a knot at the nape of his neck with a hairnet, secured by pins, much like my own hair, except that his was not braided. After that we had encountered him on deck or occasionally at mealtime on the way to the dining room. When Darn was along they had exchanged a shy greeting of, "*Kalimera*," "Good morning," or "*Kalispera*," "Good evening." The rest of us would echo the phrases self-consciously. The priest had seemed pleased by our attempts.

On the night of the Captain's dinner, on our way to bed at the end of the party, we had passed him in our corridor and when Darn had given him her usual "*Kalispera*" he had whipped up his robe, thrust his hand into some inner pocket and withdrawn it holding a watch. Displaying this to Darn with a staccato forefinger, he had said, "*Kalimera*" and they had laughed with an excess of hilarity we all of us display in order to register we have understood a joke in a foreign language. The priest was showing her with his watch it was after midnight.

Nothing in these exchanges or in the thunderous cascade of syllables in his oration at the gala prepared me for a telephone call I received five months later on the twenty-eighth of October in the Wade Hampton Hotel at Columbia, South Carolina. Answering, I heard a pleasant masculine voice with a pronounced southern accent asking if I were Miss Emily Kimbrough. Having corroborated that, I was unable from stupefaction to say anything further for some time, as I listened to the owner of the voice identify himself as the Reverend Homer Goumenis, the Greek chaplain on board the *Queen Frederica*. I could only murmur some inarticulate inanity when he expressed his regret at not being able to come that evening to my speaking engagement, because both he and his wife could not leave the children and he had volunteered to be the baby-sitter and allow Mrs. Goumenis to come. This man, in his long, black robe and hair done up in a hairnet talking to me in a southern accent of baby-sitting! I blushed at my end of the telephone remembering my toothy mouthings at him so that he would be sure to understand good morning or good evening, when Darn was not there to lead the way in Greek.

He explained as I remained in this dazed and embarrassed silence the job of chaplain for that voyage of the *Queen Frederica* had been offered, and he had accepted it gratefully because it had enabled him and his wife to take a wonderful trip, and they were still reliving it at home in Columbia, South Carolina. I managed to respond with enthusiasm about the trip, but I was unable to bring the conversation to a discovery of why he had been Greek to us.

After the priest had finished his speech on the gala night, the treasurer of the Laconians Association, the pilgrimage led by Mr. Papadakis, reported the sum of contributions that had been solicited for the relief of the city of Volos, recently very nearly destroyed by an earthquake. Souvenir ribbons were distributed to all of us as marks of gratitude for contributions.

The dancing began. The young women we had seen getting into their costumes made an entrance. They were joined by men in the audience, men of all ages and a wide variety of girth.

The Captain leaned over, whispered to me, "You see how I told you. Everyone knows these dances."

I realized from this the dancers had not been rehearsed. The men and women formed a circle in space cleared in the center of the room. They did not join hands; instead each man took from his vest pocket a handkerchief, and unfolding it offered it to the girl next to him, though he still held one corner. She took the opposite corner. This was the way the circle was joined together. The music began and the circle moved first in one direction and then another, by a series of intricate steps, expertly performed. I did not see a signal given, so I do not know what cue marked a moment when one of the young women would drop the handkerchief she had been holding in her left hand. Holding the one at her right, she danced toward the center of the circle, and performed a few solo steps that included several pirouettes under the upraised arm of the partner whose handkerchief she still held. When she had resumed her place in the circle and accepted again the end of the handkerchief she had previously dropped, the man on her right would relinquish one handkerchief and execute alone toward the center of the circle, an elaborate *pas seul.* All this while the circle continued moving, performing in unison an intricate step, though not so intricate nor in so fast a tempo as the soloist's. The soloists themselves did not step forward in orderly sequence. Sometimes a dancer across the circle from the last soloist would indicate, by dropping one of his two handkerchiefs, the spirit had moved him to an individual sally.

There was never a break in the rhythm, and the continuous flow of it was beautiful to watch. I had not seen other folk dancing quite like it. This included no jumping in the air, kicking nor staccato heel-clicking. In these figures the feet were not lifted high off the floor. They moved backward, forward, with rapidity and in complex design. In these Greek dances, too, the participants did not punctuate the steps as some folk dancers do, with shouts or stamps. The only sound above the orchestra music was a soft beat on the floor.

The last number on the program I shall remember longest. In the preceding figures some of the men had dropped out and been replaced by others from the audience. Women, unable to resist the provocative rhythm, had enlarged the circle, laughing a little self-consciously as they broke in, and then almost immediately becoming seriously absorbed in maintaining without a misstep, the even flow. Just as the Captain had promised, everyone seemed to know all the steps.

When it was announced by the orchestra leader, and translated to our group by the Captain, this would be the Kalamatianos dance, and the last one, the impromptu volunteers and all the men returned to their seats. It was the only dance of the evening given by the women without men partners. They extended handkerchiefs to one another just as the men had done. The movement was slow at first, but within a minute or two the rhythm began to quicken, and from that moment accelerated rapidly, the feet pounding on the floor, not gliding over it as in the preceding measures. Each soloist danced with a violence and abandon totally unlike anything we had seen earlier. At the end of each solo, too, the dancer instead of moving back into place and picking up the handkerchief, left the circle in a leap. In this fashion the circle narrowed until there were only two dancing round and round together, then one, dancing even more wildly than any of the others, and at the end hurling herself from the place where the circle had been.

When the tumultuous applause had finally stopped, and most of the audience had left their seats to push toward the dancers, congratulating them, the Captain leaned again to us. "It is called the Kalamatianos," he said, "and the music is the song 'Zalongo.' It does not go back to antiquity, so it is not a legend. It is a true story from the time of the Turkish occupation about 1800. There was a wild chief, a bandit from Albania. He conquer everything. Murder everybody. But he could not take Souli. Nobody could take Souli. Three hundred and fifty years the Turks were trying, and nobody could take Souli. Women learned to fight like the men, and always there was fighting. But one time, this man, this tyrant, try a trick. He asks for a truce. He signs a peace treaty. All the men from Souli come to this by his order. Then he leads them into a trap and kills all except some he takes prisoners. The women find out about this. They go out and fight. But one day they find their ammunition is finished. All is over. They know they be taken. They go back to the village. Now there is no more fighting. The conquerors come inside. The women know they are coming. Do you know what the women do? They dance. They dance this dance, only in the middle of the circle they put all their children, and when each woman finishes her special part, she does not go back to the circle. No. She takes her children and pushes them over the cliff that is just behind where they are dancing. And when she has pushed them over, she jumps after them. All of them are in their most beautiful costumes, costumes for feast days. And the last one who jumps over is Helena Botzaris, the daughter of the chieftain. Her costume is all bright, bright red. And that is what the conquerors see when they come into the village, the bright, bright red falling out of sight."

"Sometimes they sing now when they dance," the Captain added. "They sing that song of 'Zalongo.' " He translated a little.

I wrote some of it down.

> Farewell, unhappy world, farewell sweet life:
> Farewell, farewell forever, our poor Country . . .
>
> . . . .
>
> The fish cannot live in dry land,
> Nor the blossom in the salted sand of the beach,
> And the women of Souli cannot live without liberty.

The women of Souli descend into Hades—the free
city of death—
With festal dance and songs of joy.

The evening ended with general dancing, but not in couples. We all participated in the simpler of the circle dances, and when I say "all" I include Darn, Luz, Sophy and Emily. My palms moisten now from my embarrassment at remembering I even dropped a handkerchief and flounced toward the center in a skittish improvisation. So did the others. Sophy's was the most spirited. It more nearly resembled a Highland fling than anything else identifiable. Luz's was the best, but there are no people more tactful, nor warm of heart than the Greeks. They cheered us impartially.

We had very little sleep that night. We were up at dawn. We had spent ten days on the *Queen Frederica* with nothing whatever that required being done. Consequently, we had postponed packing until the daybreak of our departure. Furthermore, as Darn reminded us when she got us out of bed, we had not filled in our customs declarations. Nothing could have been more indicative of the happy slough in which we had floated for ten days than Darn's indifference to filling out a form, because hers is the most highly self-systematized life I have ever observed. I have also noted over the years there are few activities more pleasurable to her than writing things down.

We packed, that morning, before we wrote down, but when Mrs. Fidao called on us around nine o'clock, she found us sitting disgruntled on the floor. Sophy and I were in our cabin, Darn and Luz in theirs beyond; all of us unpacking the suitcases we had so recently sat on to close. She had brought us an invitation from the Master to come to the bridge for our first view of Athens, and watch from there our landing at Piraeus.

"Shouldn't you be packing?" she asked. "They'll come soon for the bags, you know. You seem to be taking things out."

"We have to," Sophy told her, and explained, the rest of us providing a background chorus of exasperated mutterings. "Darn has just found an item on the declaration slip we hadn't noticed before—tissues, of all things. So we have to take everything out to count the number of boxes of Kleenex we're taking in. Every one of us has packed them in and around other things because by themselves they take up so much more room."

Mrs. Fidao leaned against the door, and put her hand over her face a minute. "Oh, my dears," she told us, "tissue means material—yardage. If you were bringing stuff for dresses or suits, that is what you would have to declare."

Tactfully, she left at once. We repacked with very little conversation.

The Captain did not preside at lunch. Mr. Panaiotopoulos brought his regrets that he could not at this time leave the bridge. Before we had left the table another message came inviting us to the bridge as soon as we cared to come.

We cared to come at once, and Mr. Panaiotopoulos led the way. Immediately we had climbed to this exalted lookout spot, we saw the Captain in the center enclosed portion; the control room I would have called it, in a radio or television station, but I have not the slightest notion what its nautical identification is. Immediately the four of us moved to that place, I'm sure with the same idea in mind, that we must speak to our host and thank him for asking us to his party.

Mr. P. stopped us peremptorily. "You cannot go in there," he said, "and you must not speak to the Master at this time."

Subdued, we backed away to a far corner of the outer exposed section. For a minute or two we watched the Captain, seeing a man we had not known before. This was not the affable, humorous luncheon and dinner host, quick to laugh with his guests and make pleasant social relations among them. This was the Admiral, stern, quiet, giving orders in a tone so low we could not hear the sound, but we saw officers receiving them and bringing him reports that he acknowledged with a nod of the head, and not a look in their direction. He watched the scene before him and presently we watched it, too.

We seemed to have moved from a large, outer harbor into an inner one. This harbor was evidently home plate, or whatever is the marine equivalent that indicates a ship has touched base. Our ship indicated it by a giddy demonstration. Flags in streamers were threaded on lines above us; others burst out of fireworks that were set off very unexpectedly from somewhere below and behind us. Again, I thanked a merciful providence and a ship's architect who made the rail around the bridge I was backed against even higher than that around the lower deck, and solid. No one had told me there were going to be fireworks, and at the moment of the first explosion I was engrossed in taking a picture of a comical-looking, and very fat, Greek sailor, a prototype of Beetle Bailey's sergeant in the comics, who was sending aloft the trolleys that carried the little flags. The camera hung around my neck on a leather strap. When I jumped into the air, as I did, of course, at the unexpected bang of the first fireworks, the camera between my hands jumped, too, and gave me a vicious crack on the nose. But I did not go over the rail.

Little boats and big boats saluted as we neared them. The air now was dotted with Greek and American flags exploded from the fireworks, floating down toward the water on tiny parachutes. The shoreline was misty though the day was sunny. Mr. P. helpfully and eagerly endeavored over and over again to show us the outline of the Acropolis, but even with Luz's glasses none of us could find it. He was diverted by the close approach of a small stylish yacht and distracted our concentration from a shore we couldn't see clearly to the occupants of the yacht, almost directly below us. A man and woman reclined in low chairs on its deck.

Mr. P. chuckled as he pointed them out to us. "They are brother and sister," he said, "and principal stockholders of the line that owns our rival ship, the *Olympia*. They have come out to see us land. They will try to count the passengers and look over what kind of people we have."

We were indignant at such effrontery, realizing simultaneously what an aggressive loyalty we had developed for the *Queen Frederica*, and our unexpected and thoroughly quixotic reluctance to quit her.

For a considerable time before we reached the dock we could see a band playing animatedly, but we were quite close before we could distinguish any sound. The refrain that finally reached our ears was a familiar one, though I had not before heard "The Star-Spangled Banner" rendered in dreamy waltz time. The air that followed was unfamiliar to me but Mr. P., by stiffening to attention, identified it as the Greek national anthem. When the second time round of this sequence began, we were close enough to see a crowd on the dock, almost every member of it carrying a large bunch of flowers. I pointed this out to my friends as a charming gesture of welcome to those on the ship they had come to meet. Sophy's comment was she couldn't imagine anything much more unhandy than a large bunch of flowers in your arms while you were trying to show your passport, get out your declaration list and tip the porters.

We all rounded on her, urging that, in the little time left her before she landed in Greece, she endeavor to cultivate an awareness of the aesthetic.

The ship was slowly coasting into the dock when we finally and reluctantly made ready to leave the bridge, dreading to descend to the boiling turmoil of debarking that would engulf us below. The Captain came to us from his citadel and he was our friend again. We thanked him for all his courtesies and kindnesses to us, told him, truthfully, how thoroughly we had enjoyed the crossing and particularly being at his table. We assured him, untruthfully, we would of course see him often when he brought his ship into New York, knowing, as he knew, that passengers and Captain, or even shipboard friends, seldom meet again.

Mr. P. was caught up even before we were. At the very foot of the steps from the bridge he was accosted by passengers wishing to say good-by. He called out to us he would see us in Athens within the next day or so.

Once in ignorance, I poured an entire package of corn to be popped into a very small skillet for which I had no lid. What happened was closely approximated by what was going on when we reached the stair landings and the corridors leading to our stateroom. We were disheveled by the time we reached our own sanctuary. To our considerable surprise, we found it occupied by a young woman, and a young man who seemed to be an assistant to the young woman, because she not only took the lead but introduced herself and did not introduce him.

"I am Mrs. Vanvakos," she said. "I am the secretary of Mr. Papastratos. He regrets very much he must be away from the city this week, but sent me to meet you and help you to your hotel."

For a moment I was dazed by all the syllables of Papastratos, then I remembered. "He is Kakia's brother-in-law," I told the others. "She said she was going to write him but I had no idea so much trouble would be taken for us."

How little at that time I knew the Greeks and the trouble they take for a visitor.

Mrs. Vanvakos had walked away from us after introducing herself, but called back over her shoulder, "That is right. Mr. Papa-

GREECE
LEVADIA
DELPHI
THEBES
MARATHON
PATRAS
CORINTH
PIRAEUS
ATHENS
MYCENAE
NAUPLIA
PELOPONNESUS
EPIDAURIS
BOUTZEI
SOUNION
DELOS
MYKONOS
CHIOS
TURKEY
MELOS
SANTORIN
RHODES
CRETE
HERAKLION
Vasiliu

stratos had a letter from Mrs. Livanos. Many people had letters. You will see."

She had gone into Darn's and Luz's room. She came back now with the young man, who had stayed at her heels. Each of them scarcely enclosed with their two arms bunches of red carnations, a bunch for each of us.

Sophy was as cordial in her words of thanks as the rest of us, but a few minutes later when I was trying to place the flowers under my arm in such a way as to make it possible for me to carry my top coat, fur, camera, large handbag and a book written by the Captain and sent down to me that morning after the bags had been removed, I happened to catch Sophy's eye. I have never seen on any countenance a smile more benign, more smug, more expressive of "What did I tell you?" I felt an undignified and unchristian urge to whack my gift of welcome on the top of her chic hat.

Chapter Five

NO *ONE* in the whirlpool of people outside our cabin seemed to know how to get off the ship. Mrs. Vanvakos, who had appeared so competent in the stateroom, was unable to tell us in the corridor by what route she had reached us. I saw a woman in a red hat elbow her way purposefully through the crowd and I called to our party to follow her. It was not easy, but determinedly we tracked her down three flights of stairs, crowded all the way. She led us up other stairs. When we caught up with her we recognized we were in the tourist-class lounge where the gala had been held. We caught up with her because she had reversed and was heading our way.

At sight of us she stopped and said briskly, "Could you tell me how to get off the ship? I am lost."

She joined our troupe and we made our way back as we had come, to our own stateroom. I was all for going inside and waiting comfortably until we would be, inevitably, swept off with the other forms of residue left behind, but I was overruled and persuaded to keep moving. A few yards beyond the door to our extra room along the corridor, we were jostled into a ship's officer. Standing as immovably as he could, he was pointing toward our own deck only a few feet to the right of his outstretched arm. Arriving there, I saw swaying from the outer rail of the deck a fragile little flight of steps with, instead of a sturdy rail, a rope on either side, and the ropes were looped like garlands. This was our avenue of exit from the ship.

"I would sooner be lowered over the side in a basket than make my own way down this fairy trellis," I said forcefully, and reiterated my recent plan to return to my own stateroom. Again I was overridden by my friends, and also not permitted by them to sit on the top step and ease my way down to the dock in that position.

Had anyone told me as I stood wide-eyed and clammy-fingered at the head of that silly trellis I would within the month be climbing up and down even more cobweb structures, not my friends and the entire ship's personnel combined could have restrained me from barricading myself within my cabin and not setting foot out of it until I could place it on a firm gangplank down to the dock in New York. I am profoundly grateful no one did give me this knowledge.

On the dock I leaned against a stanchion until my knees should stop trembling. My three companions spotted luggage tumbling out of a large door on the ship, open at pier level, and went on the gallop to isolate our collection. Mrs. Vanvakos, her aide at her heels, went in the opposite direction to commandeer porters.

I was alone, when, happening to look up, I saw a piece of luggage, a length of rope around it, swinging in the air in a rapid descent, and simultaneously with the discovery of this remarkable sight, I identified the object as one of my own bags. I watched, spellbound, cringing with apprehension at its inevitable impact on the dock, and the effect on my belongings of the bag's demolishment. My voice could not have carried up to whoever was at the far end of the rope, and I had no vocabulary for such a crisis, whatever my lung power. My first thought was to hurl myself under the descending piece and break its impact, but my second and more practical one was that it would be more difficult to assemble me, afterward, than my belongings. Urgency, however, had restored to my limbs their ability to function, and I ran to the spot on the dock where I expected the collision to take place.

A collision did occur, but it was not between my bag and the stone pier. It was a headlong interference by me with a porter. I was looking at my bag in the air, and for a few seconds, from lack of breath after I had crashed him, he was unable to tell me why he was there. The speech he regained was of no use to me. But he got a message through by pantomime that he was one of a team of porters, that his partner was the unknown aloft, and this labor-saving device was uniquely their own invention.

This was evidently so, because at the arrival of the man I had butted, the plummeting descent of my large case had slackened, and the bag now hung almost motionless, directly over our heads.

Vasiliu

The teammate beside me diverted his pantomime from me to a two-arm wig-wagging signal, and in response to it the bag was gently eased down onto the dock. With a skillful twitch of the rope my neighbor released the sling and the rope was rapidly drawn upward again.

The ground member of the team swung my bag onto his shoulder and with a peremptory wave of the hand to me to follow, was off toward the customs house at a dogtrot. I imitated him but at an even quicker pace, and catching him by the arm indicated in pantomime he was to return the bag and himself to the place at which he had picked it up, since this was not the only piece of luggage that belonged to me. Counting rapidly on my fingers twice round, I gave him the idea that a considerable surprise was in store for him if he thought I was traveling so light.

I returned him and his burden to the spot where the rope might fall again, gave him a firm gesture I once learned in a training class for dogs that means "stay," and went to find my friends. I dared not go far because I was not sure the porter would be as obedient to my signal as my poodle had been. Therefore, I did a sort of solo Virginia reel, a few paces up the dock and back to him again, hallooing and whistling the while at my group. I attracted the attention of a goodly number of passengers from the ship who were making their way toward the customs house, but it was some time before I caught the notice of the ones I wanted to reach.

Darn was the first to heed me. Once she had attracted the attention of the others to my inexplicable choice of time and place for indulging in a dance, they all came on the run. They were, if anything, even more alarmed than I had been to learn that ours were the bags selected by this pair of inventors for displaying their unloading device. The unloader on the dock in our midst was a little alarmed, too, and more than a little surprised, twenty-four times, when each one of this number was identified as ours. After the twenty-fourth, the member above signaled this was the end and disappeared.

It was a pity, I thought, that Mrs. Vanvakos returned with two porters, and of course her aide, at the moment we were enjoying from our porter and his mate, who had joined him, a lifelike imitation of a donkey as the only carrier possible for such a mound of luggage. Our twenty-four pieces were distributed among the four porters under Mrs. Vanvakos' supervision, and I naïvely supposed we would now proceed without further interruption to the customs house. We had gained only a slight yardage when Mrs. Vanvakos was addressed by two young men, one of them carrying a camera. Mrs. Vanvakos stopped, and since she was leading our procession we all stopped.

She brought the two young men down our line to Luz. "Miss Taylor," she said, "here are a reporter and a photographer. They would like to make some pictures of you and ask a few questions, with your permission."

Luz groaned. "Oh no," she said, "not again. I am *not* Elizabeth Taylor, the motion-picture actress."

The reporter understood English but he looked bewildered. "Oh no, madame," he said, "I do not know about your motion-picture actress, but my paper has been told you are the commander of all the women in America."

Luz was less astonished than the rest of us. The young man's identification of Luz had pictured for me a form of government in our country of which up to that time I had been totally unaware. Sophy was bridling a little and muttering, "She's nothing of the sort."

Luz spoke soothingly, though she looked a little agitated. "Oh no," she said, "you are mistaken. But I think I know what you mean. I am simply a member of a national committee appointed by our President to look after the welfare of all the women of my country who are in any branch of our armed services."

Sophy grew calm. We all looked proudly at Luz.

The young man was obdurate. Whatever Luz chose to call herself was her affair. He had been told by the editor what she was, and certainly the editor of his newspaper knew more than any American tourist. He couched this verdict politely, but he brooked no further argument from Luz. He leveled his camera sternly, and Luz yielded, insisting only that we all be photographed. He was magnanimous about this.

Next day the group photograph appeared in the Athens newspaper and the caption, translated for us, identified Darn, Sophy and me as companions to the "Commander."

The photography completed, we were not interrupted again until we reached a long counter in the customs building. This interruption was scarcely more than a pause. It may have been the words Mrs. Vanvakos murmured to the man behind the counter, but I am more inclined to believe it was the sight of twenty-four pieces of luggage on a steaming hot afternoon that made him put an official stamp of approval on each piece without so much as a look inside, and wave us on. In spite of his obvious impatience to be rid of us we paused voluntarily at the sight of His Excellency and Mme. de Romero. We had not seen them in the hurly-burly of leaving the ship and wanted to say good-by.

They were talking to a strikingly beautiful woman with blond hair, fair complexion and blue eyes as dark as cornflowers. Mme. de Romero introduced us to her, and I was profoundly thankful that when she pronounced our names she repeated the name of her friend. As I heard the repetition of "Mme. Pothamianos," I clutched at its syllables in a desperate effort to keep them together in my memory, though I was somewhat distracted by the realization that up to now I had assumed all Greeks to be dark-haired and brown-eyed.

Mme. Pothamianos was evidently not baffled by the combination of syllables that identified us. The instant she heard them she said in English, engagingly, "You are the new friends I am going to meet. I know about you in a letter from Kakia Livanos. I am coming to call. These," she indicated the de Romeros, "are very old, very dear friends. Now we are all friends. That is lovely, isn't it?"

"And so are you," I thought to myself, as we left with promises all around we would meet soon again. "And so are all the Greeks; warm, hospitable, thoughtful, like Mr. Papastratos sending people to help us off the boat."

When Mrs. Vanvakos sorted us into a car sent by Mr. Papastratos and additional taxis rounded up efficiently by her gentleman assistant, I was ready to approach all Greeks not with a clasp of hands across the sea, but an affectionate fling of arms around the neck. Approximately three minutes later I was damning all of them, and to a special purgatory the driver of the taxi in which I was riding, the behavior of other drivers we encountered, the pedestrians, who paid not the slightest heed to our maniacal advance on them, and Mrs. Vanvakos. Each time I begged her to tell the driver to go slowly, and my entreaties followed so close on one another as to be a continuous chant of supplication, she made a sound that was to my ear a derisive chortle of pleasure. I learned this is the word for "slow." It is spelled "*a-r-g-h-a*." In answer, the driver shook his head negatively. The gesture means "yes" in Greek. I didn't know these things at the time.

Mrs. Vanvakos, luggage and I took up the whole of the taxi in which we rode. My friends were in the other cars. I had no one with me whose background in automobile transportation was the same as mine. I was an alien and these were hostile people. I did not like any better the scenery through which we flashed, nor the people through whom we threatened to flash. The road from Piraeus, the port of Athens, to the city proper is not attractive. The Germans cut down all the trees that formerly lined it, and those in the immediate vicinity, in order to have an unrestricted view out to sea. The road goes for a time along the shore. The total distance from Piraeus to Athens is about ten kilometers. On the side of the highway away from the sea there are houses that have once been handsome, but are now in disrepair, tumbled down; a row of blowzy slatterns.

Close to the city there is a neighborhood of recent, modern houses. Almost all of these are white, and there is little or no planting. The road is white and dusty, and the glare from this and the houses is almost intolerable. What comes after that section I had no idea on that first day.

When "we picked up trolley tracks," as the old automobile guidebooks used to say, and our driver looped among and around them, whether they were proceeding ahead of us or coming toward us, I closed my eyes. I did not open them again until a second or two after we had come to a convulsive stop. When I heard no screams and felt nothing falling on us, I opened my eyes to a prince charming who was bending over me, identifiable more explicitly by his uniform and the lettering on his cap as the doorman of the King George Hotel.

The King George Hotel would be starred by Baedeker as first class. It is not quite so fashionable as its next-door neighbor the Grande Bretagne. They are both on Constitution Square, an excellent location because every section of the city radiates from this center. Therefore, the sightseer, like the man in the song who had a shooting box in Scotland, is never far from home. If he is, like me, an innocent when it comes to a sense of direction—and I use the word "innocent" as it was used in the Middle Ages to denote a want-wit—even he can find his way back to Constitution Square, and start off again along another spoke.

We had planned originally to go to the Grande Bretagne. At one time in our planning we had every reason to believe we were going to be there. Letters had been exchanged, reservations made and accepted. At this point in the negotiations, friends of ours wrote to friends of theirs who were of executive status in the Grande Bretagne, asking we be given very special consideration. That put the kibosh on the whole thing. I knew it would, but this was a phenomenon so peculiar to me I could not have made it plausible enough for my friends to keep their helpful hands off.

It is a phenomenon I cannot rationalize to myself. I only know it exists. In the course of a year, and this has been true for the last ten years at least, I make a considerable number of trips since, in the fall and the early spring, I go on a lecture tour. The lecture bureau makes hotel reservations for me at each of my stops. Occasionally, I make my own reservations, and I do it undemonstratively like the lecture bureau. When I arrive at the appointed hotel, the reservation, whether made by the lecture bureau or me, is thoroughly satisfactory. I have the kind of accommodation I have requested. It had never occurred to me there could be a variation of this pattern until friends interested themselves in holiday trips I told them I was contemplating. The friends happened to know the owner or the manager of the best hotel in the place to which I was going; certainly I must stay there. After such a letter, or letters, as he would receive, the owner or the manager would see that I had the handsomest space in the whole establishment. This is when the phenomenon took place, and this is what the phenomenon is: The moment a manager, or hotel owner, receives word from his friends that I intend to visit his hostelry, he calls for sweepers and cleaners and orders the attic made ready. I am a Sara Crewe in any hotel at which special attention has been requested for me. The attention I receive *is* very special. Fellow guests in the places where I am living under the eaves have not known of the existence of such a room as mine.

The Grande Bretagne wrote rooms would be available for us on the dates we requested. Scarcely more than a week later, just time enough for airmail letters from this country to have reached them, and I know they were sent, I had an airmail letter from the Grande Bretagne. The management regretted deeply the best accommodations in the hotel were already booked, therefore there were no rooms for us. The last things in the world we wanted were the *best* accommodations, at corresponding prices, but that is what friends had wanted for us. Therefore, we were out on the street and in next door, at the King George Hotel, as close to the roof as it was possible to be. This, in turn, was because, through our Greek friends in New York, and friends of Luz's in the American Embassy in Athens, a number of people, learning we were coming there, had visited the King George Hotel, asking we be given very special consideration.

We had four rooms, two on each side of a narrow, dark corridor that started at the elevator and ended at a blank wall. There were a few other rooms on the corridor, two or perhaps four, but at the moment of our arrival these were unoccupied, waiting, perhaps for guests like us with special recommendations. There was nothing about any one of the four open to us that required drawing lots for first choice. Each accommodated a single bed, a shelf above the foot of it and hooks beneath, a bare table allowing the imagination full range to identify it as either a desk or a bureau, a straight-backed chair pushed as far under the table as the chair back would allow. If it was pulled out it hit the side of the bed. With the chair pushed under to its extremity, it was possible by sidling between the table and bed to reach an armchair by the one window of the room, and that looked out on a court. At the other end of the room were a bathroom, and facing it a shallow clothes closet. Each room accommodated this much, but it did not accommodate luggage in such quantity as we carried.

This was so evident to the porters carrying it they made no effort to prove it, counting their services accomplished when they had made of the separate pieces a compact mound in the center of the corridor. Mrs. Vanvakos told us what to pay them. We gave them what she had advised, and then stood braced for a hullabaloo of protest to crash around us. We knew what happens when you tip a porter in France. Nothing in the least like what we had anticipated came from the porters in Athens. They thanked us cheerfully, happily, and urged us through Mrs. Vanvakos' interpretation to let them know if there were any further services required, particularly to call them when our bags had been emptied. They would find places in our rooms to store them. We doubted this, we said to one another, but through Mrs. Vanvakos thanked them in turn for their kind offer and high hopes.

Without recommendation from Mrs. Vanvakos we gave her silent assistant an expression of our gratitude, in drachmas, for all his help with baggage and taxis. This not only evoked for us an assurance that he had the power of speech but a power of oratory. With flushed cheeks, misty eyes, hand on heart and considerable head and hair tossing, he thanked us, I suppose, and probably wished for us a happy stay in Athens. Mrs. Vanvakos murmured he was somewhat carried away because we had given him the equivalent of more than half his monthly salary. Persuaded by a few words from her, he brought his declaration to an explosive end. While he wiped his eyes with his handkerchief and then smoothed his hair with both hands, Mrs. Vanvakos told us she was going down immediately to speak to the management about our accommodations. She could not understand how such rooms could have been given us considering what the management had been told.

Alarmed, I did my best to deter her, but I could not make her understand that any further communication with the management on our behalf would bring us up on the roof, housed in tents or down on the street with no housing whatever. I could not put into understandable terms to Mrs. Vanvakos this peculiar allergy generated in a hotel management by a heralding of my coming, and so I had to let her go on her errand. But on my way back into my own room, I said gloomily to my friends it would be just as well to unpack only what we needed immediately. We would probably be dispossessed shortly! Someone was speaking for us again.

Hanging up my topcoat and fur in the clothes closet, I discovered the equipment for my wardrobe comprised three sagging wire coat hangers, drooping on a sharp slope from the weight, undoubtedly, of layers of clothes hung by previous inhabitants. I know now that one of the most valuable items to include in luggage for a trip to Greece and Yugoslavia is a case that contains a set of folding coat hangers. I had one of these given to me as a bon voyage present on several previous trips abroad, and each time, having thanked the owner, I had put the little object in a box I fill during the year with Christmas and other holiday gifts for which I can see not the slightest use. The following Christmas I use them to fill out the stockings for my family and as presents for those not included on my list but from whom at the last minute, on the day before Christmas, I have received a present. I had in the box at home four cases of folding coat hangers. Casting my eye along the dismal objects in the clothes closet of my room at the King George Hotel, I would rather have had my hand on at least one of them at that moment than my arms around both my dear children. My wardrobe was considerable, not in preparation for a giddy social whirl but for a wide variation in climate. The wire slopes in front of me would not hold up the smallest part of it.

The closet included a set of narrow shelves and I concluded I would have to store my clothes there, dresses and even suits, folded to the narrow measurements of each shelf. I would hang other garments on the hooks under the shelf at the foot of my bed. Neither of these storing places would improve the shape of my costumes when I wore them. They would either be creased in the pattern of a checkerboard or humped between the shoulder blades in the mold of the clothes hook. That was how it was going to be, I concluded, and returned to the hall.

I found my friends there burrowing into the pile of luggage to extricate their own pieces. Each pilgrim reported her storage equipment precisely like mine and her conclusions about the disposal of her garments those at which I had arrived. We also agreed on a system of unpacking: one bag at a time carried in, opened on the bed, contents emptied, empty bag pushed under the bed, and when that space was filled, a call to the porters and a dare set up to them to find additional space.

When these decisions had been reached there was little further conversation exchanged among us. An occasional news announcement called out with profane embellishments from one of the rooms that the largest of our bags would not go under the bed, and once a horrifying series of expletives from Sophy, prefacing her announcement that the hook of one of her three hangers had broken off from the body from the weight it was sustaining. She was now left with two hangers and a mound of clothes on the floor.

We happened to have converged on the diminishing luggage pile in the hall when La Belle Hélène, as we had heard Señora de Romero address Mme. Pothamianos, called on us. We heard the elevator door open. We thought porters had come at our summons and were considerably startled to hear behind us the clear, cultivated tones of a lady announcing her presence. She brought flowers with her for each of us. I knew the instant she extended the bunch for me I would not take her into my room. She could not avoid seeing there the red carnations I had received on the ship, hanging over the rim of my wastepaper basket and very dead.

Sophy invited us all into her room and we persuaded Mme. Pothamianos to sit down there. Only one person could, since the bed and the straight chair were covered with what had recently been on the floor of Sophy's closet. Mme. Pothamianos was dismayed to find us in such rooms, and said so frankly, adding she would speak at once to the management about it. She had personally requested a suite for us, including a drawing room looking out on Constitution Square. She would find out why we were not ensconced there and make sure of our removal to it instantly. I groaned and held my head in my hands, but at our caller's inquiring look in my direction found myself once more incapable of communicating to her the urgent desirability of leaving well enough, though it was far from well, but whatever it was, leaving it alone. I did implore her not to take any further trouble on our behalf, and my friends echoed my pleas fervently. But La Belle Hélène was charmingly insistent it was no trouble whatever and she would see to it at once. She rose at this, and added she would telephone us the following day. She wished to take us on some excursions, wanted us at her house, wished her husband to meet us, and their friends, and as she left, put into my hand a large box of candy.

I have not eaten candy in years for reasons apparent to anyone who has seen my figure, but after the departure of La Belle Hélène, I pushed out of the way the things that had been on Sophy's bed. There couldn't be any noticeable difference, I told her, between objects that had been on the floor once and those that had been there twice. I sat down on the space cleared, and was promptly joined there by Darn and Luz. Sophy with the courtesy of a perfect hostess cleared the straight-backed chair of the clothes on it, and sat down. The four of us went through half that box of candy with scarcely a word exchanged. I do not remember anything that has brought me such comfort in an hour of need as those sweet, chocolate-coated, pistachio sticks. When each admitted feeling a little sick, we closed the box, left it in Sophy's room and went our separate ways back to the unpacking.

I do not know how much later it was when Sophy called my name from the corridor. I had been plodding from bed to shelves in a dreary, discouraged monotony that had dulled my awareness of the passage of time. But there was a lack of dullness and discouragement in Sophy's tone that made me respond immediately to her summons.

"Will you come with me?" she asked. "I've found something I want to show you."

She led me to the elevator, turned to the right there, passed it and a serving pantry. French doors immediately ahead of us were closed. Having opened them, she stepped to one side, motioning me without speaking to go ahead. We were on what was evidently a roof garden. Tables were stacked upside down, their legs in the air and chairs were piled on top of one another in the same way. There was a wall around the rim of this area, and again Sophy indicated without a word for me to go to it. She was unusually quiet, almost as though she were holding her breath, and I caught something of suspense and anticipation from it.

I walked to the wall and leaned my elbows on the broad surface of its top. The roof garden faced Constitution Square and I first looked down at that, realizing it was late afternoon and citizens going home from work were lining up for buses. The square below was full of activity. I could see people at little tables on the sidewalk in front of cafés. The buses were along the side street to my left and my attention moved slowly from them to the bustle in the square and the pleasant sight of the cafés and their occupants. By now my range of focus was a little to my right. Perhaps Sophy willed me to lift my head there, maybe God told me this was the place and the moment to look at what I had come to Greece to see. And I saw it. I saw the Acropolis in the yellow light of the late afternoon sun. I said,

"Why, it's a crown."

In spite of all the pictures of it I have seen, I had not had any conception of its compactness, its entity, its separateness. Leaning on my elbows because I was trembling a little, I thought, "This is my crown. This is the crown of the whole Western world. Every single one of us lives under this and because of this. This is where we've got our way of life, democracy, human relations, political patterns, sculpture, literature, theater. Why, this is coming back to where I came from. This is home, my home, the home of everybody in the world I know about."

I put my head down on the top of that wall and cried.

Sophy was standing beside me. After a little while, she put her arm around my shoulder and said briskly, "Now I've got something else to show you."

I pulled myself together, whatever that means, and followed her once more; this time to a corner of the roof a little to the left of where I had been standing, but with the same view. She pointed with justifiable pride to a table there, upright on its legs, with a white tablecloth spread over it.

"Wait a minute," she told me; but before the minute, the French doors behind us opened again.

A young girl in maid's uniform came through them toward us. She carried a tray with glasses on it and a bowl of ice.

"This is Koula," Sophy said, in as proprietary a fashion as if Koula were Sophy's own Galatea. "She's our chambermaid, and she's brought the things I asked for."

"Good evening," Koula said in a soft voice with scarcely any accent. "I have brought napkins, too. Can I serve you anything else?"

"No, thank you," Sophy told her. "I have everything else we need. I'll get my shoebag and my other friends."

Chapter Six

LUZ, Sophy and I each had a camera. Darn had not brought one. This was not a matter of forgetting, she had explained, as though anyone who knew her would have conceived it possible for methodical Darn to forget anything. The reason for her omission of such a basic accessory to a tourist was she preferred writing down what she saw. Furthermore, she said, by her observation of them, travelers spent so much time squinting into their view finders or at their light meters, their outlook was as narrowed as though they wore blinders like a horse, not to mention the times they had to absent themselves altogether from the passing scene to crouch in the darkest place available, while they changed a film.

Sophy had admitted the validity of much of Darn's argument but had then contended it was based on too narrow a range of observation. "Because," she had insisted, "you evidently haven't seen people with cameras like the one I carry. I doubt you'd be likely to when you're traveling. Mine is the kind usually given to a child to learn on, and it suits me fine. It cost about $9, I think, and it takes wonderful pictures, color and black and white. You don't see me fiddling around with gadgets on it, because there aren't any. No distance regulator, no light adjuster. I just look into it, see what I want to take, push a button and it's done."

I had upheld Sophy, both as to result and method. Her pictures of any trip we had been on together were wonderful. Mine were wonderful, too, I had admitted, and I had used almost precisely Sophy's method, though my camera was a Stereo-Realist that took three-dimensional pictures to be seen through a viewer. The camera had many of the devices Darn deplored, but I didn't bother with them, adding hastily, before anyone of the three could say it, they were beyond my range of competence. I also owned, I had admitted, a pretty collection of light meters, each one a Christmas gift from either or both of my two sons-in-law, always presented with a message on the Christmas card to the effect that here was a meter I would surely be able to operate. All of them were carefully put away in a box at home.

Luz had taken no part in this conversation. When the rest of us had made our separate contributions, we had turned inquiringly toward her. Luz had fidgeted a little and then admitted apologetically she had brought along a brand-new camera, one she had got from Germany, of so new a design it was not yet on sale at home.

Darn had wagered it had every known gadget and some extra ones.

Luz had conceded all of them, including a built-in light meter as one of its extra features. She had justified her possession of such an infernal machine. "I like taking pictures," she had said.

It had seemed to the others a frail reason but I had amplified it. "Don't forget," I told them, "Luz used to fly her own plane. Once I was shown the panel board of an airplane. I expect her camera is just about the same, and she likes it."

After that summing up the conversation had drifted to other topics.

On the morning following our arrival in Athens we gathered after breakfast in my room to discuss plans for the day. Early as it was, the day had not been uneventful. I had got shut in my bathroom and only the happy accident that before entering I had pushed the bell that would bring a maid with my breakfast had provided a rescuer. She had summoned a workman of some sort. He had discovered the door was not locked. I had been endeavoring to communicate that bit of knowledge to him and the maid, but I had not the vocabulary for it. The only pantomime I had evolved on the far side of a closed door, had been to rattle the knob and call, "No, no, no," then hurl myself against the door and say, "Yes, yes, yes. Stuck."

This charade had not got through to the maid and the workman. When the door was finally pried open there had been faulty reception, too, of my urgent plea to them to get out of my room, allow me to come from behind my bathroom door, put on some article of apparel, and bestow in the corridor outside my reward for services rendered. I had finally got through to them by extending one bare limb as far as possible around the corner of the troublesome door behind which I crouched, kicking it several times in the direction of the exit to the corridor, and saying sternly with each kick, "Shoo! Shoo!"

Sophy had also experienced a ruffling, though a different sort of obstruction. Ordering a breakfast from the maid she had summoned, Sophy had confused the words Darn had taught her for "please" and "orange." Instead of requesting *portokali* she had said "*parakalo*," which is "please" and the maid responding politely "*efharisto*," which turned out to be "thank you," had stayed where she was, waiting. Sophy had repeated the word for "please" the maid had answered "thank you" and waited. When this exchange had grown tiresome to Sophy, she had abandoned speech for a pantomime so vivid it had evoked a burst of spontaneous applause from the maid, and a glass of tomato juice.

Luz had been advised in dumb show by her maid to telephone her order direct to the serving pantry on our floor and so expedite her breakfast. Whatever our rooms lacked in comfort and equipment, and that was a good deal, the service that went with them included three chambermaids. Luz, misinterpreting the message from hers, had picked up her telephone thinking she had been told there was a call for her. This had resulted in a spirited altercation between her and the telephone operator about a caller who was not being put through, until the maid had taken the instrument from Luz's hand, replaced it on the hook and fetched her breakfast.

Darn had had a delightful conversation with her maid, "All in Greek, of course," she emphasized.

She checked our rude comments with a list she had made out while waiting for her breakfast. Things, she said, we ought to do at once.

"Marathon," I prompted, "and Delphi."

"What about the Acropolis?" Luz put in. "After all that's *in* Athens."

I hadn't forgotten the Acropolis, but I hadn't mentioned it. I had thought to grow a little more accustomed to having it around before I ventured foot on it.

Darn was shaking her head impatiently. "No, no," she interupted us. "I'm not talking about places. I mean things to do before we start seeing, like coat hangers."

We were in agreement on that.

"And I'm going to order calling cards." She looked up from her list defiantly. "I did *not* forget them. It didn't occur to me to bring them, but with La Belle Hélène calling on us while we're still out in the hall, it stands to reason there will be others, and there we'll be . . ."

"In our Maidenform bras," Luz murmured.

Darn shook her head impatiently. "I'm afraid we'll have to have them printed. Otherwise it would take too long. But," she added anxiously, "do you think anybody rubs a finger over a card any more to see if it's engraved?"

Although it was only a little after ten when I came out on Constitution Square, there was already a fair number of customers seated at the sidewalk café of the King George. There were scarcely any women, and for the most part the men sat alone. Here and there I saw two at a table, but not more. This was evidently not a social hour, simply a pause in the day's occupation. Almost every customer was drinking a demitasse. I learned later this was thick, very sweet Turkish coffee. In mid-morning and afternoon the drink would be lime or lemonade; before lunch and dinner a liqueur glass of Ouzo. Cocktails, or whiskey and soda would be set down only in front of tourists. I found out, too, that Ouzo tastes like licorice and that I do not care for it.

There were vendors walking back and forth in front of the tables, weaving their way among them. They ranged in age and size from very old men to very little children, and they sold pistachio nuts in transparent paper bags about the size of a fat cigar. I bought a bag. These pistachio nuts are the most delicious I have ever tasted, much crisper than the ones we know at home. I watched and copied from the café customers the expert's way of opening them. The shells are not so tightly closed as the ones at home are likely to be, but the expert's way of opening is to pry apart one, then use an empty shell as a lever.

I left the square and strolled down a side street, looking in the shop windows I passed, listening with pleasure to the sounds of Greek in conversations of passers-by and sniffing with pleasure to catch the particular smell of Athens. I like to store in my memory the individual smell each city possesses. I know now, however, not to be so open-nostriled in Athens. I drew into my lungs an impact of garlic that made my eyes water. It was not difficult to discover the source. A man had approached and was abreast of me, carrying over his shoulder a thick plaited rope of it. He, too, was a street vendor but I thought little of his merchandise. The sponge merchants were more to my liking. I passed any number of these peddlers, their faces and much of their figures almost eclipsed by the strings of sponges in every size and shape, strung around their necks and over their arms. I could not discover for myself what was on the slips of paper other vendors carried in cleft sticks. I know now they are lottery tickets.

Less than half an hour away from the hotel, and I was walking slowly, I found myself in narrow streets, houses and shops squeezed together, and nothing in the shop windows resembling the chic merchandise displayed in the windows around Constitution Square. I recognized from Kakia Livanos' description of it that I was in the Plaka. This is the oldest part of Athens, forming a belt around the base of the Acropolis. Now it is the Greenwich Village of that city. The tavernas are here, the houses are close together, and as in the Village, all sorts of people live in them from admirals to artists. After a little tour there I turned back. On the fringe of the Plaka I came into a narrow, cobblestoned street, where shoes on strings framed the doorway of every shop. This was Odos Pandrossos, Shoe Lane, a street where only shoes are sold. There are other lanes, I had been told, as exclusive about their wares as this one, but I did not investigate them that morning.

During my wandering I had bought coat hangers, talcum powder and other oddments that included an assortment of large, wooden cooking utensils. I had not the slightest idea what these were for though I had enjoyed the explanatory pantomime of their salesman, but I thought they would make interesting additions to a collection of cooking tools one of my sons-in-law is gathering. I was encumbered by enough parcels to make me look not unlike the sponge merchants. I had walked a long time, and the morning that had begun pleasantly cool had increased its temperature along with the hours, until now at midday it was uncomfortably hot. I knew there was a street in which only materials were sold, those "tissues" we had once thought meant Kleenex, and another street for antique shops. I could scarcely

Vasiliu

have seen, much less examined their merchandise because of the load I was carrying.

I started back to the hotel and thought I was retracing my steps, but I came unexpectedly to a dear little church, set in the middle of a busy street and endearing because it popped into view so suddenly, like a mischievous child who jumps from around a corner and says, "Boo!" I had to pause long enough to discover this is the church of Kapnikarea and that it dates from the ninth century.

I was back in the stylish shopping district again and presently I was at Constitution Square, facing the large, handsome building that is now the House of Parliament but was formerly the royal palace. On my left was the King George Hotel.

I was the first of our four to reach home, but the others came soon after to my room, each one of them hot, great with bundles, but happy. Darn was only a little disgruntled because shop doors had been closed to the front and behind of her, as she had tried to enter or been urged politely, but firmly, to leave. She had been told politely, and equally firmly, twelve-thirty was closing-up time. They would open again around half past four. She brightened, however, even as she told us this at the prospect of a happy time ahead after four-thirty, and in the meantime, lunch.

We all revived immediately from shopper's fatigue at the suggestion of eating and congratulated ourselves and one another that not one of us was indifferent to food.

"In my opinion," Sophy said, as we separated to wash up, "people who do not like food are not likable people."

It is one thing to like food, more of the same thing to want it acutely when you want it, but it is an impossible thing to get food in Athens if you want it at half past twelve. The doors of restaurants or hotel dining rooms will not open until half past one. If you go in at that time, in all probability you will be the only occupants of the room. It will not begin to fill until two. We learned this by stages that day.

First, we asked the elevator boy to let us out at the second floor. He did, giggling. We wondered only a little at this as we left the car. We knew the dining room was on the second floor so we couldn't have made a mistake about its location. We knew, too, that the elevator boys giggled a great part of the time. They were very young, the oldest of the ones who had carried us had looked to be thirteen, the youngest around eight. I do not like to remember my trip with that one. My four-year-old grandson would have had the same kind of fun playing with the levers this child had, with the difference that my grandson would not have been given permission for such happy experiment, much less a snappy uniform of authorization.

As we walked across a ballroom that separated the elevator from the dining room I gave an opinion that the reason the elevator boys giggled when we were in their car was not our appearance, nor even Darn's conversational sallies in Greek, but simply their technique for extending a spirit of good will over the barrier of language.

We reached the dining room; the doors were closed. We retraced our steps, found the elevator door open, the little boy waiting for us, giggling. By the time he had got us all in and closed the door, he was fairly doubled over with mirth.

Luz, eying him, remarked, "It doesn't sound like good will to me. The message I get is that he considers us a parcel of old fools."

We inquired from the clerk at the desk the name of a restaurant he would recommend for lunch. He raised his eyebrows. "You do not lunch here? This is semi-pension, you know. Breakfast and one other meal is included. This is the best place for you."

Perhaps I sounded patronizing. I did think it stupid of him not to know more about his own hotel than he seemed to. "We would be delighted to lunch here," I told him, "but your dining room does not serve lunch. It is closed."

I learned from him how to sound really patronizing. When he had finished conveying to us what rustics we were, I suggested we move on out to the street, anywhere rather than remain in his neighborhood or subject ourselves again to the patronage of an elevator boy of twelve. That was how we came to have an *apéritif* at the outdoor café and to discover this is practically what everyone else does at midday. At my suggestion, and because we were ravenous, we bought packages of pistachio nuts.

From that day on when we were in Athens I had a "limonade" and pistachio nuts before lunch. Some of the waiters spoke and understood a British English, and for them it was a "limon squash" with soda. We lunched every day at something after two. Pistachio nuts provide a splendid restorative for a twelve-to-two faintness.

In Athens, afternoon life begins at five. From noon on there is scarcely any sign of it on the streets. The sensible thing, therefore, is to conform to this. We found the conforming to be very pleasant indeed. We wrote letters, brought up to date our travel notes. Darn, in addition to these things, always washed white gloves, but we all of us took a long nap. This is a pattern I recommend, with or without glove washing. The silly folk who try to make every minute count, and I really don't know what they were counting, succeeded only in beating against closed doors, feeling sick and acting cross in the midday sun. We saw some of these before we acquiesced to the Greek ways.

The Greek way is to start the day very early, end it very late, with a long siesta between. This proves to be not a quixotic effort to be different from other folk but a sensible adaptability to climate. In the beginning, just as we had done at lunch on the first day, we four yokels presented ourselves for dinner a little after seven. Again the elevator boy giggled and the hotel clerk was patronizing. We are women who learn by trial and conspicuous errors. In Greece one dines at half past nine, ten, or even later.

The night we learned this, we took to the streets as we had done at lunch, but we did not pause at the sidewalk café. We had had our shoebag hour on the roof. After this evening, the hour was stretched to an hour and a half, from seven-thirty to nine. We strolled about our section of the city and found a considerable portion of its citizenry taking a promenade. The shops were all open, doing a brisk business. Darn, who is a great one for asking questions, shared with us the information she had got by this method: that there is no uniform closing hour, but that no one shuts up shop before nine, and many stay open until half past ten; if business is good, even later.

Someone had suggested we try the Averof Restaurant at Number 2 Churchill Street. We agreed this evening of involuntary exile from the hotel was a good time to visit it, though we had not the slightest idea how to find it. Sophy prefers walking until she drops to asking directions. Darn prefers asking questions to almost any other occupation. That night Sophy was in the lead as usual. She was annoyed with herself because she had not brought a map of the city. She had bought one at the hotel but had left it in her room, thinking we were not going out for dinner. Nevertheless, she insisted, she was sure she could take us to the restaurant.

I was dubious about this. Many trips with Sophy have taught me to be aware and wary of a peculiar talent she possesses. It is not a homing instinct. I do not know how to classify the sense that takes her unerringly, by car or on foot, to the slummiest part of a town into which we have come as strangers.

I gave to my companions illustrations of Sophy's peculiar talent as we followed our leader, but during the anecdotes, Sophy quickened her pace wishing, she said, to be out of earshot of such tiresome irrelevance. She was considerably ahead of us when Darn saw a policeman and with the hopefulness in her voice of the child who says, "Would you like me to get us all an ice-cream cone?" suggested, "Would you think it a good idea for me to ask directions of that officer?"

Darn enjoyed the satisfaction of asking, but none of us derived either satisfaction or information from his answer. He spoke only Greek, but Darn said it was not the accent of her Berlitz professor. By pantomime, he seemed to us more of a weathervane than a signpost.

A young couple walking by caught my attention as I was endeavoring to follow the loops and whorls of the policeman's right arm in the air. The couple stopped. The man came to us and asked in good English, with Greek accent, if he might help. We told him we were trying to find the Averof Restaurant. He said he knew it, spoke a few words to the young woman with him and, at her eager nods of acquiescence, offered to show us the way there. In spite of our protests, this is what they did though the restaurant turned out to be in the direction opposite the one in which they were moving when they had seen us. They insisted this was not out of their way. We had to ask our guides to wait while we rounded up a stray.

We found Sophy some distance away but she came back tractably. When our Greek guides told her she had been headed toward a section of the city that was most undesirable, I was not surprised.

As we entered the restaurant Darn surprised us by asking us to let her order the dinner. When we had been seated she explained her request. Her teacher had urged her to try a Greek *specialité*. It was eggplant stuffed with ground meat and rice, flavored with spices and covered with a rich sauce. He had told her the name for it.

Pausing only a moment at the threat to our figures of a rich sauce, we urged her to say the word.

When the waiter came to take our orders we waved aside the menus he proffered. Darn told him what we wanted, pronouncing it carefully, with an emphasis Mr. Panaiotopoulos would have deplored. Since she did not know how to make a sentence, she put nothing with it.

To our surprise, the waiter started, drew back a step, looking anxiously from Darn around the table at each of us. I said, "I don't think he understood you. Try it again."

Darn gave him the word a second time, articulating it even more meticulously than her first exposition. The waiter seemed even more dismayed and after a slight pause inquired hopefully, "*Éna?*" meaning "one."

We all understood that and shook our heads in unison. Darn held up four fingers. "*Ohi*," she answered, meaning "no." And then, "*Téssera*," the word for "four."

At that the waiter wrung his hands a little and, turning on his heel, left us. We saw him a minute later conversing with another man who looked to be the proprietor of the restaurant. We waited, wondering what was causing this delay in filling our order, Darn murmuring, "It's a very well-known dish."

The two men came to our table, the proprietor a little ahead of the waiter. He identified himself and then indicated to Darn a request to tell him what she had wanted. He bent over her a little and watched her closely. Again she gave the word.

The proprietor straightened and turned to the waiter, a look of mutual dismay passed between them; each shrugged his shoulders, the waiter with particular emphasis as though to indicate this was how he had said it would be. The proprietor turned back, and as the waiter had done asked in a tone of hopefulness, "*Éna?*"

By this time we were a Greek chorus. Each holding up four fingers we chanted in unison, "*Téssera*."

The face and shoulders of each man drooped, a pitiable sight. Almost simultaneously we turned to one another and said in effect obviously the restaurant didn't have it that day. Obviously too, they were unhappy at not being able to provide what we wanted. We had learned already it is intolerable to a Greek not to make possible anything the visitor may require. Certainly we would order something else and put the two men out of their misery. Almost simultaneously we pointed to the menu the waiter still held in his hand. At this gesture a look of astonishment and relief crossed the face of each man. They both leaned forward. The proprietor, pointing to the menu tremulously, wished in pantomime to know if, by any chance, it was something to eat we required.

It was our turn to be astonished, and we looked it. Certainly this was what we required, we communicated to him by vigorous nodding. What on earth else?

We learned.

The word for the eggplant dish is *moussaka*. What Darn had ordered, with painstaking care of each syllable was *moustakia*. A *moustakia* is a gentleman with a black moustache.

Afterward we conjectured their hopeful inquiry of "*Éna?*"—"one"—must have been prompted by their acquaintanceship with one individual in the neighborhood who would meet our requirements, but to provide four such gentlemen exceeded the social circle within their call.

Chapter Seven

ON THE morning of the fourth of May, we went to a special ten o'clock service at the cathedral held in honor of the Laconian pilgrimage. Mr. Papadakis, its chief pilgrim, had invited us. He and his wife, the erstwhile Miss Greece, were staying at the King George, in a suite, he told us, that was magnificent: high ceilings, spacious rooms including a drawing room, furnished in royal splendor. He asked politely about our accommodations, but we were evasive.

We left the hotel close to ten o'clock, though we had planned to make an earlier start. I was the one who held up the others. I am always the one, they complain, and my answering plaint is that I have to braid long hair which they do not, and this throws me out of kilter. Luz suggested mildly I might ask a priest at the cathedral how he fitted his coiffure to his schedule. The others thought this very funny. Darn would as soon appear without her white gloves at any function as be late to it, therefore she was fretful. By way of apology, accordingly, I suggested and secured a taxi, though we had been told the cathedral was only a short distance away.

Soon after our arrival, Darn whispered she need not have been so anxious. This was our initiation to the Greeks' idea of time. We had experiences throughout the rest of our stay that substantiate my assertion there is no such thing in the Greek mind as an idea of time. I do not mean by this that the Greeks are always late. I mean that time and the Greeks provide the very essence of relativity. A guest may arrive an hour early or an hour late at a party. That in itself has no meaning because the hostess has not set a specific time for her party. If you ask the hour of her dinner she becomes distressed. She does not wish to be so rude as to impose restrictions on you, so she murmurs reluctantly, "Oh, nine-thirty or perhaps ten. Whatever is convenient."

It was evidently not convenient to hold the special Laconian service at the cathedral at ten o'clock. We were the first of the congregation to arrive. Inside the church we saw through an open door into a little side room a group of priests sitting round a table drinking the customary morning demitasse, as men all over the city at that hour were drinking them at outdoor cafés. Darn immediately volunteered to carry out Luz's suggestion to me by joining the coffee drinkers in order to ask how much time they allowed for their hairdos. I dissuaded her.

We had made a slow and thorough tour of the interior before anyone else arrived. The others came, for the most part in small groups; the greater number were women. We could hear them talking and laughing as they approached the door and when they had stepped inside they did not lower their voices nor check their laughter. The gossiping, if that's what it was, continued as the newcomers circled the church, pausing at each icon to kiss it and make the sign of the Cross a number of times. There seemed to be no uniformity in the number of times each person made the sign of the Cross. Very few of the women wore hats. When one group converged upon another at an icon there were mutual recognitions, followed by introductions and handshaking all around. Some men came in. They came individually; most of them carried a brief case. Each one made a brisk round of the icons and then took a seat.

A little after half past ten the Laconians arrived in a body. After a considerable shuffling about and shouted directions plainly audible from inside the church, they formed a procession and marched up the center aisle. They were led by a church official in bright blue with knee breeches, white boots and a sword in a scabbard. The congregation rose to honor the procession and it was only then we four discovered we had chosen to sit on the men's side of the cathedral. We had not noticed, heretofore, there was a cleavage of sexes. It was too late to change.

The doors behind the altar opened to admit three priests, tall, dressed in magnificent robes of cloth of gold. They began a chant and their voices were excellent, a chant that was echoed antiphonally by a boys' choir in balconies high up in the church, on either side of the altar. The service that followed was impressive and the music beautiful. The *décor* of the church was strange to us, but when the priests in their magnificent gold appeared, the whole blended into a stunning mass of splendor.

At the conclusion of the service, the Laconians marched out of the church and from there to the grave of the Unknown Soldier on which Mr. Papadakis was to place a wreath. We had made our excuses to him, however, and slipped away from the wreath-laying ceremony.

We wanted to explore further, and that is what we did happily the remainder of the morning, strolling up and down the streets, pausing to look in shops, purchasing incidentals here and there for the sheer fun of it.

In the midst of this happy aimlessness, I realized by a similarity of display in succeeding shop windows we were on the street of "tissues" and called the attention of the others to the row on either side of the street, of shops, as far as we could see, that sold only fabrics. It was a sight that reminded Sophy, suddenly, she had come with a commission to find and purchase some raw silk for a friend at home. The very mention of this commission was an inspiration to Darn to ask questions. Begging us to leave it to her, the deputy trotted up and down and across the street we were on, darting in and out of shops, reporting at each exit with a shake of her head to us waiting on the corner, so far no luck. Almost at the end of the block she found success and returned with him, a pleasant gentleman who had, he told us, beautiful materials he would be delighted to show us at another time, but he would not detain us at this moment since we were in search of raw silk. He knew where this was to be found and if we could grant him time to lock up his shop he would be delighted to take us.

I thought I was becoming accustomed to the spontaneous offer of Greeks to take almost any amount of trouble for a stranger, but all of us were staggered by such an amount as this man proposed: not only to relinquish us as possible customers for himself, but to close his place of business to any others, whilst he would show us the place of a competitor. He walked rapidly; we scuttled after him and came to a halt at Number 24 Hermes Street.

This is the shop of I. Tzanetogleas, and what beautiful stuffs he has, all of it handwoven by Mme. Koula Karaoula. We met her. She had come to deliver a new batch of her making. She is like the core of an apple that has been eaten: brown, wrinkled, showing the bites of time and hard work, but crisp and strong. She told us by pantomime she not only weaves but spins the materials. Though the color varies only in shades of "natural," from just off-white to an ecru, there is a wider choice in texture and bulk; some are very fine and close woven, others coarse and of looser weave. We bought the fine for shirts for the men in our families; the heavier, coarser weave we took for summer coats, trousers for them, suits and dresses for ourselves. We became a little out of hand in our pleasure over these fabrics and quite a little out of pocket, but we knew we would not find anything like these beautiful stuffs at home. Furthermore, they would last nearly a good, full lifetime. Among us we took the entire supply of one weave and wanted more. Mme. Karaoula, when this was communicated to her, was far from daunted. She clapped her hands, went into a pantomime of rapid spinning and assured us she would provide all we needed within ten days.

The rival merchant who had been our guide shared the pleasure of Mme. Karaoula and the shop owner in our invasion. He took the key to his shop from his pocket, displayed it, returned it with a hearty slap against his thigh and with a shrug of his shoulders indicated to us his business could wait while he devoted himself to our transaction. He measured yardage from the bolts and the amount required for trousers and coats from the figure of the shop owner, who seemed a little dazed as his visitor twirled him around, flipping a measure across his shoulder and down his trouser leg. I think it more than probable the voluntary assistant collected a fat commission after we had left. I would pronounce that justifiable.

When we had shaken hands all around and made our departure, leaving our erstwhile guide to his private transaction, we confided a mutual reluctance to visit any more shops until our buying fever should have dropped.

At a hint from Luz that we turn our attention to sight-seeing trips, since after all that was what we had come for, the executive and her deputy were off like beagles with the smell of rabbit in the wind. They were going to find the tourist bureau Mr. Panaiotopoulos had recommended to us, Sophy tossed back over her shoulder. Luz and I agreed they were making it evident they would prefer not to have us with them. They liked to create and present what in the entertainment vernacular is called a "package deal," arrangements made, contracts signed, without interruptions or suggestions, only approval and applause. Luz and I, wanting to share a little of the planning too, managed to keep them in sight and caught up with them in the office of the Etea Organisation Tourisme at Number 8 Avenue Venizelos, diagonally across the street from the Grand Bretagne.

We are agreed this is one of the best organizations of its kind any of us has encountered: efficient, knowledgeable, its personnel charming and patient. We talked first to Mr. Nicholas, the manager, a widely traveled and experienced gentleman, who then turned us over to "Miss Alice" for details of the excursions we had requested and those he had suggested. I do not know Miss Alice's last name, but she is competent, humorous, understanding and speaks English so effortlessly it was a surprise to learn she is actually Greek. She was tolerant of our suggestions and the manager's, except for his proposal we engage a guide.

"No, no," she said. "That is not necessary. I will give you explicit directions. Pieces of paper are much less trouble and take less room in a car than a guide."

We left her working on Delphi, Epidaurus, the Aegean Islands, Olympia and our final exit from Greece a month thence, by the Dalmatian Coast. On our way back to the hotel Sophy announced with deep satisfaction she considered the morning well spent. Luz's comment was that from the amount left by each of us in the silk merchant's shop, she considered the term unfortunate. Furthermore, her legs were so tired she doubted her ability to stand on them much longer no matter what sights to see were even immediately in front of her.

Pistachio nuts and *apéritifs* at the King George's sidewalk café revived us somewhat, and lunch was a complete restorative.

That afternoon we took no siesta. We had an important engagement. This was our second day in Athens and we had been moving toward the engagement with eagerness, certainly, but slowly. We would not have been so presumptuous as to burst in without introduction and the introduction itself required, at least in our opinion, an observance of protocol. One is not presented to royalty by whoever happens to be at hand. We did not wish to be presented to the Acropolis by someone with less stature than royalty requires.

We were indebted to Mr. Papastratos for the person of proper rank, scholastically. She is Lily Litina, who lives at 60 Vatatzo Street, Athens 7, Greece. She is young, she speaks English well. She is a classical scholar, with sound knowledge, meticulous accuracy and a glowing enthusiasm. She does not permit herself to become fulsome, but for all her intellectual approach, she cannot prevent revealing her love for and dedication to the antiquities of her country.

We had changed from street clothes to cotton dresses and sneakers when we met Miss Litina at the hotel. Though this is not the costume required for a garden party at Buckingham Palace, it is suitable for a visit to the Acropolis. Anything more stylish from heels to tight skirt is improper equipment and an obstacle to moving about, if not a real peril. A car can go only as far as the outer gate, where tickets of admission are to be purchased. From there on the journey is a climb on foot.

I do not suppose anyone thinking about the Acropolis has the foolish notion that one could see it by car! At the same time I doubt that the novice tourist has visualized beforehand what difficult walking it is. Since the word "Acropolis" is a synonym for "citadel," its location on a vast rock high above the city was for the purpose of defending and protecting the city that sprawled below and around it.

The ascent from the admissions gate to the actual gateway, the Propylaea, is up a flight of steps, on either side of what was once the central avenue where the great processions on feast days once moved, and animals were led to be sacrificed. Now the center roadway of marble is far below the threshold of the Propylaea; the modern pedestrian must go by the stairway. These are blocks of marble and each step so massive it seemed to me about three feet in height. I know they required a giant leg reach.

The Propylaea, though the word means a great entrance, is not an entrance as one thinks of doors, gates or an arch. It is in itself a magnificent building comprising a central portico and a wing on either side. In the central portico there are magnificent columns in a double row on each side of the stone roadway and there is open space between. In this sense the great structure is an entrance, the pillars blocking the space only sufficiently to frame it and so emphasize by its restriction the vast scene ahead, of the Acropolis proper.

Standing between two of these lofty pillars, I patted one surreptitiously, saying to myself foolishly, "This is Doric." I moved to another row and patting one of these said, "This is Ionic." As I did this silly thing I knew why. I had a sudden recollection of a story a friend of mine had told me. The first time she had taken her little boy, and he was very small at the time, to Ringling Brothers Circus, he had turned to her while the band was playing, the animals were performing, all three rings filled with dazzling activity, clowns tumbling about the outer rim, and had said fiercely and imperiously, "Sing 'Three Blind Mice.'" His mother, though she could not possibly make herself heard above the din, had endeavored to oblige, because she understood, after her first start of astonishment, the child was so overwhelmed he had a sudden urgent need for something familiar. "Doric, Ionic" were "Three Blind Mice" to me. I saw myself at Miss Faulkner's School drawing laboriously a column with flutings but no base and with no ornament on the capital and printing underneath the label "Doric." And then another, with a base and a capital with spirals on either side, one within the other, "ram's horns" I called them, but had learned the name for them, "volute" and underneath I had printed "Ionic."

There is an inevitable sequel to my recognition and recollection of something I have learned. I have almost never experienced a sense of intellectual familiarity with something, that I have not immediately afterward experienced a dismal realization that another thing with which I should have had intellectual familiarity is a stranger and a surprise to me. In the long program of a conventional education I was taught a great many things. Evidently I "took in" a discouragingly small proportion of them. Of course I was taught the Parthenon was a temple to Athene, and as such was a treasury. I would not expect that portion of Fort Knox where our supply of gold is stored, nor the United States Mint to be constructed like a peristyle open to the winds, rain, sun, and robbers. But since in photographs the Parthenon is open, so that in many of them there is even a view visible between and beyond the pillars, I have always thought with happy certainty that was the way it was built. I like it as it is without the solid

EK
Vasiliu

wall behind, that once safeguarded the towering gold and ivory statue of Athene, forty feet high, and the gold in the treasury vaults.

Miss Litina's face turned bright red when I admitted first my ignorance, and then my pleasure. I could not tell whether anger or embarrassment for me had provoked this rush of color, but I did not risk it again and shared no further confidence with her. I kept my own counsel and my sharp delight at remembering the word *entasis* and that what it means is "true." There it was under the hand for proving. It is the term for a bulging in the middle of a column for the purpose of making the column appear to the eye undeviatingly straight. I could not feel for myself but I accepted Miss Litina's corroboration of what I had learned too, long ago, that the columns taper toward the top and that they incline slightly inward. Furthermore, the corner columns are slightly heavier than the others. They taper and incline inward just as they have the bulging, to make them look straight, and the corner ones are heavier in order to seem to be exactly like the others.

With a brashness that is the hallmark of the untutored I presume to assert I find deeply satisfying the Caryatids, the six beautiful maidens who support on their heads the rich entablature and give to that section of the Erechtheum the name "The Porch of the Caryatids." I have read and I have been told they outrage the Greek standards of taste, both by an intrusion of sculpture into an architectural plan, and by such a conception as would allow them to be portrayed serene, and unpressed by the weight of the structure on their heads. I say this is quibbling and consign it to the textbooks.

The Erechtheum is, like the Parthenon, a temple to Athene, but the Parthenon is to the virgin Athene and the Erechtheum is to the Athene Polias, meaning the Athene of the City, the Protector. Smallest of all is the exquisite Temple of Athene Nike, the Athene of Victory. Tucked around the corner of the Propylaea, it is a lovelier jewel in this setting, because it is out of the way of the dazzling splendor of the Parthenon. The myth is that the wings of this Athene were clipped so that Victory could never depart from Athens.

To move from one temple to another on the Acropolis is not in itself an easy strolling about. The terrain is deeply cracked and there are sizable fragments to be got over or around. They are monuments themselves commemorating, involuntarily, the siege of Athens by the

Venetians. The Parthenon had become in 1687 under the Turkish occupation a storage house of ammunition. The Venetians fired on it and scored a direct hit. It is little short of miraculous that as much of the Acropolis as is standing today should have withstood this bombardment.

Making my way over and around the fragments I turned vehement champion of Lord Elgin. I am, I know, partial to carrying a banner for something or someone, but heretofore I had not picked up a standard for Lord Elgin. I knew he had transported to London much of the frieze of the Parthenon, the sculpture of the east and west pediments, and other fragments. I had seen the Elgin marbles in the British Museum there, but I cannot say that at my first sight of them in 1923 and in the years between I have been concerned about their right to be in the British Museum. Sliding and slipping over what remains on the acreage of the Acropolis, I gave myself, with apology to the Greeks I hold so dear, to the rights of Lord Elgin. Who could have said in 1801 when Lord Elgin was in Athens as British Minister to Turkey there would be no future bomb hit to destroy what remained then of Pericles' Golden Age? And even then, much of what had not been destroyed was being carted away by citizens to use as building materials. Lord Elgin won permission from the Sultan of Turkey by way of a handsome payment to remove the pieces he selected. He was only partially recompensed by his own government. I have heard suggested several times since my self-appointment as Elgin champion that England could make a gesture of good will to Greece by returning the marbles to the place from which they were taken. In my position as an unknowledgeable but talkative defender, I have answered I would consider the gesture generous but not obligatory.

We stayed on the Acropolis three hours. It is open daily from sunrise to sunset, and three nights in the month until midnight: the night before the full moon, the night of the full moon and the night after. Those were dates ahead of us and ringed on our calendar.

Chapter Eight

DURING the next two days, under the guidance of La Belle Hélène, we saw some of the work to which she and a large group of other volunteers are dedicated. We visited a rehabilitation center a few miles out of Athens on a hilltop with a view of the mountains. Our hostess pointed out to us Pentelikon, the peak from which much of the marble comes that is the most widely used building material. It had been startling to us and one of the things we had first noticed in and around Athens that marble is the material for floors and staircases in every building we had entered. Brought up on "I Dreamt I Dwelt in Marble Halls" as a symbol of the summit of luxury, we had thought so much marble flung about was sumptuous but perhaps profligate. We learned, however, that marble is very nearly the cheapest building material, and lumber the most difficult to obtain. During its periods of occupation, Greece has been stripped of its trees, though now there is a vigorous national campaign for reforestation with even school children making voluntary contributions toward this project.

Our hostess at the rehabilitation center was Miss Willis, an American passionately devoted to Greece and her work there. She told us she was retiring after twenty-five years and coming home to America, but added smiling, she doubted she would find it home. She would probably come back after a visit, to retire in Greece. The center houses and trains men and women, boys and girls, almost all of them victims of land mines; many are recent victims, because, we were told, much of the land is still peppered with mines. These physically disabled occupants of the center are being trained in trades they can carry on after their return to their native villages: shoemaking, weaving, watch repairing, tailoring, dressmaking. The men and boys put on for us an exhibition of gymnastics and, with the girls, a program of dances, astonishing evidences of the physical rehabilitation that has been accomplished along with the vocational guidance. The plant itself is pitifully simple, the simplicity of poverty. They live and work in sheds, sleep on army cots in rows. An old and rasping victrola is their entertainment. But the atmosphere was one of sparkling courage and gaiety reflected from the indomitable buoyancy of Miss Willis and her co-worker, a Greek—warm, humorous, indefatigable Mrs. Despina.

We drove out from Athens in the opposite direction, to Voula on the coast just beyond the airport. Mrs. Vlachoustikos took us, another friend of Kakia Livanos, to whom Kakia had written. Voula is the site of a hospital for children with tuberculosis of the bone, and there are many of these. The disease is a souvenir of their undernourishment during the wars. The beds at Voula are in pavilions, roofed but open at the sides and looking out to the sea. There are women patients, too, in separate buildings. We were amazed by the exquisite needlework these patients had produced, since most of them were in heavy plaster casts, and many of them unable to assume a sitting position. Mirrors had been attached over their heads to the beds, to enable them to see the work they were doing. We bought some of this on sale in a shop run on the grounds of the hospital, and found no more exquisite workmanship anywhere. The new drugs are working miracles, Mrs. Vlachoustikos told us, and the head nurse corroborated this. Patients who came to live out their lives, and it would not be a long term, leave Voula cured. These drugs come from and are being provided by the United States, under specifically the Marshall Plan.

We went to the Red Cross Hospital, the largest in Athens. It has had substantial financial aid from the United States. We would not have called the equipment luxurious. The beds are little more than army cots of a height backbreaking to a nurse when she is ministering to a patient. They lack, too, the mechanical device we take for granted that enables a bed to be raised and lowered to the patient's comfort. We were shown, however, a system for dealing with emergencies that seemed to us both ingenious and efficient beyond anything of its kind at home. Each hospital in Athens is allotted a day in the week on which it must be prepared for emergency. An operating room is set aside, additional nurses put on duty. Newspapers carry the name of the hospital of that day, the police and fire departments know the table of rotation. Therefore, when an emergency occurs, a motor accident, a fire, whatever, the injured are taken at once to the specific hospital where everything is in readiness for immediate care.

Mr. Georgacopoulos is head of the Red Cross in Greece. A charming gentleman, he evoked within a few minutes of our meeting him an active spirit of competition among us. Sophy won at a walk and smirked annoyingly when he asked her to sit beside him at lunch. Defeated, we turned back to our women companions and elicited from them further information. I was delighted to talk with Miss Messolora, who until her recent retirement had been the head nurse of the hospital for many years and was, I heard from the others, a distinguished and widely beloved woman throughout Greece. Even after her retirement she had chosen to live at the hospital and to work in an advisory capacity. She was dressed, when we met her, in a kind of uniform, a long, severe robe. Just before we quit the hospital for lunch she left us for a few moments. When she rejoined us, she was wearing all her decorations, and there were many of them, across her chest. I asked her as we drove away from the hospital about the volunteer workers like La Belle Hélène, Mrs. Vlachoustikos, and others we had met.

We were in the back seat of a car at the moment. She turned to face me, took both my hands in hers as though to emphasize what she wanted to tell me. Leaning toward me, looking at me with deep earnestness, she said, "Madame, how can I say? I pray I have enough English to tell you in the right way about these volunteers. They are not like volunteers I am sure anywhere, because *they* do not say, 'I will come this day in the week and perhaps an hour or two on another day.' They come year in and year out, all their time. And that is how all this work is done. You see we are so poor in Greece, we cannot pay people except the technical ones. But these volunteers have become technical ones, too, by experience. And so we can run our hospitals and our services on money you could not believe in other countries, it is so small. This is the volunteers. They do not give us hours. They give us their lives."

We lunched at the Royal Yacht Club of Athens. I am better qualified to judge a yacht club than a yacht though it could not be said I am familiar with anything having to do with boats. Nevertheless, as a club this one in Athens has the most glorious location of any I have ever visited. It is on a high promontory between Piraeus and Athens with a view of the city to one side, the harbor, immediately below, dotted with boats of almost every size and description, the King's sailing yacht among them; to the right, the Aegean Sea and the mountains. The day was sunny, and a sunny day in Greece produces a clarity of atmosphere, a piercing quality, unlike any I have experienced. This light in Greece is an unearthly translucence. It is not the blinding sunlight I have known in California or Florida. This creates the illusion that moving in this light you are not earthbound, you are in a stratum of purity; there is no dust, no haze, as though all the impurities had been somewhere else, put through a strainer and rejected, and only the essence of light retained. Any traveler there who tells himself this is all a flight of fancy has only to take pictures in that atmosphere. His camera will tell him. His usual accuracy in allowance for light is out of line here. I have seen more than one photographer so baffled he has shaken a light meter as though it were a watch that had stopped.

One of the luncheon guests spoke of this. I had learned from other guests she is one of the owners of an Athens newspaper. She had been with us at the hospital. She had talked interestingly, factually, authoritatively, with a charm of manner but a briskness, too, that indicated a woman who would be impatient of the inaccurate and of the indefinite. She was the one who at lunch said to me, "I do not know, madame, whether you are religious or not; that makes no matter. I assure you I am not inquiring into your personal belief. What I want to tell you is this. There has to be something in Greece to give us strength, to stand firm against our disasters. Our religion alone could not do this. But do you know what it is? It is our extraordinary sunshine, and the wonderful light it gives us. Each day we wake up to our sun and that makes us have a renewed desire to live and to work, and that is the most important of all, because we *must* work. If we were in a dark climate without this Greek light, we would not survive. I know this."

She asked if I had been shown Mt. Hymettus. I said one of the first places I had asked to have identified was the mountain from which the honey of Hymettus came. She was a little impatient with me.

"Yes, yes, of course," she answered, "everyone knows the honey of

Hymettus. But do you know the light? That is what you must watch. You must watch at evening the light on Hymettus that turns it lavender, and all the country around. This is why Athens is always called the lavender city. Did you not know that?"

Across the table Mr. Georgacopoulos was talking to Sophy, of course. But for a moment she graciously allowed those of us seated near him to be included in what he was saying.

He spoke in French. He had explained when we met his English was so poor it was distasteful to him to hear it. His French was exquisite. He spoke it lovingly, rounding each syllable with careful enunciation; his selection of words was a poet's. He was talking about religion and architecture when we listened. I heard him say the spires of Gothic cathedrals were the expression of a yearning for the light because early Christians, persecuted, had had to live in darkness, hidden in catacombs, always having to shrink from the light of discovery.

"In Greece," he said, "we have suffered from nature, our dreadful earthquakes. But our Greek light has never been taken from us, and that is how we will always survive."

Before we left the Yacht Club I took some pictures. Luz's beautiful camera was in her hands again, returned from the repair shop. She took it delicately from its case and we walked across a terrace where we had eaten lunch, to a parapet from which we agreed we could get the best shots of the harbor below. Before I turned to my own picture taking I watched with interest and admiration her knowledgeable twiddling of one button after another on her machine. With astonishment, I saw her within a minute fold up the camera and return it to its case. I foolishly asked what on earth she was doing.

"I don't think it's a view that will show up much in a picture," she answered.

I won a silver medal once from *St. Nicholas Magazine* for a snapshot, but I do not lean on this as support for my ability to select as well as photograph a subject. However, when a scene below the photographer comprises aquamarine water with white-tipped ruffles on its surface like the edging on children's panties, polka dotting of little sails, red, blue, green and yellow, and soft hills in the distance, and the film in the camera is for color, then no one can tell me, not even Luz with all the buttons on her camera, there is nothing in the scene worth taking.

"Luz," I said, "is your camera out of whack again?"

She twitched a shoulder with as spurious a nonchalance as I have ever seen recorded. "It's nothing in the least important," she answered, "just the . . ."

She said something I had never heard of on a camera and saw no point in remembering.

She went back to the others, who had remained at the lunch table waiting for me to take my pictures. As I was focusing for my second or third shot, I noticed for the first time a terrace below the one on which I was standing. It was little more than a platform walled around. A small group of people in comfortable chairs sat on it. What had caught my eye was a sailor on this platform who was preparing to run a flag up a mast that was placed at right angles to the balcony and extending beyond its outer wall. The sailor was picturesque in his white uniform and round cap and I focused on him. Bending over and putting my elbows firmly on the wide top of the low parapet I was facing, I held the camera steady. At the instant of my snapping the picture, a cannon went off from the terrace below. I gave an involuntary demonstration of the way leapfrog is played that very nearly sent me out over the heads of the people below and on down to oblivion. The cannon was a little brass miniature, not more than a foot long. The sailor was running up the flag to mark the start of the weekly sailboat races of the club and the cannon gave the signal.

All this, my luncheon party explained, rushing from the table to rescue me, when I had already recovered my balance and had tottered to a chair a few feet on the safe side of the parapet. Darn reminded me I had been photographing a sailor, running up a flag on the *Queen Frederica* when I had very nearly dropped my camera and myself over the bridge because the fireworks had gone off at the instant of my snapping of the picture. I was grateful to her for this reminder.

"I'm no longer interested," I told her, "in photographs of sailors putting flags on masts."

We dined that night at Vassili's, Number 14 Jan Smuts Street. It was a delicious meal, that cost $6 for the four of us and included a bottle of lovely wine called Kava Camba.

Darn called our attention to a container on our table filled with toothpicks. The sight reminded her, she said, of the Greek restaurant owner and his friend who had been table companions to her and Luz the first day out on the *Queen Frederica*, and who had given them lessons in the etiquette of the toothpick in America and in Greece. She wondered what had become of them and if they were having a pleasant time in the homeland they had told her they had not visited since their emigration to America, nearly forty years before. Sophy's surmise was they had probably not spent much time in Athens, but had gone direct to some one of the islands from which they had undoubtedly come. Every Greek, she asserted, comes from an island. Ask anyone in this city if he was born here and invariably he will say no, he comes from one of the islands. He never says what island, either. Having delivered herself of this traveler's note, she took a toothpick from a container and applied it. To our protests of astonishment and remonstrance, she retorted she believed in adopting the customs of a country.

Our waiter was deeply interested in Darn's use of his language. He was not troubled by it as Mr. Panaiotopoulos had been; he seemed to find it highly enjoyable. When on departing she led our chorus of "*kalinihtas*" he urged her to substitute the word "*yazoo*." He indicated this was a friendlier, more colloquial term for "good-by."

We had not gone fifty feet from the door of the restaurant when we saw coming toward us the Greek restaurant owner and his friend, of whom Darn had spoken nostalgically only fifteen minutes earlier. They identified Darn and Luz at the same instant, and rushed forward calling out their names and incoherent greetings. Luz described to them how recently they had been the subject of conversation among us, and indicating Sophy, added, "This lady was sure you would not still be in Athens, you must have gone to one of the islands."

The two men looked searchingly at Sophy, scowling a little. The restaurant owner inquired somewhat truculently, "Why must I go to islands?" "What is at islands?" He slapped his chest. "I am Athenian. My friend is Athenian. Why you think I go to islands?"

By way of apology and distraction, Sophy extended toward him her right hand with closed fist. Opening it she revealed the toothpick she had secreted there after our remonstrance.

The mentor of Darn and Luz bent down to identify what Sophy was displaying, but having ascertained it was a toothpick he stood erect again. Scowling a disapproval even more formidable than his dislike of being relegated to the islands, he directed a stiff arm and rigid forefinger toward the object on Sophy's palm and said to Darn, "That is not proper. People in society never bring toothpicks out on street, only inside. And in Greece, like I tell you, this way."

Sophy and I were privileged to witness a demonstration we had got before only by hearsay. When he had finished his performance Darn thanked him on behalf of all her friends and assured him we would take his lesson to heart. His geniality was restored. He smiled at all of us, and patted Darn approvingly on the back.

We began the ceremony of departure. Whatever our shortcomings about toothpicks we would not shame Darn and Luz, I thought to myself, by a swift American leave-taking. We had learned the Greek way. We suggested we must leave, then spoke of how beautiful the weather had been; proposed again we must take our leave and said how much we were enjoying our stay in Athens; intimated it was getting late and that perhaps we were detaining the two gentlemen and said how hospitable we had found the Greeks to be, how delicious their food. This made three times around the subject, so now we could start shaking hands. We did this twice around. It paved the way to actually saying good night. This, we also knew, would have to be said several times over before it took the effect of allowing us to move on. Accordingly, we gave it several rounds, one taking up where another left off, much like singing "Frère Jacques." Now we could move. Our moving was gradual, more a shifting of weight than an actual step.

This was the moment Darn chose to introduce to society the friendly farewell she had so recently learned from the waiter. "*Yazoo*," she called, loud and gay, and in her pleasure at her own advancement, grasped once more the hand of society's advocate and wrung it.

The owner of the finest Greek restaurant in Pasadena, California, withdrew his hand. "That is not a nice thing to say, is not society talk," he pronounced. With a stiff bow, echoed by his friend, the reunion was ended.

Back at the King George on the way to my room I paused at Sophy's open door to say good night. She was standing in front of the wastebasket in her room. I saw her drop into it a toothpick.

Chapter Nine

ON SATURDAY, May 7, we visited the Acropolis by moonlight. Everything else in the day was incidental to that, of course, though the day itself was not without incident. The first was a radio broadcast at half past nine. That four middle-aged American women would do a broadcast over a Greek radio was such a preposterous notion we had laughed lightheartedly when the first request had arrived by mail. We speculated during a good part of one shoebag hour on what mistaken identities had caused such confusion until Darn suggested perhaps the request had been accurately directed on account of Luz being Commander of All the Women in America. Luz protested we were being unfair. Darn retorted we were entitled to a righteous indignation because Luz shouldn't have been on a committee with such a fancy name; it was bound to cause confusion abroad.

The day after this discussion took place, a gentleman from the radio station called on us. He clarified the invitation. Word had got around, he told us, that one of our number had prepared herself for this trip by learning modern Greek. The officials of the government radio were confident it would be an inspiration to the women of Greece for this tourist to give them, at the conclusion of the program, a message in their own tongue. Darn became very nearly violent.

But at nine-thirty on Saturday morning, we gave the broadcast and Darn delivered a message to the women of Greece. The composition was not her own, though she graciously told the young man who had written and translated it for her she endorsed the sentiments it expressed. The author was the same young man who had called on us. He was nervous in Darn's presence. She herself was not fortified by the presence of Mr. Panaiotopoulos in the studio though the rest of us were as delighted as we were astonished to meet him there.

He explained his surprise visit. The head of the studio was a friend of his and had happened to mention a forthcoming broadcast with four American women. Mr. P. had identified us immediately from his friend's description though he refused to tell us how, and had volunteered to be present in order to help us in whatever way we might require.

Darn assured him he would be of tremendous help to her personally by removing himself from her sight before she began her message. "It's not my idea of reassurance," she explained, "to see you flinch and screw up your face at every word I say. I want to look at someone in the control room who's not so sensitive."

Mr. Panaiotopoulos walked back with us to the King George after the broadcast.

"On the condition," Darn had exacted, "that you make no comment about my message."

Mr. P. shaking his head agitatedly had answered, "No indeed, I will not."

He apologized on the way to the hotel because he had not called on us as he had promised at our leave-taking on the *Queen Frederica*. We assured him we had expected him to be overwhelmed with work on his return and unable to get away. We thanked him for the flowers he had sent, eying one another furtively to make sure no one of us betrayed by tone of voice or dejection in the face the despair we shared and the groans of dismay each of us sent out in the corridor when flowers arrived. In our narrow cells there was no room for turning, let alone placing another vase of flowers, and never were there such flower senders, we had agreed, as the Greeks.

Mr. P. told us he had not been swamped with work. On the contrary he had been given a few days' leave and had used it by taking off immediately with his wife on a quick tour of some of the islands, looking for a place to spend the summer close enough to the mainland so that he could join his wife and small child for the weekends, in addition to his summer holiday, and where he could also find good spear fishing. That had become his engrossing hobby.

I asked if many Greeks went in the summer to the islands and he told me they were the favorite holiday places. Mykonos was very popular; Rhodes had always been fashionable. Spetsais was a favorite, and Corfu. As we left Mr. P. at the hotel Sophy asked hopefully, "I'm sure you were born on one of the islands, weren't you?"

"Not at all," he told her, surprised. "I was born in Alexandria. I am Greek, of course. My parents lived in the Greek colony there." As he left us he paused a moment. "Greeks are born all over the world, you know. But they are Greeks."

Within a quarter of an hour we were on another excursion.

Mr. Papastratos sent his car to bring us to his cigarette factory in Piraeus. I think we missed very little of it under his enthusiastic direction, and we found most of it deeply interesting. I do not know in acres or miles the area encompassed by Mr. Papastratos' cigarette factory, but the tour of it constitutes quite a tramp. Mr. Papastratos told us they employ twenty-four hundred workers, and when he added 80 per cent of these were women, we four feminists beamed and congratulated him. He told us, too, in 1922 over four and a half million Greeks were repatriated from the countries in which they had been living and returned to Greece, a million and a half of these from Turkey. This presented, of course, a backbreaking problem of employment, housing, food, et cetera. The Papastratos factory at that moment was about to replace its equipment by modern mechanized machinery, but under the urgency of the sudden increase of population, it retained the old equipment and so absorbed a greater number of workers, three times more than mechanization would have required.

The factory is a pleasant place in which to work—light, spacious, airy—and Sophy with pleasure made a note of its schedule of work that included a forty-eight-hour week, and shutting down at noon on Saturday the year round. Sophy's pleasure in the working conditions at Mr. Papastratos' factory was genuine, but certainly not passionate. The pleasure in the cigarettes from Mr. Papastratos' factory was both.

When we had completed the tour Mr. Papastratos led us to a room something like a board room for directors of a company with a large table down the center and chairs all around it. There was an ashtray on the table in front of each chair. It was not a board room, we discovered; it was a place in which to try tobacco blends. Since Darn does not smoke, this part of the excursion was not of particular interest to her, but for Sophy, who likes only Turkish tobacco and has some difficulty at home keeping herself supplied, this was as delectable as dessert to a child. The knowledge that all around were thoughtful, understanding, generous working conditions provided a lavish heaping on of chocolate sauce.

All the time Luz, Sophy and I were trying the various brands Mr. Papastratos presented to us, he was telling us about the tobacco industry itself. I was learning at the same time that, when testing a cigarette, one is not expected to smoke all of it, but only a puff or two, like the delicate sip of a tea taster. Until this technique was tactfully revealed to me, I had made myself giddy in the head and queasy in the middle, by an intensive inhaling and non-stop consumption.

Mr. Papastratos told us tobacco growing as an industry is increasing in Greece though by far the greatest amount is still imported from Turkey. But, he said, the Greeks themselves were not fond of strong Turkish tobacco; they preferred it reduced to a mild blend. The heavy brand was entirely for export, principally to Germany. It was much too strong for the Greek palate. This was the brand Sophy chose. Mr. Papastratos could scarcely believe when she told him it was a serious choice, but when she had convinced him this was actually her taste, he presented her with twenty-five packages, the first of this brand, he said, he had ever given to a woman. Sophy was all the more pleased.

Mr. Papastratos had invited Mr. and Mrs. Kapsalis to join us for lunch at the Royal Yacht Club. Mr. Kapsalis, we learned, had until the recent election been Minister of Co-ordination. He and his wife were charming, interesting people who spoke excellent English. This reduced me again to a self-contemplation of a tongue-tied yokel. Along with this self-contemplation I vowed that returning to America I would talk long and loud, wherever anyone would listen, about the urgency of overcoming at home the apathy most of our young people feel toward learning to speak a foreign language, and the failure of all too many of our educators to instigate a change of system in the teaching of modern languages from reading and translating to a flexibility of tongue. This last would be best achieved by including a modern language in the curriculum of primary grades.

Back at our hotel after lunch, we four allowed ourselves only a brief siesta. We had engaged the car and chauffeur, Marino, Kakia Livanos had urged on us. Our first excursion was to be to Daphni. He was to come to the hotel for us at four o'clock.

Our hearts warmed to Marino from the moment of our joining him at the desk of the King George, from which he had sent up a message he was at our service. His services to us proved to be prompted by thoughtfulness, concern for our enjoyment and comfort, executed with efficiency and competence. I recommend him heartily and with deep gratitude to him.

It is my own fault I am unable to speak so warmly and enthusiastically about Daphni. I wish we had allowed ourselves a longer siesta and not gone out the nine kilometers of dusty road while the afternoon sun was still hot. If the grounds and the interior had not been invaded by a line of buses emptying their noisy cargo of schoolchildren as we drove in from the main road, I could have seen more of the architecture without, and the mosaics within. I know Daphni is one of the great Byzantine churches. I know that finer mosaics of the eleventh century are not to be found anywhere. I know other travelers will give their personal endorsement to the praise bestowed whenever Daphni is written about. I could scarcely see the Christos for a trellis of scaffolding over my head, workmen perched on it here and there, engaged in restoration. I could not move through a mob of chattering children. I was hot, disgruntled, frustrated. I made my way out of the church, tried to walk around the outside in order to have firsthand contact at least with the architecture. The grass was high; nettles concealed in it tore my stockings. A young baseball player engaged in a game with other children narrowly missed the side of my head with a splendid inside curve pitch. A bee stung me on the ankle. I went back to the car. When my companions joined me they told me the mosaics were superb. I'm sure they are.

We went up on the Acropolis that night with Cuthbert Lamb. Cuthbert is a friend from New York who had reached Athens only that afternoon by boat and by plane, racing the moon. She joined us for our shoebag hour on the terrace that had become our very special property. We had learned that as a roof garden it would be ready and open to the public in June. Meantime it was our own and because of it we would not now have exchanged our cells for the handsomest suite in the hotel. When Cuthbert was seated at our table—the only one on the roof right side up—and had been directed to our own particular view, she said after a minute or two she would count her journey well taken for this sight alone.

We dined at the hotel as soon as the dining room opened. At a little after ten we were on the Acropolis. We moved about on it separately. We sat on the wall, and then again on one or another of the broken pillars that lie in such tragic number on the ground. Sitting on a column watching shadows change as the moon came up, I remembered the talk at lunch a few days before about the light in Greece, and I knew for the rest of my life I would think of light when I remembered Greece. In the late afternoon when we had watched from our roof the sun setting, the stones of the Parthenon had been golden with such warmth of color as to make one believe it would yield to a touch of the hand. In that late afternoon it had looked a friendly place, protecting benevolently the city below it. But when the land was white with moonlight, the Acropolis was awesome, remote, austere; cold temples to remind an Athenian looking up that these were the houses of gods to be placated, worshiped with sacrifices and in fear. I think in that Golden Age of Pericles, a citizen on a night when the moon was full must have trembled a little if he dared lift his eyes. At midnight, when we came down to the city, I did not look back.

At eight o'clock on Sunday morning we were on the road to Marathon, Marino at the wheel. We were learning to start early on any excursion in order not to be caught in the middle of it by the noonday sun. By the time we left Athens, after a month, eight o'clock had come to seem to us almost the middle of the day. I was anything but silent as we traveled to Marathon. Each of my friends pointed this out to me, at the same time reminding one another wistfully how untalkative I had been the night before on the Acropolis. I begged them to be forbearing.

I must say aloud the story of Marathon. I overrode their indignant protests. I didn't doubt they knew the story as well as I, though I did doubt it could have been such a favorite tale in their childhood as when my mother, at my insistence, had had to say it over and over to me. I only begged them to let me tell it this time, in order to convince myself that right now, on the morning of the eighth of May, I was actually on the road to the Plain of Marathon. No wonder I count them my dear friends; such patience, tolerance as theirs is a rare quality. They interrupted me only to point out such things as ice delivery wagons remarkable to us because they were little carts drawn by diminutive donkeys, or May Day wreaths faded but still hanging on the doors of the houses we passed, in the fashionable suburb of Kephissia, and, in the country beyond, families of gypsies on the road, their possessions packed on little donkeys, the donkey scarcely visible. Sometimes they nudged one another's attention and mine to the thick ruffle of scarlet poppies on either side of the road we traveled, or a hillside so covered with mustard it was of solid gold.

I told them, nevertheless, about the battle of 490 B.C. between the Persians under Darius and the Athenians under the great General Miltiades, on the Plain of Marathon that is only twenty-two miles from Athens. I said aloud, remembering how the story went, that when the Athenians heard the Persians were coming they marched their troops out to Marathon, but before leaving, the generals dispatched to Sparta, Pheidippides, one of the best runners in Athens. He reached Sparta, that is about 140 miles from Athens, in two days, and when he had arrived, he made an impassioned speech to the rulers, begging them to come to the help of the Athenians against the barbarians. But the Spartans had a law that forbade them to march out of Sparta until the moon was full. They sent back word they would come as soon as the law and the moon permitted.

Meanwhile the Persian fleet was directed to Marathon by a traitor named Hippias, who had been banished as a renegade from Athens. He instigated the battle at Marathon because he had had a dream in which he had lain in his mother's arms, and he had interpreted the dream to mean he would be restored to power and his possessions in Athens. When the fleet had anchored, Hippias led the troops on shore, but no sooner had he himself set foot on land than he sneezed so prodigiously one of his teeth fell out. He immediately halted the troops in order to retrieve the tooth, but it had disappeared in the sand. From that instant Hippias began to have forebodings about the coming battle, because, he said, "All my share in this land is the portion that has swallowed up my tooth." Therefore he felt his dream had been both fulfilled and denied.

Meantime the Athenian generals had fallen out of agreement about the strategy of the battle, some feeling they should delay until they were sure reinforcements would come, because the Persians so far outnumbered them. Others, Miltiades particularly, urged they fight at once. To settle the matter, Miltiades went to the man who was the head of all military matters, the Polemarch, imploring him in a fine speech to cast the deciding vote in Miltiades' favor.

The Polemarch gave the deciding vote in Miltiades' favor. The other generals—they commanded in rotation—relinquished their authority and put themselves under Miltiades as the supreme commander. He set up his battle front in a long line, thin in the center, but with a depth of many ranks in the wings. These wings were not all on the flat, open plain but partially concealed by low hills that form its boundaries.

When the proper sacrifices had been made and the soothsayers had pronounced the time propitious, Miltiades gave the order to attack. The Athenians rushed at the Persians, who prepared to meet them with great self-confidence because this was the center line advancing and the Persians saw it was thin, a mere handful of men. But while the Persians were occupied with the center line, the wings came in full strength on either side. They chased the Persians into the sea, but many were left dead on the battlefield. The survivors pulled up anchor and in a desperate last stand sailed as fast as the wind and their skill would permit toward Athens, hoping to reach the city and burn it before the defending troops could return from Marathon. The Persian fleet went round Sunium, but when it came to Phaleron, about four miles from the city, the leaders learned the Athenian army had about-faced and on the double returned to defend their beloved city. Once more the Persians hauled up anchor. This time they sailed away from Greece.

"That's the way the story was told me," I ended.

Darn said she hadn't minded hearing it but knowing the story pretty well herself questioned my saying Pheidippides was the runner who had gone to Sparta for help. She had thought he was the runner who brought the news from Marathon to Athens of the Victory, and it was in commemoration of him and his feat the Marathon races were held. I told her I thought the torch races were in his honor, but it was because when he got back to Athens after delivering his message to Sparta, he told the Athenians on the way to Sparta he had been stopped by Pan. The god had told him to ask the Athenians why they were so neglectful of him, for he had always been friendly toward them, even helping them in their need and would help them again. It was because of this meeting the Athenians erected a temple to Pan just below the Acropolis and established the torch race, honoring both Pan and Pheidippides. I added, remembering at that minute, the postscript to the story, that the Spartans had arrived when the moon was full but the Battle of Marathon was over. Nevertheless, they had marched on to view the battlefield and had come back full of praise for the Athenians and awe at the number of Persians slain.

"Over two hundred thousand Persians," I said, "only ten thousand Greeks, and of these only one hundred ninety-two Athenians. What a sight."

Sophy's comment was I must have been a ghoulish child.

I admitted this.

"Nevertheless," I said, reiterating a fact they all knew, "those hundred and ninety-two Athenians are buried in a mound that is there today."

Darn returned to the discussion of Pheidippides versus the unknown runner. She is as tenacious about an argument as I am about telling a story. I asked Luz to be like the Polemarch and cast a deciding vote, but she started a little when I spoke to her and said apologetically she was afraid she hadn't been listening very carefully.

She was sitting in the front seat beside Marino and I realized she had for some time been bent over something in her lap. I had vaguely assumed she was looking at a map, but I leaned forward with a sudden suspicion. She was not looking at a map. She had taken her camera out of the case and was surreptitiously twiddling and pushing the little nubbins on it.

"Is it working?" I asked.

And Luz, who among all my friends is the Abou Ben Adhem of gentleness and sweetness of disposition, answered, "Shut up!"

I leaned back, but not for long. The car was slowing down. We had left the highway some time before for a narrower road, but now we were on a sort of lane, a passageway at any rate, so narrow two cars could not pass. There were pedestrians on either side moving in the same direction as ours, and ahead of us a line of buses. "We must be there," I said, and found I was breathing hard.

The passageway led and widened onto a bridge. We had traversed, perhaps, a quarter of its length when Marino stopped the car, got out, opened each of the rear doors and the front one on Luz's side. When he had helped us all out, he said, "Is Marathon."

We had discovered one little flaw in our chauffeur, who in all other ways was as close to perfection as the human frame can encompass. Marino could speak only a few words of English and these totally unrelated to one another. With pantomime and Darn's Greek, more successfully I'm afraid with the former than with the latter, we had surmounted the barrier. This time there was no need of either. Marino had said clearly, "Is Marathon."

We walked to the rail of the bridge and looked around us. Within our view there were a body of water, not large, a meadow, small, hills in the distance, low. These were the mountains that look on Marathon and Marathon looks on the sea; only the sea was not visible to us, just a little lake. Not one of the four of us spoke. I doubt I could have spoken, not because of excitement but because of sick disappointment and rage. Rage at the writers from Greeks to Byron who had distorted and exaggerated a banal landscape to a panorama of heroic size. I wished I had not come to Marathon. I thought of the Acropolis just in time to keep from wishing I had not come to Greece.

I turned my back on the silly scene and walked toward the car. I heard Luz say, "My camera's working perfectly but I don't see much of a picture here."

Darn put a hand on my arm to stop me. "Look here," she said, "can you figure out how all those thousands got into that space, dead or alive? It certainly must have been hand-to-hand combat, face-to-face, I should think."

I hadn't the heart even to take my camera from its case, though Sophy was snapping away. "It may not show up as much," she explained, "but at any rate it's Marathon."

I had reached the car. Marino was standing by the open door to see me into it. "Is Marathon," he repeated, echoing Sophy's last words. "Marathon, Athens' waterworks." He pointed to the rail of the bridge. "Marble."

We fell over one another getting back into the car, though Luz paused to take a picture. "I want to remember it," she said. "I hadn't expected to see the Athens waterworks on my trip to Greece."

Marino spread his arms wide. "World!" he said.

Darn solved correctly this cryptogram. "Marathon is the largest waterworks of marble in the world."

Having seen this wonder, we suggested, would it be possible to visit probably a lesser sight, but one where a great battle had taken place?

Sophy's charade of the Battle of Marathon was a pleasure to watch. Marino enjoyed it and understood it. He clapped his hands softly. "Marathon," he said, pleased and astonished, as one who has recalled a long-forgotten memory.

Immediately, he realized the mistake he had previously made. He was humiliated, ashamed. He clasped and unclasped his hands in distress. We comforted him, we reassured him, we promised him this was a sight we would never forget: a dam and a bridge of marble.

He started the car, drove on across the bridge so that he might turn around. He indicated by pointing, and again he was apologetic, we would have to retrace our steps almost to the outskirts of Athens and then turn off at right angles to the way by which we had come.

We approved this with sounds of encouragement and reassurance. Darn likes to have statistics properly docketed. "Well," she said, happily, "Marathon is the name of the waterworks. We should have said, 'the Plain of Marathon' or 'the Battle.' Now we know."

We knew that for Darn knowing something specifically and accurately gives her deep satisfaction. So we were all happy and we sang a little as we rolled along, softly in deference to our dignity we tried to remember, and our age we tried to forget. It was a refrain we had adopted on another trip* to mark the setting out on an expedition that promised well. "We're off to see the wizard," we sang, "the wonderful wizard of Oz."

We went through a few little towns and marveled to one another at the technique of their single, white-helmeted traffic policeman, who performed incomprehensible gestures, with violent exertion. The locust trees were in bloom, and between the little towns we drove through miles of vineyards, pruned low but wide-spreading. We passed, too, a number of *tavernas*, outdoor eating places, with tables and chairs set under trees. In front of one of these we saw two men standing at either end of a spit, on which they were turning a whole lamb.

Sophy was the first to catch the sight, the first of its kind we had seen in Greece, or that I, for that matter, had seen anywhere. She

* *So Near and Yet So Far.*

was all for stopping then and there, but when Marino had halted the car at our request we held a consultation. Realizing it was not yet noon, we decided to go to Marathon first. We conveyed this to Marino. Here again Sophy's delineation was remarkable. Graphically, for Marino's benefit, she devoured the lamb from the spit, patting her stomach smartly to indicate how keenly she anticipated such enjoyment. Marino was all sympathy, but by means of his wrist watch indicated we would go to Marathon and return just as the lamb was cooked to a turn. A pat on his own stomach indicated the perfection of its cooking at just the proper time. We continued on our way.

The curving road straightened; the end was the foot of the mound on the Plain of Marathon where the Athenian soldiers in 690 B.C. had been buried. We climbed to its top. We looked down on the plain below and to the sea beyond; a wide, wide plain with hills on either side of us, just where they should have been to hide the wings of the Athenian army; directly in front of us the island of Evia. The Persians had anchored just off that island. Except for that interruption, there was only the blue sea all the way out to the horizon. Behind us were the mountains, and they did look down, as we were looking, on Marathon. I was not sorry I had come to Greece.

Something went wrong with Luz's camera so she was unable to get any pictures of the real Marathon.

When we had come down from the mound and walked on the plain itself we took to the car again and drove along a dusty lane that followed the sea. This road, too, ended about a mile further. We left the car and walked on the beach past a taverna set a little way back from the water. Tables and chairs were under a grape arbor there. A radio was blaring out jazz in a roar of sound. We walked away until we could hear only faint music in the air; to our relief, not recognizable. But we recognized aloud to one another that we were walking along the shore of the Bay of Marathon.

Back in the car again we stopped along the highway to buy flowers from a group of ragged, wistful children on the roadside. There was nothing wistful about their salesmanship or their competition to dispose of their wares. There were seven or eight children in the group. One little boy, the only shy one among them, offered calla lilies. Each of the others had sweet peas in a bunch so large it could scarcely be held in two hands. Marino leapt into the scuffle, making himself a bulwark between the salesmen and us and acting as moderator. There was no moderating such shrill persistence. We bought the entire lot though Marino deplored our lack of sales resistance. We needn't have taken the calla lilies. We bought them because the little boy withdrew from the fighting group and stood sadly off by himself. We wanted Marino to tell the little boy and the others the reason we had bought his callas was because he had been so polite and hadn't tried to push. Inasmuch as we had bought all the others as well

from the children who did push and fight and yell, we decided the logic was too difficult to communicate to Marino, since it was scarcely clear to us.

We drove off in a car that now looked something like one of the head carriages in gangsters' funeral processions I have seen in Chicago. The scent in such quarters under a hot midday sun evoked from us an atmosphere of waspish irritability at ourselves and one another, over our spineless expenditure of about a dollar on such overpowering merchandise.

When we pulled into the taverna we had marked on our way to Marathon, we saw at once the same two men still turning the lamb on the spit, and it had the soothing effect on us that the sight of food, as we had found, always produces.

Luz said as we climbed over and around the floral display to get out of the car, "Aren't we really charming people when we are eating or about to?"

We hunted out the proprietor of the taverna and found him inside the little whitewashed building. We indicated to him we would like very much to have lunch and certainly some of the lamb cooking outside. He was delighted we had chosen his taverna. He led us back outside to a table under the trees, seated us there with a flourish at each chair, spread the table with a clean checked cloth, and then, rubbing his hands in that gesture characteristic of headwaiters when proposing a particular succulence, asked us something. We knew he was asking something because his voice rose at the end of the phrase. We turned expectantly to Darn.

"He's asking us something," she said.

A fine-looking elderly man approached us. We had noticed him a few minutes earlier sitting between two women under a tree at a table not far from us. He asked if he could be of any help. He spoke English well, though slowly and with a heavy accent. We told him, thanking him, we had asked for lunch but we did not know what the proprietor was asking us.

Our visitor explained. "He wants to know if you would like a bottle of wine now while you are waiting for the meat to be done."

Sophy looked stricken. "Imagine my not understanding that," she said.

Our interpreter continued. "He will give you fresh ripe tomatoes, too, and cucumbers and our Greek olives. He will cook you potatoes in olive oil, not greasy," he added quickly. "I know in America you like them dry. This man prepares them so the olive oil is only a little flavor, not a wetness."

When I spoke I found my voice was husky from hunger and yearning. "I haven't eaten potatoes in years," I told him, "but I didn't come to Greece to diet. Tell him potatoes by all means."

Our interpreter translated this.

The proprietor in a rush of happy approval leaned over and patted my shoulder.

"Fresh bread," the interpreter continued. "It is baking now. And cheese."

Darn stiffened. "He did not say cheese," she protested. "I would have gotten that. And," she added belligerently, "I could tell you a lot of other things he didn't say."

The proprietor left us to fetch the wine. We invited the friendly stranger to join us in a glass. He said he would take a little to drink our health and a pleasant stay in Greece. While we waited he told us he had been chief engineer on the United Fruit Company boats, and had visited America many times. Now he was retired, living in Athens. Every Sunday during the spring and summer he and his wife came out to this taverna, bringing their maid with them for an outing. They liked to come early, he said, sit under the tree, have a glass of wine, watch the lamb cooking, and the people going by.

"It is a pleasant occupation for us," he added apologetically. "We are not sophisticated people."

The proprietor brought a bottle of wine, a dish of olives, and another of Feta cheese. Greek olives are small, brown and wrinkled, like the ones I have eaten in Italy, but I prefer the Greek ones. They are saltier. Even in the time we had been in Greece we had begun to eat them as one does salted peanuts at home. The proprietor at our request brought two additional glasses, one for our visitor and one for himself. The two allowed their glasses to be only half filled, and each in turn, stiffening like a soldier, proposed our health; the engineer welcoming us to Greece. The proprietor, as translated, pledged this tree, under which we sat, would always be waiting for us.

We urged our translator to bring his wife and the maid to join us, but he shook his head, smiling a little. "You will excuse her, please," he said. "My wife is shy, and she has the blood pressure. Strangers are not good for the blood pressure when one is not sophisticated."

He shook hands around the table, but before he left, the proprietor requested him to tell us one more thing, and the engineer obliged. "He will bring you the bread now from the oven if you would like it with your cheese and wine, or perhaps wait for the lamb."

We told him we would like it immediately. I asked if I might see it brought from the oven. Our host led me across the road. A little house was set some distance from it, but almost at the edge of the road—and this was a highway with a considerable traffic of buses and cars—there was an earthen oven, round and painted white.

As we approached it a woman with two small children clinging to her skirts came toward us from the little house. The children were clean, but their clothes were pitifully shabby and sparse. The young woman was pretty; clean, too. She wore a bright yellow coif over her head. Her dress was cotton, faded almost threadbare, so there was scarcely any distinguishable color. The proprietor indicated she was his wife and those his two children. I tried to shake hands with the children but they hid behind their mother. She carried a long-handled wooden shovel, and, in front of the oven, bent down, slid the shovel in and drew it out carefully with a loaf of bread on it. Her husband picked up from a small pile nearby a flat stone and very carefully transferred the bread from the shovel. It was obviously too hot to hold in the hand.

We brought back across the road two loaves, each on a stone. When it had cooled barely enough to touch we broke it with our hands, the innkeeper laughing at our gasps and our hands waving in the air. He put down on the table a mound of sweet butter set in grape leaves in an earthenware bowl. We eyed it a moment, but I voiced, I think, the sentiment of the group when I said, "I'm eating potatoes. I consider it quibbling to turn down butter."

Sophy's way of endorsing this pronouncement was to order another bottle of wine.

When we had arrived the only other customers had been the engineer and his household, but along with the arrival of the bread, cars began turning in from the highway and the tables around us were occupied. It was now a little after two o'clock. Evidently that is the timing for lamb roasting on spits outside tavernas, because the other customers came in a rush. Simultaneously with their arrival, the two men stopped turning the handles and, under the supervision of the proprietor, cut and served the meat. There was no finicky nonsense of slicing. A solid piece was cut off, put first on a scale we had not noticed before hanging at the foot of the spits close by the door into the taverna. From there it was transferred to a platter and brought to the table. The meal was priced according to the weight of the piece of lamb served.

We were given a considerable section of the hindquarter. We laughed at the sight of such a mountain of meat, saying to one another we could not possibly eat half of it, but we explained hastily to the proprietor, with gestures of approval, we were laughing only with pleasure at such a beautiful sight. We ate every morsel of it, and every one of the succulent crisp, brown potatoes.

There were other customers who sensed the time for serving and joined us. They included a large, black dog with a small, black puppy, a brown dog, two cats and a rooster. In a nearby field six donkeys gathered in a compact group and set up a piercing bray. Swallows appeared, flying agitatedly in and out through an open window of the taverna. With some small differences it was not unlike a banquet at which Henry VIII might have presided. I pointed this out to my friends as I tossed over my shoulder, to the animals, bones and morsels of lamb.

The lamb was the most delicious, I am sure, I have ever eaten. It had a subtle added flavor we could not identify. Sophy called across to our friend, the engineer, asking what it was.

He was pleased. "I hoped you would notice it," he said. "It comes from the smoke of the fire, because it is cooked over wood from grapevines."

Darn took this opportunity to ask what was in two bags hanging from the limb of a tree above us and one like it attached to a telephone pole a few yards away from us at the edge of the road. We had only noticed them as we were eating.

"Buttermilk," the engineer said, "for the cheese."

There was no doubt about it, Sophy affirmed, this was the way to eat, in the very heart of production, lamb on one side, bread across the road, and cheese in the making over our heads.

The bill for all this was $4.50 including a lunch for Marino.

We asserted a need for exercise after the meal, and the engineer pointed out a path at the side of the taverna. It would lead us to the sea, he told us. The path took us steeply downhill through lovely woods. A short distance behind the taverna we saw a row of huts made of closely woven rough boughs, roofed over but with one whole side open. Darn had been looking for them. Her professor had said she would find them a characteristic and picturesque feature of the Greek landscape. They are corrals where sheep are kept in winter. We were to see them when we motored on remote steep mountainsides we would have thought uninhabitable by men or domestic animals. They are like quotation marks, indicating in every landscape, "This is Greece."

Vasiliu

An old woman came out from behind one of these sheepcotes. She was stooped, dirty, ragged. She carried a staff in one hand and over her other arm a basket of eggs. At sight of us she quickened her pace to an astonishingly vigorous trot, caught up with us and importuned us with gestures to buy her eggs. In spite of our regretful but emphatic refusal, she followed us for some time. At length we gave in. When Luz reminded us what the climb back up the hill would be for the poor old soul we could not bear for her to come farther and knew she would follow us as long as we walked. We gave her money. With rapturous gestures of gratitude that would have included kissing our hands all around had we not backed away, she set the basket of eggs down at our feet and turning round trotted up the hill, kicking her heels behind her like a young goat.

Darn was the first to speak. "The eggs will fit in nicely with the sweet peas and calla lilies," she said, and added bitterly, "I wish I'd given her my shoes." The old woman had been barefoot. "They'd finish that heel kicking for her."

We came to the sea and walked along the shore for a few minutes. It was beautiful, but our hearts somehow did not respond to the charm. The basket of eggs lay heavy between whichever two of us carried it.

Darn's shoes, she said, weighed heavier and more painfully on her feet with every step she took. "Walking shoes," she said, "that's what they told me in New York these were. That's the last thing I can do in them. They'd be good in China for binding women's feet."

She started up the hill with the shoes off, tied around her neck. "If that old woman could do it," she asserted grimly, "I can."

We followed more slowly. She was sitting on a rock when we caught up with her.

She looked up at us from the sole she was contemplating. "I may bleed to death now," she said somberly. "They're cut to ribbons."

Luz and Sophy offered to make a basket seat for her with hands crossed, but she would have none of it.

"You're no more fit for that," she told them, "than I am for walking barefoot."

In the end she forced her shoes back on and we climbed the path with frequent stops.

Reaching the taverna we dissuaded Darn from offering the shoes to any taker among the remaining luncheon guests at their tables. Luz pointed out gently that a path to the sea was one thing, but the path from our car through the lobby of the King George Hotel was one not to be trod barefoot. Neither did we tread it with a basket of eggs and a carload of flowers. We left these souvenirs with the proprietor. He expressed himself as grateful but seemed dazed by the floral tribute.

The engineers' party had left. We agreed this was just as well. A presentation from us, we were sure, would have evoked from him an oratorical display that might have kept us well through the afternoon and we were ready now to go home.

That night at nine o'clock, with Mr. and Mrs. Vlachoustikos and their son, we went to the Acropolis again, and for three hours, with scarcely any talk among us, we looked and wondered at it under the full moon.

Chapter Ten

EARLY next morning with suitcases in the trunk and Marino at the wheel, we were on our way to Delphi. Our road first followed the shoreline along the Bay of Salamis; when we had left that we drove through miles of olive groves. We saw almost no houses but a number of little churches, whitewashed, most of them as small as a woodshed at home. Later we learned these were, so to speak, private churches; that is, a fulfillment by an individual of a vow; not, therefore, places of community worship, but individual shrines. Why they should be placed so remotely from any settlement we did not discover. Along the roadside there were white icons on standards, and each of these had four tiny windows, many of them hung with lace curtains. Each, too, had inside a candle or lamp; most of these were burning as we passed.

Presently we left the olive groves and began to climb. From then on my view of the passing scene was sporadic, because a great part of the time I had my eyes shut, and at other moments looked only through latticed fingers held in front of them, ready to block out the scene completely when it became unendurable. The scene itself, around and over mountains, was magnificent but I am a craven. I am nervous in a car, and I am made giddy in the head and violently disturbed in the middle by looking down from even a modest height. I was now in an automobile skittering among mountains.

Mr. Papastratos had told me as he was driving us to the Yacht Club for lunch, a few days earlier, the reason foreigners could not drive their own cars in Greece was because they lacked the touch of insanity in their blood that made them able to understand what a Greek motorist was likely to do.

Darn was a little squeamish on the Delphi road; Luz and Sophy not at all.

What vistas when I looked! Most of the way snow-capped Parnassus emerged from clouds and disappeared into them again, directly in front of us. We passed no farmhouses, though in the valleys between the mountains there were fields under cultivation. But the people live clustered together in villages where most of the houses are bright pink, with gleaming white doors and window trim. On the roadside to and from the villages we passed workers coming in from the fields or going to them, a man, a woman and a donkey, generally the man riding. In the wheat fields on either side of the road women were in bright-colored dresses. With the wind rippling the grain around them, they might have been standing knee deep in a gentle sea. Their heads and faces were veiled in a manner so like that of Moslem women, we said to one another seeing them, it must be a holdover from the Turkish occupation. We learned later it was nothing of the kind; simply the most practical way of protecting themselves from the sun. All Greek women are proud of a fair skin. This pride goes back to antiquity as a symbol of caste. I thought of these veiled women in the fields when our guide in the Palace of Knossos pointed out on the wall paintings that young men of royal blood were depicted as dark-skinned in evidence of their participation and prowess in outdoor sports, but a woman shown with dark skin symbolized a peasant or servant.

I cannot remember a motor trip on which I have gone direct from the point of departure to my destination. I am a serpentine traveler, working my way in a series of loops around whatever my eye or the guidebook tells me is provocative. Happily, my friends are also inquisitive. So we did not go straight to Delphi, as though anyone could go straight along that mountain highway.

From Athens we had followed the sacred way, the Hiera Hodos. This is the road created and named for the sacred processions that went from Athens to Eleusis, where the mystic religious ceremonies were held, called the Eleusinian Mysteries. Festivals and processions took place there in honor of Demeter and Persephone. At Eleusis, accordingly, we made our first loop, a small one, since what there is to see is no great distance away. There is a cut in a hill that was made, the legend says, by Pluto when he carried off Persephone. There are the remains of a Propylaea, but the columns were destroyed by an earthquake and are scattered over the ground. The Propylaea itself was built in the time of Hadrian. There is the Hall of the

Mysteries, a narrow rectangle in which there are rows of benches, and this is where the mystic rites were held, rites that today are as secret as when they were named the Mysteries. No scholar has found a written record of them. There is the view of the lovely Bay of Salamis, but there are also factories in the way of it.

In the city of Thebes there is less to see. The satisfaction to the sightseer does not come from what is to be seen but from an inner exultance in being able to say to oneself, "I'm in Thebes," remembering stories of that powerful and rich city where Oedipus once was king. We told Marino to drive on, because the village of Thebes today has no particular distinction.

We made another loop at Levadia, a loop of eight miles and back to see Alexander's lion, the lion of Chaeronea, a city he destroyed. It is a magnificent statue of heroic size, a memento left by the arrogant conqueror to mark the scene of his conquest, since nothing else remained. The lion is superbly framed now, in a half circle of cypress trees, a gift from our one-time ambassador to Greece, Lincoln MacVeagh.

We reached Delphi in time for lunch. I was not surprised to find our hotel, the Delphi, was even higher than the top of the main village street that is in itself a sharp ascent. Only a stretch of level road would have surprised me. The hotel is one of the Tourist Inns built by the Greek Government. This was the first we had visited, but we stayed in a number as we continued our trip and found each of them of excellent quality in both accommodations and food, but none with quite so breathtaking a location. We were given two adjoining rooms, each with a balcony, and from these we looked down across a wide swath between towering mountains. This cleft that runs to the sea is so solidly planted in olive trees it is like a great, dusky green river. When the wind blows over the treetops, as it does most of the time, the river seems actually to be flowing down into the bright blue water in the distance. It is called the gorge of the Pleistos, with Mt. Cirphis on its left. The winding stream of olive groves flows into the Gulf of Itea.

It is misleading and inaccurate to say, "When the wind is blowing," because in Greece the wind blows all the time. I think I am not making too sweeping an assertion when I say this. I know from first-hand discomfort it blew every day of the month we were in

Greece in whatever part of the country we were, and I learned from people who live in that country the year round there is nothing "unusual" in this kind of weather. "Fair with moderate to strong winds," is average. Lady tourists would do well to take note of this when assembling their traveling clothes.

Darn was providing the rest of us with a vivid illustration of the kind of dresses not to take. This was irony raised to whatever that ratio is in mathematics that denotes the ultimate. Darn, the forehanded, the careful planner, the heeder of details, had clothes trouble from foot to head, and because of this her dear friends were having considerable trouble in persuading her to keep the wardrobe she had assembled. She had scattered shoes as though she were throwing pennies for diving boys. After our first trip to the Acropolis, she had tried to give away several of her dresses. She had been thwarted in this by a ruling of the hotel that forbade an individual chambermaid to receive a donation of any sort from a guest, from tips to garments. Everything bestowed had to be turned over to the housekeeper, and distributed equally among the corps of workers. Since a garment could not be divided, its approximate worth must be paid into the pot by the maid who had received it. This was not a quixotic ruling of our hotel. It is evidently an old Greek custom. We had discovered it first on board the *Queen Frederica.*

Darn's is a generous and an equable nature, but her threat to scatter garments from the window if she were not allowed to give them away was prompted by the wind. Darn's is also a conservative nature, and only the wind blew her so out of character as to declare she would sooner dress like Raymond Duncan, from scandals to burlap togas, than go sightseeing in Greece with her skirt up over her head. That is what the wind did to her skirts. With sober forethought she had had them made to her own design, in order to be sure they would be as full as she needed; she had been told there would be climbing. The dresses were made of nylon, or a like material, dark blue, not so vulnerable as lighter shades to dirt, yet easy to launder when necessity demanded. Nylon, or its equivalent, is a billowing material. On the Acropolis it billowed over and around her head. Even on the modest burial mound in Marathon, she had been engulfed in nylon. She was still under the tyranny of the nylon skirts when we traveled to Delphi, because our crowded schedule in Athens had not allowed her time to hunt out conventional clothes, burlap for togas, or whatever would cling. The tyranny demanded that in order to keep her skirts down she must tie by the sleeves a sweater around her hips, and under a Greek sun sweat it out.

The rest of us, all haphazard planners, were adequately equipped. The dresses the other three had brought for country motoring or sightseeing were cotton, cool and full-skirted, though not so full-skirted as Darn's, and heavy enough to withstand impertinence from the wind.

Kakia Livanos had told us we must wear hats, not for conformity to custom and style but for preservation from the intensity of the sun. "Take cotton hats," she had advised, "the kind golfers or tennis players wear. You can roll them up and carry them in your bag or a pocket, but never forget to put them on your head when you are out among the ruins."

How we blessed her for this advice! My hair is long; I wear it an old-fashioned way in braids around my head. I do not wear a hat, principally because of vanity, since no matter what the model, when set down on my braids, it looks as though I had acquired it from the late Queen Mary's collection. Though there are many ways in which I wish I might resemble that splendid and awesome queen, a selection of hats is not one of them. I have never felt the need of protection against the cold of winter nor the heat of summer, but I think I might have been stricken down by the Greek sun had I not been covered by a shape in cotton that pulled over my braids, dropped about my face in involuntary scallops once it had been folded, and in no way resembled anything the late Queen Mary would have placed upon her marcel waves. A scarf will do, but a hat with a brim is better. Dark glasses are indispensable.

We ordered fish for lunch at the Delphi Hotel, and when we had ordered, knowing we must wait a little time for it to be broiled, Darn and I went moodily to a little shop off the lobby where we had seen postcards for sale. We returned to the table with a considerable collection. Neither of us, we said, was likely ever to see any of these places or, for that matter, any place other than Delphi, for the rest of our lives, because nothing under Heaven would induce us to go back over the road we had just traveled. Since there

GUIDE
GRÈCE
S
EK
Vasiliu

seemed to be no other way of leaving Delphi, we would endeavor to grow reconciled to our St. Helena. Perhaps our children, braver than we, would visit us one day, and perhaps bring their children for us to see. Darn suggested we might take up a handicraft, weaving she thought, since that was a Greek specialty. Sophy observed she had never known me able to use any tools except a knife and fork. Darn's answer was in that case I could read aloud to her while she wove.

The fish arrived, firm, sweet, a lovely golden brown, and with it a bottle of Samos Sec, the first we had had really chilled. At the end of the meal over cheese and the last of the wine, Darn and I consented to see Delphi, and even to leave it.

We took a siesta first, but at five we were ready when Marino brought the car. We drove back down the steep village incline and along the road past the museum and the entrance to the shrine. Around the next bend in the road—the road is all bends—we left the car. By a path and steep steps we descended to the Temple of Athena, moving aside, at one point, to allow an unobstructed passage for an old lady driving a reluctant donkey ahead of her, down the steps. She crossed the site of the temple as we watched, and disappeared up the hill on the far side.

We stood at what was actually the Precinct of Athena Pronaia, a name that means "before the temple." Athena Pronaia, the guardian, was one of the patron goddesses of Delphi. The reason this was called "before the temple" was because it was a shrine for pilgrims before they reached the great Temple of Apollo on the summit of Delphi. In this precinct there were, formerly, numerous sacred buildings and there were also memorials to heroes. The temple proper of Athena Pronaia is of the Doric order, probably dating, the guidebook says, from the sixth century B.C.

When we had climbed back onto the highway we saw considerable traffic approaching us, just as we would have found at home a traffic rush around six o'clock when people are returning from work. This traffic was a procession of donkeys, scarcely visible under the loads of hay they carried, and frequently, in addition, a passenger. The passenger was generally a man. A woman trudging alongside, directed the donkey by smart taps with a stick in her hand. When a woman did ride she sat sideways on a pack saddle of wooden slats. Because of this traffic the drive back to the hotel took considerably more time than had been required to reach the temple.

At dinner I speculated on the possibility of shipping home for my grandchildren some of the endearing little donkeys, such as I had seen on the road. Darn, consulting her notebook that she is never without, read off that to date I had announced my intention of taking home with me: Yolande, a stewardess on the *Queen Frederica*, Koula, my dear chambermaid at the King George, and a little orphan at Voula, cured of tuberculosis but with no family to which she could be sent. Darn added to the list a cluster of donkeys.

I woke next morning with a paralyzing sore throat. Swallowing was painful, well-nigh impossible. Luz and Darn came from their room as we had arranged the night before, for an early breakfast on our balcony. With Sophy they went into a head-waggling consultation over my condition. They prescribed a gargle of salt and warm water. Sophy volunteered to bring salt from the dining room. When she returned she was palpably flustered. She was followed by the desk clerk and two chambermaids.

Sophy addressed Darn irritably. "Tell them," she said, "I want salt."

"What did you ask for?" I whispered.

Sophy rounded on me. "I didn't ask for anything. I don't know the word. I couldn't show them; the dining room isn't open. So I gargled. The idiots think I was braying. They're getting donkeys for us. Stop them, Darn!"

Darn wrung her hands. "I can't think of the word," she moaned. "I'm rattled. Wait," she added, "I've got my vocabulary list. Hold them. I'll be back."

She ran from the room, Sophy barred the door to the donkey messengers. Darn returned, panting a little and thumbing rapidly the leaves of a notebook. With a restraining hand on the arm of the gentleman, Darn gave him the words for, "good morning, good appetite, how much? what is the price?" as she read down a page.

Finally she shouted at him, "*Alati, alati.*"

As if on cue, each of my three dear companions and helpers, to indicate the reason for the request, clutched her throat with one hand, pointed to me with the other, threw back her head and brayed or gargled urgently, according to the viewpoint of the onlooker.

They stared wide-eyed, backed a little toward the door, then nodded in sudden comprehension and burst into voluble speech.

When my companions were convinced we were all of us as one in understanding, Sophy permitted the hotel delegation to leave.

The chambermaid returned almost immediately with salt for me, a teacup filled to the brim with it. I gargled again and again, but I missed Delphi. All that terrifying ride, and nothing, I thought, to compensate for it. I had a compensation, however. Certainly not full payment—nothing could offset the bitter disappointment of missing the navel of the world, as the ancients had called it—but it was a soothing palliative.

I was roused from a stupid half sleep that fever induces by the sharp, clear note of a cuckoo clock. Drowsily I thought, smiling to myself, how that cuckoo clock must have come to this remote Greek village. Perhaps a sailor, returning from a voyage had brought it back as a novelty to his mother or wife, and it was probably the pride of the village. It did not at the moment strike me as unlikely that a Greek sailor would have made port in Switzerland. At the instant I reached this involved conclusion I realized I had unconsciously been counting the hours the clock was indicating, and at that very instant heard it strike thirteen. I was sitting bolt upright when it struck fourteen. On the stroke of fifteen I was saying aloud, "It's a bird. That's a cuckoo!"

I can scarcely boast I am the only one who has heard a cuckoo sing, but I shall not forget I heard that blithe spirit singing on a May morning from an olive tree in Greece.

I could not stay in bed after that. As I dressed I realized I felt too light in the head, too wobbly in the knees, to attempt the climb I must make to reach the stadium and the other treasures, but I would certainly visit the museum.

Members of the hotel staff at sight of me in the lobby endeavored in some consternation to shoo me back to my room, but finding me adamant, returned to their original misconception and volunteered a donkey.

To have heard a cuckoo for the first time had been one thing, but to ride a donkey for the first time, feeling as I did, was a thing I did not care to attempt. I was fervently communicating this point of view to my well-wishers when Marino walked in. My companions had sent him back, Sophy explaining afterward she had distrusted my assurance I would stay in bed. He drove me to the museum.

I hear in wondering pity now of tourists who say they went to Delphi from Athens, and back, in one day. I wish we had stayed a week. As I entered the museum I felt sure, had we carried out our plan of the night before to spend the rest of our lives in Delphi, Darn would not have had to take up weaving. The village itself is delightful. Every house down its steep, single street had flowers blooming around the doorway, either in a garden or in containers that were probably war souvenirs, old gasoline or oil tins, but painted white, pink, blue or yellow. On a terrace at the far end of the street there were groups of people at little tables having coffee. It was still very early morning.

When I left the car at the entrance to the museum I waited outside several minutes listening to the birds sing all around me. I did not hear another cuckoo, but what beauty I saw! Brilliant wildflowers in the fields across the road and a view down to the valley below and up the mountain beyond, that stretched the eye to encompass. And what treasures I saw that morning in the museum!

Almost immediately inside there is a large mound of marble like a beehive. The exterior is sculptured. This is thought to represent the Omphalos, which is the navel, because Delphi by the Ancient Greeks was believed to be the center of the earth. At the end of the room to the left stands the famous charioteer, dramatically placed. This superb bronze figure was once part of a four-horse-chariot group. The eyes are onyx, and eyelashes are included in the sculpturing. These give a startling effect, but I came back again and again from the other rooms to look at the feet. They are strong but supple, wonderfully fashioned. To me, this museum was one of the most rewarding of all I visited in Greece.

At the end of two hours I came out. Marino had gathered up my friends. We went back to the hotel, packed and at ten o'clock were on our way to Athens. My companions were subdued by the magnificence they had seen. They talked sporadically. Darn mentioned eagles that flew above the stadium. She said, too, it was good to go to the stadium and the theater early in the morning when the air was cool and fresh. I had heard people talking at the hotel before I left for the museum. They had gone up at six and had just come down for breakfast. Darn also said it was good to take the by-path by the museum to reach the theater, and that a very good path to the stadium leads off from the left of the base of the theater. She also advised against climbing to the top of the theater to find the path, emphasizing that the good one was at its base, to the left.

I do not remember ever before rejoicing in temperature and a sore throat. I cherished both on the way to Athens. They made me relaxed, indifferent to the passing scene; I even dozed around a mountain curve.

I roused as we were driving through the main street of a village. Marino said the name of it was Arachova, at least that is the name we decided on after he had said the word patiently several times. I saw hand-woven bedspreads on display outside a shop and asked the others if they would mind if we stopped to explore a little. They didn't mind though Darn was a little irked with me for sleeping on mountain roads, leaving her to shudder all by herself, and then waking up on a straight village street, just because we were passing an antique shop.

She bought things, too. We all came out of the shop laden. Marino was becoming accustomed to our mode of travel. He had the trunk open and was standing beside it, waiting. It was not exclusively a shop of antiques, we discovered, but of native work, some of it very old, but many articles new. I bought a pouch bag made of beautiful embroidery that had once been the bodice of a wedding costume, two hand-woven bedspreads, and a pair of sleeveless jackets, for Sophy's little granddaughters, who love costumes. These were the traditional knee-length, wasp-waisted overtunics that Greek women wear on special occasions. They are made of very heavy and coarse lamb's wool in the natural color, embroidered in red and black, and worn over a straight pleated undergarment.

The curious thing about almost all the embroidery we saw in Greece, old or new, is that the patterns are strikingly similar to those of the American Indians. When I brought home to Lillian, my Finnish cook, a hand-woven tablecloth, she hugged it with startled affection and said, "This is like home. This is Finnish."

The shop owner and his two sisters, who were his assistants, came to the car to see us off. We persuaded them to pose in front of their shop, with the pieces of peasant work that had first attracted our attention a colorful background behind them. Sophy and I took a number of pictures. Luz snapped one that I heard, but when I turned to ask her how she was setting her camera for light, I saw she was climbing into the car.

I heard Darn ask brightly, "Busted again?"

I thought to myself, "Darn's love of asking questions is going to get her into trouble one of these days, possibly right now."

But Luz has a forbearing nature, and apart from not answering, showed no antagonism.

I did not sleep again. I was feeling much better. Sophy, noticing this, observed that had they been able to find an antique shop in Delphi, I might not have taken to my bed at all. We were not as yet out of the mountains, and I shared shudders with Darn, so that when we emerged at last into the valley, her good spirits were restored and everyone was in high humor. I think Marino must have felt better when the curves straightened out and I left off prodding him in the back.

We stopped again at a little taverna. We had seen on the edge of the road a spring bubbling up in a stone trough and necks of beer bottles visible over the top. This was the sight that had prompted us to stop. As we left the car we saw close by the taverna a stone monument and walked over to see what it commemorated. There had been a village here, we learned from the monument, Korakolithos. The monument recorded the names of 134 men, the total male population of the village, killed by the Germans in 1944 in revenge for the death of one German officer.

We sat on benches at a table under a big tree. The proprietor brought us beer from the spring, deliciously cold. As we drank it we watched two women a few yards away washing clothes in a stream, and beating them with large, flat stones. A handsome old man sat under a tree not far from us; we exchanged smiles and nods. Two little girls came down the road toward us, one about six years old, the other perhaps three or four. They were brown-skinned, pink-cheeked, pretty and clean. They were driving before them a goat with her kid. At sight of the old man they all ran toward him, children, goat and kid. The goat nuzzled under his outstretched hand and he patted it; the two little girls swarmed over his lap. The kid, to our astonishment, after frisking about for a minute, rushed toward a tree and actually climbed it. The older of the two children scrambled down from the lap of the old man, went up the tree after the kid, caught it, brought it down and carried it over to the patriarch. The baby on his lap reluctantly yielded her place, and he sat holding the kid instead. The proprietor told us these were his children, and the old man, his father.

Sophy and I took pictures of all of them, including the two women at the stream, his wife and his sister, we learned. Luz and Darn waited for us in the car.

We were back in Athens in time for lunch at three o'clock. I went up to bed. The others reported the hotel dining room more crowded than they had seen it, evidently because we had heretofore been so unfashionable as to lunch before three.

They held a conference in my room about plans for the afternoon. My plan was to stay where I was, Sophy's, a siesta. Luz muttered she had an errand to do and we did not inquire its nature. Darn was more communicative though somewhat defiant in her announcement. She reminded us she had secured from Mme. de Romero one day on the *Queen Frederica* the address of a *couturière* in Athens. We had teased Darn at the time about this but she had persisted. "I like writing things down," she had said. And this, we had agreed, was the God's truth. She was going now to that address and order new clothes.

"By the time I leave," she told us grimly, "I'll be equipped with the kind of clothes I ought to have had when I arrived."

Sophy pointed out perhaps this would not be just the equipment for the *Queen Mary*, on which she was sailing home, but Darn was not to be deterred.

Next day I was completely recovered, but at lunch Sophy said she felt unaccountably heavy-eyed; she would take a long siesta. Stopping for her later, on our way to a cocktail party, we found her in bed, held there by the same symptoms that had pinned me down. Pausing at the dining room on our way out I sent up to her, without any difficulty, salt for gargling.

On the way to the party Luz was communicative about her errand of the day before. Her expedition had proved so charming it had broken down her reluctance to mention her camera. The man at the camera shop had admitted, she said, he could not repair this last misfire, whatever it was. He had recommended her to a special camera mechanic.

Armed with the address she had set out but had been unable to find the street. Seeing her obviously searching her way, a young American in the uniform of the Merchant Marine had stepped up to her and asked if he could help. Taking the card from her hand at her grateful acquiescence, he had led her a few blocks and on the way told her he came from Cleveland but was of Greek parentage. The address turned out to be in a little arcade that the Merchant Marine seemed to know very well, and the mechanic doubled in brass by running as well as a camera, a shoe-repair shop. The Merchant Marine proved to be an excellent interpreter, speaking Greek fluently, though this, he had told Luz, was his first visit to the country. After the transaction had been accomplished, the mechanic assuring Luz he could make the repairs with no difficulty, her new friend, the Marine, took her farther down the street into a bakery shop. He knew the street well, he revealed, because the bakery shop belonged to his brother, and he wished Luz to visit it. They had a pleasant time, she reported, munching sugar cookies as they talked.

The cocktail party was in the Grande Bretagne. The upper corridors of that hotel are constructed much like the maze at Hampton Court, with the added obstruction to finding one's way that the hotel provides rooms on either side, numbered with a disregard for sequence that is both capricious and baffling. On our third or fourth time around, when unexpectedly we had come back to the elevator from which we had started, we saw one of these doors a few feet ahead open, and determined to ask for help from whoever was about to emerge. The person turned out to be His Excellency, Señor de Romero, whom we had not seen since our farewells on the dock at the landing of the *Queen Frederica*.

We had a happy interlude with the de Romeros, Darn particularly delighting in the coincidence that had brought us to their door so soon after her visit to the dressmaker Mme. de Romero had recommended. When we left them, reluctantly, His Excellency delivered us to the suite of our host, Mr. Shelby Carter, admitting, as he pointed to the number we had been seeking, that the only intellectual triumph he had achieved over Mme. de Romero was his mastery of the labyrinth of the floor on which they lived. She had achieved only the triumph of forcing the management to change their suite to one in view of the elevator, because she had been unable to find her way alone to the one originally allotted them.

While he was greeting us, Mr. Carter led the way through his little sitting room saying, "I've a surprise waiting for you on the balcony."

The surprise turned out to be two old friends, Grace and Neil Phillips, who told us they, with friends, had chartered a yacht to cruise the Aegean Islands. There was room on it for two more. They begged two of us to leave our group of four, if only for a ten-day cruise. They could not crowd in all four, but wouldn't we draw lots? The thought of such an expedition was so tantalizing Darn, Luz and I looked at one another with a wild surmise, each, I know, picturing to herself the bliss of sailing at leisure on one's own boat, stopping as long as one wanted at an island, and then lying on deck in the sun, sailing over the blue Aegean.

Neil, who is a retired Admiral of the United States Navy, said he had made sure the members of the crew were experienced sailors. There was only one drawback! Not one of them spoke any language other than Greek.

"But," Neil said, "we'll get along. A good sailor is all I ask. I didn't hire them for conversation and the owner of the boat guarantees these are top men. How can you resist such a trip?"

It was not easy, but we did resist it. Though we had set no fixed itinerary, each of us preferring to be flexible, we decided a ten-day separation would hold back the two remaining from making trips they felt all four would enjoy, and that since we had set out together, we would keep our original formation.

Chapter Eleven

THE road to Nauplia goes through Corinth and Mycenae. It is also the town nearest to Epidaurus. Travelers setting out from Athens have visited these four places in one day. If a crowded schedule makes this the only way possible then certainly it is better than not seeing them at all, but we four on that excursion more than once dropped a word of pity for those who must rush it so.

We left the King George Hotel at nine and drove slowly, partly because of pressure from me, but also because there is so much in the Greek landscape that is a delight to see. Marino, a perceptive man, appreciated both my idiosyncrasy and our pleasure in the passing scene, and drove now without prompting at a leisurely mileage.

Our departure had been delayed for at least a quarter of an hour by the unexpected appearance of a bellboy from the hotel, just after our bags had been stowed in the trunk and the lid dropped. The unexpected factor was a man's white shirt the boy brought us. It was spotlessly clean, perhaps it had just come from the laundress; it was not wrapped in any covering, certainly it was not part of the traveling equipment of any of the four of us.

After a fervent exhortation from the boy, Marino opened the trunk and placed the shirt on top of our bags. Watching this procedure, we decided the shirt must belong to Marino. But Darn, not one to accept speculation, inquired directly if this were so. Marino, startled, assured us it was not. We therefore requested him to remove the shirt and return it to the boy, but the boy would have none of it. We gathered he had been instructed by someone to put it in this particular car. No expostulation, nor entreaty from us, gave him so much as a prick of doubt that he was carrying out precisely his instructions. He corroborated this by turning on his heel while all four of us were gesturing. We were left with this extraordinary *souvenir de voyage*. I said perhaps it was a token from the management like a St. Christopher medal for protection on our little trip. The others thought this unlikely but offered no more reasonable explanation. Whatever its source and significance, we included this unsuitable appendage to the luggage of four middle-aged women.

We always drove with the windows of our Chevrolet sedan wide open. All four of us constantly pointed out through the open window objects for the others to see, even the one in the middle, leaning across one or the other of her neighbors. To anyone we approached, the car might have looked to be transporting some representation of Lakshmi, that Indian goddess with four arms.

Luz pointed out in a gypsy train we passed a monkey on the shoulder of one of the band, but it was Darn, the practical one, who a minute later called our attention to the extraordinary cleanliness of the road. We had not realized heretofore how characteristic this is of every road in Greece. What made the cleanliness extraordinary, we said, was the fact there is scarcely a time in the day when the roads are not being traveled by animals. The particulary gypsy train we had just passed had included seven or eight donkeys. We learned later this cleanliness is due to the urgent need among the Greeks for fertilizer. All animal droppings are carefully and eagerly gathered up immediately. This is what makes possible motoring with open windows in a country where the wind blows constantly.

Just as I associate Italy with swallows, white bullocks and scarlet poppies, I shall always think of Greece as rows of olive trees, framing a vista to a bright blue sea. There are eucalyptus trees, too, along the roads, and fields of wheat, yellow here, rippling like a golden river under the wind. On the road to Delphi it had been a flowing of green; the wheat had not ripened there. Here, too, the olive trees were in bloom, a solid, impenetrable mass of blossoms.

The Corinthian Canal is a dramatic sight, so narrow and so abruptly steep there is no view of it from a distance. We had no indication of our nearness to it until we were stopped by a guard at our end of the bridge that spans it. He told Marino, and Marino conveyed to us, it was forbidden to take photographs there. We looked inquiringly at Luz.

"Yes," she said grimly, "it's in perfect working order."

Vasiliu

Marino parked the car at one side of the road, and we walked out on the bridge. The cut is over 260 feet deep, straight down in solid rock. Marino, counting by fives on his fingers, communicated to us it is 75 feet across at the bottom. The optical illusion at this depth is such it looks scarcely broad enough to accommodate a small sailboat.

I stood with stiff spine at such a height and eyed the descent with only a gingerly inclining of the head. As I eyed it as askance as was possible, and still see it, I thought how my father and grandfather, brother and uncles, in my family of engineers, would have marveled at this magnificent construction. I thought, too, how preposterous that it should have been, of all figures in history, the Emperor Nero who conceived of this idea of a cut across the isthmus. That bawdy figure, visiting Greece in about 38 B.C. to participate in games and festival, had proposed the idea, but it was A.D. 1893 when the canal was opened. I could not avoid thinking, too, of the terrible years in the recent history of this place, when the British tried to hold it in 1940 and were driven off in bloody defeat; the dark days that followed until liberation by the Allied forces in 1945.

As we drove on we talked about ancient history. We were in the Pelo*ponn*esus, that peninsula of southern Greece that for forty odd years I had called the Peloponn*e*sus, and I was learning, too, to say Sa*lon*ika as a replacement for a lifetime of Saloni*k*a. The aspect of ancient history we talked about that bright morning on the way to Corinth was transportation. From now on, I said, I would consider the symbol of Greek history to be the labors of Hercules. What manner of men and what number of men had brought to the Acropolis the material for its buildings? The others begged me not to mention the Acropolis in the same breath with Delphi, pointing out I had not climbed its summit. They had, and found a camera almost too much to carry. Arriving, spent of breath, they had looked at remains of vast structures, every piece of it carried to that peak. We knew now, we agreed, whatever variation there was in style and design, the location was not variable. It was always the highest point in the Greek landscape.

Sophy diverted our conversation from buildings to ships. She reminded us that in the Peloponnesian War, when there was no canal on which to float the vessels, the entire Athenian fleet and that of the Spartans, as well, was *rolled* across the isthmus there. And later, the Emperor Augustus, vengefully pursuing Anthony and Cleopatra, had accomplished the same maneuver.

"And you," Sophy concluded, turning abruptly on me, "fuss about traveling a mountain road in a car. Picture yourself setting out from Athens on foot to consult the Oracle at Delphi."

I made a mental leap from the Peloponnesian fleet to myself as a Delphic pilgrim, and asserted I would have preferred that method of transportation; but I begged Darn, who likes to share whatever information she has gleaned, not to communicate this to Marino, next to whom she was sitting at the time. I did not want his feelings hurt.

Corinth is only a little more than fifty miles west of Athens. Even at our pace we reached it by eleven.

We changed shoes before getting out of the car; Darn put on for the first time new ones bought the day before in Athens. She found she had been given one of one size, one of another.

We stood between two massive Doric pillars of that ancient temple, said to be the oldest in Greece, and looked down across the fields to the blue Bay of Corinth; a scene of brightness and light that, conjured up in the memory, will make my heart leap on the darkest winter day.

My three companions, who challenged one another frequently on feats of map reading, were baffled by the map each held of the ancient city of Corinth in relation to what we actually saw. As I was the first to point out later to my friends, I excel in providing help in time of need. The manner of help may, at the time, seem irrelevant, but it proves efficacious. What I provided at Corinth in lieu of a map was a young American girl. I saw her while the others were fussing over diagrams. She had flowers in her hair, rags and a bottle of liquid in her hands. She looked American and she was, by curious coincidence of name, Elizabeth Taylor, an archeological student from Radcliffe. At my request she was charmingly polite about substituting herself for the printed page. She identified for us streets, shops and dwellings of that once great, rich city. As we walked over the stones of its streets, we reminded one another this was where Paul had come.

We pressed ear to stones and heard the sound of bubbling water. This was the Fountain of Peirene. Pausanias wrote about it, and

Pausanias of the second century was a considerable forerunner of Baedeker's guide for tourists. The water does not come from a spring below the ground but from springs high up above the spot on which we stood.

The Acro-Corinth, the Acropolis of Corinth, is nearly two thousand feet above the ancient city itself. Our guide told us its summit can be reached by an hour's hard climbing, and from there is to be seen one of the widest and most glorious views of all Greece. We took her word for it. Through Luz's field glasses we could see the wall that surrounds the Acropolis. From a guidebook we read that Pegasus was browsing in a meadow on that summit when Belerophon saw and captured him. In the struggle, Pegasus endeavoring to escape his captor pawed the ground wildly with his hoofs, causing springs to gush, those springs that feed the Fountain of Peirene.

Our guide asked shyly if we would like to see the place where she was working. She led us to a Roman house and showed us the mosaic floor of one of its rooms she was interpreting and chronicling. The equipment she was carrying was for a bit of scrubbing to be done. She was working that summer, she told us, under the direction of the American School of Classical Studies. When we had examined, with interest, her mosaics, she took us to the museum, a little distance away. This building, we learned from her, was a gift from an American. It houses an interesting collection of pieces from the Corinthian ruins.

The place to lunch is at the Tourist Pavilion, one of the hostelries established by the government, though this one does not accommodate overnight guests. It is a charming spot, with a superb view over the water and in the distance Mt. Parnassus. We had an excellent lunch.

The road from Corinth to Mycenae took us through olive groves again, all in bloom. By finger count Marino told us the olives would be ripe in November.

The road to the Acropolis of Mycenae is bordered by tall, old eucalyptus trees. Oleanders were in bloom at their base. There is a Tourist Pavilion, where the traveler who does not pause at Corinth can lunch.

To anyone who has read *The Bull of Minos* by Leonard Cottrell, the inn called La Belle Hélène will have a meaning other than an association with our friend in Athens, Mme. Pothamianos, or the Trojan War. *The Bull of Minos* is absorbing reading, whether or not one visits Greece, but it would be a great pity to visit Greece without having read this account of the great discoveries at Mycenae by that dedicated eccentric, Heinrich Schliemann.

I do not know first hand the view from the Acro-Corinth, but the sight of the Argos Plain from the Hill Mycenae would take one's breath if it were not already taken away by the climb. In the distance beyond the plain is the blue water of the Bay of Nauplia in a cup made by the enclosing mountain. On that climb, however, there is no indication of the vastness and the grandeur of the citadel itself until the very entrance is reached, the wonderful Lion Gate. There within is the City of Agamemnon and his Queen Clytemnestra. Here is the palace where Orestes, Electra, and Iphigenia, the youngest and loveliest, were children. Here Agamemnon was murdered by Clytemnestra's lover Aegisthus, and Clytemnestra murdered by Orestes. It was from here Orestes fled pursued by the Furies because of his awful deed. These were the people and this the place recorded by the great Euripides and retold over and over again by writers down through history.

We put our feet in the grooves made to carry chariot wheels up a ramp. We looked down on the mysterious Treasury of Atreus, that has been called the Tomb of Agamemnon and the Treasury of Athens, and is still not indubitably identified other than that it is one of the greatest of all the products of the Bronze Age. Like the Omphalos in Delphi, though this is far larger, it is in the shape of a beehive. This one, the guidebook told us, is fifty feet across, and fifty feet high.

We were driven down from Mycenae by the sun. Although we saw it, explored it, put our hands and our feet on its stones, we did not sit as we had sat on the Acropolis, letting the place seep into our memory, and peopling it again from what we already knew of its rulers and their deeds. We should have waited in the pavilion until half past four or five, but we visited it at three when the day was close to its peak of heat. Next time I shall not be so impatient and I shall stay longer.

Nauplia is only nineteen kilometers beyond Mycenae. This is the town closest to the great theater of Epidaurus and the shrine of Aesculapius. We spent two nights here, but only one of these at the hotel on the mainland. On our arrival, Marino drove us to a dock, where he blew the horn unceasingly until we saw a little launch put out from what looked like a fortress in the middle of the Gulf of Nauplia, that is itself an arm of the Aegean Sea. We had been urged by Miss Alice at the travel agency in Athens to stay at Bourzi, but she had not explained to us what this was. We know now it is a hotel unlike one any of us had ever visited. It has a history that could scarcely be paralleled. As a hotel it is charming, comfortable, clean (that is an adjective that becomes redundant in Greece). The rooms are so small as to be monastic, but each one has a balcony that hangs out over the water and looks to the mountains beyond. The food is excellent.

The history of the place is anything but charming. Bourzi was a retreat for retired executioners. The executioners were themselves convicts under sentence of death, but they were released, not into freedom, but for the performance of the duties of an executioner. This was a duty so abhorrent to the Greeks only those under the most stringent compulsion would perform it. When his term of office was ended, the executioner was not acceptable to any community. He was therefore confined for his retirement to the hangmen's retreat of Bourzi.

We found no gruesome souvenirs of its former occupants, nor did we hear ghostly sighs or clanking chains during the night. What I did hear as I stood on the balcony off my room was a familiar voice calling, "Is that you, Emily?"

Craning out over my balcony railing at some peril to my equilibrium, I looked up to find Grace Phillips, at a perilous downward angle over the balcony rail above.

At Mr. Carter's cocktail party, where we had met, no mention had been made by any of us of an intended trip to Nauplia. We had been too absorbed in the tantalizing proposal of the cruise on a yacht. They were on their way to Olympia, she said, making this a stopping point for the night. I asked them to join my group for the shoebag hour.

When I went in to tell the others of our unexpected neighbors, I found Sophy and Luz about to go for a swim. Darn stayed behind to wash white gloves, she told us; an unnecessary statement, we pointed out. I followed the bathers with my camera. I am not one,

I told them, to go plunging off a dock, or whatever leads to water over my head. Sophy answered it was as unnecessary an explanation as Darn's that she was going to wash gloves. No one who had known me for thirty years was unaware of my method of swimming. Sophy's mother once told me the only people she had ever seen employ my technique were the Irish maids whom they took up to Maine for the summer. They went in a step at a time, and at each step scooped up water, patting it on their wrists and the backs of their necks, and squealing at each application. I did not deny then the similarity, and I have not changed my way of approaching a swim.

The swimming at Bourzi is by way of a flight of steps, hewn from the rock that forms its base. The steps go down from a charming, broad stone terrace, not easy to find in that astonishing fortress. We had gone through, in single file, a number of passages before we had the happy surprise of following one corridor that actually opened onto it.

A man and woman smiled at us as we came through the door. We were saying aloud to one another our pleasure that we had at last found the right one. They were sitting in low chairs near the outer edge of the terrace where the late afternoon sun still shed a patch of warmth. The man spoke gravely. "The white rabbit just went by," he said.

I am absurdly shy about making conversation with strangers, only because I do not know how to begin. But anyone who refers to *Alice in Wonderland* is no stranger to me. "Oh my stars and whiskers," I answered, "was he late for the Queen?"

The man nodding several times affirmatively and contentedly, stood up, inviting us with a gesture to share their sunlight.

The woman was in a bathing suit. She left her chair, saying to Sophy and Luz she had discovered the steps that led to the water. She added she was glad they had come along; swimming was much pleasanter in a company.

I sat down with the man and we fell into easy conversation, talking at first a little about our mutual love of Alice and her adventures, and then about Greece, swapping places we had seen in the manner of all travelers, confirming a little cursorily the places each had visited, but emphasizing with loving possessiveness those spots the other had not seen, as though they were rare and exclusive stamps in a private collection. We talked, too, of the Greek language, found we both had once studied classical Greek, and agreed this was far more a frustration than a help; frustrating because it enabled us to read a little, and yet had provided us with no speech equipment. I confessed that a few days before in Athens, in a desperate effort to establish congeniality with Greek friends, I had seized paper and pencil and written down the first lines of the *Anabasis*. This had been socially about as satisfactory a gambit as communicating to a group of Americans a little phrase from Chaucer.

"However," my companion said, "I do think it's a very helpful thing for anyone planning to visit Greece to learn the Greek alphabet. He can at least spell out the words on signs."

I agreed, adding that if the fourth member of our group were there, she would write this down at once on her list of helpful hints to travelers. A minute or two later he had given me two gems to add to a list I myself have made over the years of Helpful Phrases from Language Handbooks. One of these he had got from a Guide to Spanish. It read, "Waiter, please bring me a knife, fork and a beehive." The other he had found in India. "Please hand me my lavender shantung pantaloons."

I took pictures of the swimmers from the rim of the terrace. The water was so clear I could see every tiny pebble on its sandy bottom. I would have thought it scarcely two feet deep, but Sophy demonstrated how mistaken I was by holding her arm straight above her head and dropping below the surface until even her fingertips were submerged, and still she had not touched bottom. Luz was indulgent to me, too, when I asked for a close-up picture of her. She posed with one foot on a step, the other braced against the rock, her head just above the water.

We were dressing for dinner in our separate rooms when Luz came into Sophy's and my room. One foot was bare and she was limping.

"I seem to have stepped on something," she told us, "but I can't get the sole of my foot around enough to see what I've done."

She held it up for our inspection.

We were not happy, and I was particularly unhappy to have to tell her that, by posing amiably for my picture, she had braced her foot against a sea urchin on the rock. The wretched creature had left its imprint like a round pincushion, and one stuck with pins, on the bottom of her foot.

Sophy is not only the executive and the sommelier of our traveling group, she is also the official apothecary. In addition to her shoebag of specifics, she carries a separate traveling case filled with everything she deems necessary for the physical well-being of travelers. On every trip we have made together, we have left the selection to her, and on every trip nearly all the remedies in her kit have been used at one time or another. On this little two-day excursion, and the only time such a thing had happened, Sophy had left her bag of medicines at the King George Hotel in Athens. With all the things she might have brought, and I include a list as a suggestion to other tourists,* she had not so much as a Band-aid with her. I have seldom seen her so exasperated as she was that evening, but she is resourceful.

"I've a bottle of Ambrosia," she said, "stuff I use to clean my face. It's pure, it's got considerable alcohol in it, I think, and I have cotton pads to swab it on with. I'll make a compress of it."

This is what we did when we had decided among us it would be risky to try to probe the pricks the tentacles had made, lest that spread an infection. The treatment was thoroughly successful. The foot was painful for a few days Luz admitted afterward, but there was no infection. Sophy sacrificed her bottle of Ambrosia, a large one, applied a fresh compress every few hours and washed her own face with soap and water.

Some weeks after Luz's accident, when she and Darn had gone back to America, and Sophy and I were in England, Sophy read *The Crack in the Column* by George Weller. She was reading it in bed one night, and I heard her give a sharp exclamation. A minute or two later she had come into my room.

"Listen to this," she said. "It's about Bourzi." She read aloud: " 'Look out before you dive, sir!' cried Walker. 'Look out for the sea urchins.' . . . Clinging to the face of the wall under the surface, spiny and red.' "

Grace and Neil joined us for the shoebag hour in Sophy's and my room. We accomplished a seating arrangement by utilizing beds,

* See page 306.

floor and balcony. Passage was possible by moving sideways, one at a time. One at a time each of us sidled to the balcony in order to look at the sunset colors on the water below and the brilliance of color over the mountaintops above us. We counted it a special favor to us that the *Stella Polaris* on a cruise had dropped anchor off Nauplia that afternoon. She is a beautiful ship, all white, and because she is not large she did not throw her weight over the bay but nestled into it.

There were six people in our room at half past six, but I was the only one of that group leaning over the balcony rail when the *Stella Polaris* fired her cannon in farewell to Nauplia. It very nearly marked as well Kimbrough's farewell to the world. At such a sound on the *Queen Frederica*, and at the Royal Yacht Club, I had leapt toward extinction. There are a great many things I have learned to stay away from, but a cannon is not one of them.

Before five o'clock next morning, I was on the balcony again. There was no cannon, thank goodness, to salute the sunrise, but the sunrise was trailing clouds of glory over the mountaintops and their reflection was in the water. There were boats in the water, as well, one of them immediately beneath where I stood. An old man had anchored it there in order to fish. He was fishing with a spear, and because the water was so clear, even from the height at which I stood, I could see the sandy bottom as I had seen it the afternoon before. I watched intently the spot he was watching, and at the moment he plunged his spear, I saw it impale an octopus.

The old man heard my involuntary shout of excitement. He only nodded his head once or twice, in acknowledgment of my tribute. When he had drawn his catch into the boat, however, and detached it from the spear, he held it up by its squirming arms for me to see. I could only call "*Kalimera*," but I said it with such fervor I hoped he would understand it as "Good for you!" I think he did, because as he sat down in the boat he bowed at me and called back thank you, "*Efharisto*."

Chapter Twelve

IT WAS not yet eight o'clock when we left. We learned that Grace and Neil had been on their way to Olympia for two hours, but we were joined on the landing stage by the couple we had met on the terrace the afternoon before. We chatted a few minutes as we waited for our boatman.

I found them as delightful as they had been the preceding day. This prompted me to ask spontaneously if they would join us for cocktails that night at the mainland hotel. We had already learned from them they had been members of a bus tour when the bus put in at Nauplia, but had been so enchanted with the place they had abandoned the tour. The sum they had to forfeit was not too dear a price, they asserted, for learning never again to walk into the trap of a rigid schedule. Like us, they could get only one night's accommodation at Bourzi on such short notice, and like us were spending the second night at the tourist hotel, The Amphitryon. They accepted my invitation. A minute or two later it occurred to me that since we would, of course, have drinks in the room of one or the other of us, since we disliked bars, our guests would have to know our names in order to inquire for our rooms. Up to that time names had been unnecessary to our conversation. Explaining the necessity that had arisen, I introduced my friends and myself.

We had known from the beginning by their accent they were both British, as they had undoubtedly recognized we were Americans. When I had finished my introductions, the gentleman told us his name.

"Smith," he said, though that was not the name he gave. But he did not say, "John Smith," nor "Mr. Smith," simply "Smith." He bowed to the lady and she spoke for herself. "Mrs. Jones," she announced.

I have not seen what might have been an awkward situation handled so deftly and so easily, nor with such delicate courtesy.

He left a choice to her of identifying herself as Mrs. Smith, or doing what she did, with composure and dignity as well as honesty.

Sophy, who was sitting farthest away from Smith and Mrs. Jones, put both feet into the delicate situation. She protested afterward when we had rounded on her she had not heard either of the names that had been given. Of course this was true, or she could not have made the comment that she tossed brightly in their direction.

"We're much luckier than you," she said. "We have imposed four names on you, and you've only given us one name between you to remember."

The conversation for the rest of the way to the mainland was an incoherent babble among the three of us, endeavoring to cover up Sophy's gaff, and an amused silence on the part of the two British traveling companions.

Marino was waiting for us with the car at the dock.

Epidaurus is an hour's drive from Nauplia. The road goes through a few little villages where again we saw, in front of the cottages, old oil tins painted white and filled with bright flowers.

As the car climbed, we marveled again at the distances the ancients traveled. I should have thought having seen it, I said, to visit Delphi once would be a feat of a lifetime. On the contrary, according to the records, the Greeks were constantly traveling there to seek counsel from the Oracle, as though she dwelt in a suburb of Athens. Now our car was taking in second gear a road early travelers had worn up over the mountain, coming to a drama festival as though it were no more of an expedition than for a New Yorker to visit the Lewisohn Stadium for summer concerts. Even more nearly impossible to visualize was the picture of the pilgrims who came to Epidaurus not for the great dramas, but for the healing therapy from the shrine of Aesculapius. These people were ill, crippled, misshapen. Those who were able had carried on litters the ones unable to walk.

We sissies got out of the car only after Marino had driven it to the farthest point to which a vehicle could travel. From there we climbed on foot to the base of the stadium, and sat down panting under trees to rest.

This marked the beginning of a red-letter day for Luz. She took pictures of us there, gingerly at first until, intoxicated by the steady click that responded to each press of the button, she snapped giddily everything that was in range. She even coaxed us to the top of the stadium over our protests that we could see it perfectly from where we sat.

Of course I am glad we made that extra effort under Luz's goading. It is the only way to apprehend the size of that glorious theater. From the top, too, we proved to ourselves the miracle of its acoustics. An actor on the stage far below could speak in a whisper and be heard distinctly at the very top. This phenomenon, in comparison with the magnificence of the sight itself, is in the ratio of the size of the coin a guide drops on the stage to be heard by tourists on the top row, to the size of the theater. The reward for the climb, and it is actually *not* a bad one, is such beauty, dignity and simplicity, in spite of its overwhelming proportions (it seated fourteen thousand spectators), as cannot be approximated, even by a camera such as Luz's. It can be truly revealed only in the eye of the beholder.

We found the museum rewarding, too, and spent a long time there until we were driven out by three busloads of young girls. We learned from one of them who wanted to try out her English on us they came from what she called the Domestic High School in Athens. We were delighted the high schools engineered such excursions as this, but the actual bulk of it obstructed our view.

We moved on to the ruins nearby, of temples and hotels that had flourished at this spa. There are traces of Roman baths. Luz photographed them and everything in their neighborhood. Sophy and I took pictures, too, but more conservatively.

When her film ran out we were able to coax Luz back into the car for the return trip to Nauplia. On the way she revealed the pitch of intoxication to which her success had carried her when she advised us earnestly, "I think everyone ought to bring three cameras, one always loaded for black-and-white pictures, one for color, and a motion-picture camera."

"If you were tinkering with three cameras out of order," Darn began, but I pressed her foot heavily. She left her speculation unfinished.

Since the road back to Nauplia is downhill, I saw a good deal more of the scenery on either side of it than I had ventured to peek at on the way up. This is an unreasonable distinction, I admit, but it is one on which I operate. Therefore, I saw a little cottage with wheat spread over its roof to dry. In front of it an old woman was minding a few goats and at the same time, with rapidity and dexterity, twisting rough wool wound on a stick she carried upright in one hand onto a spindle she twirled with equal rapidity in the other. We stopped the car and photographed her, waiting for Luz to change her film. The old lady seemed pleased; she put down her implements to wave us good-by, using the gesture we had found characteristic of Greek handwaving—with the back of the hand extended, the palm turned inward.

We lunched around three, at the Amphitryon in Nauplia, took a brief siesta and got into the car again to be driven down into the village. It had been Marino's suggestion. We had thought he was taking us to some distant spot. The village itself is within easy and pleasant walking distance of the hotel. We separated the instant we were out of the car. This is an instinctive scattering when any of us wants to browse. But within a few minutes we were assembled again by coincidence in a food shop, the prototype of a general store in any American village. We would have liked to buy a considerable number of things to eat we saw there, but we agreed most of it would neither keep nor be usable in a hotel. We eschewed such things as Feta cheese offered in such bulk it was kept in a barrel, but each of us bought a paper sack of ripe olives. Though we scattered again on leaving the shop, it was not difficult from that point on to trace the path of any one of us by means of the meandering trail of olive stones in her wake.

When we met at the car again we were laden with packages. We were not surprised to learn one of Darn's contained a pair of shoes, but we regretted having missed the transaction when she told us half a dozen people wandering in from the street had participated in it. Each one had felt her toes within the shoe and advised her on a proper fit.

I was the object of some derision that I chose to interpret as an expression of envy when I revealed one of my purchases. This was a pair of heavy leather straps each with a bright buckle and gaudy ornamentation of bells down its length—horsehair dyed red and woven in patterns, and an intricate pattern of bright colored beads. In Greece these straps are buckled round the neck of a donkey to ward off evil spirits. I intended them for belts my daughters might wear. The derisive opinion of my companions was that the weight would be insupportable. I am happy to report my daughters both supported and loved them, and furthermore, a few days later at a party in Athens given by some members of our State Department, I saw two American women wearing as belts duplicates of the ones I had purchased.

We were making arrangements for our cocktail party, moving in and out from the balcony off Sophy's and my room, when a voice called down from above, "Is that you, Emily?"

I have come to believe there is some quality in my voice that carries over a considerable distance without benefit of the acoustics of Epidaurus. I recognized the one that floated down to me, though I had thought its owner was in Olympia. "Grace," I called back in identification, and relayed the news to the others.

We learned by intercommunication between balconies that Grace and Neil had returned to Nauplia instead of following their original itinerary of going on from Olympia, because the drive to Olympia had been so hair-raising even Grace, whom I had heretofore classified as intrepid, had been too unnerved to continue it. My verdict after what I have heard is this road is for the Greeks. There is another road, but at the time it was under repair and closed.

When the Phillipses came down for cocktails, Smith and Mrs. Jones were already seated on our balcony. As I started to lead the way to them Darn appeared from the balcony and blocked our passage. She put up her hand like a traffic policeman and shook her head in violent negation. Somewhat surprised, Grace, Neil and I stopped, interested in her pantomine. Sophy and Luz were filling glasses at the bureau on which the bottles had been arranged. They turned, aware the little procession had stopped, and joined Darn's bemused audience.

She walked toward Luz and Sophy, calling over her shoulder toward the balcony, "I think I know exactly what you want. I'll have it in just a minute." Under her breath she muttered at us something we could not catch. She then walked past us, still muttering this curious chant we could not translate, and at intervals calling reassuring messages back to the balcony, such as, "You don't like much ice, do you?" Or, "I'm just getting another glass." All the while she was tramping up and down, past our spellbound group. She might have been doing maneuvers on a parade ground, except that she was talking in a hoarsely whispered repetitive chant.

At last my ear caught it. Bless her heart, she was doing her best to cue us.

"Lord Smith," she was muttering entreatingly. "It isn't Mr. Smith, it's Lord. That's why he didn't say 'Mister' or 'John' or anything. It's Lord. Do you get it? Lord!"

We got it, at last. But Darn's apprehension had been so great that for the remainder of the cocktail party she prefaced every sentence to the gentleman with his title, and accompanied it by an anxious look around our circle. We dined together and then said good-by. We were all starting early next day on separate ways.

The introduction that morning must have gone deep into Sophy's inner consciousness. Sometime in the night I wakened. A street light shone through the uncurtained and wide-open doors of our balcony. I saw Sophy sitting bolt upright in her bed across the room, her arms folded across her chest. As I looked, she spoke. "You can always count on me to do the right thing," she said, and lay down again.

At six the next morning, Sophy, Luz and I went for a swim. We followed the road past our hotel as it curved around and beneath a high, jutting rock. We walked perhaps half a mile before we came to a place from which we could descend along an easy slope to a sandy beach. The water was, like the little bear's porridge, just right in temperature, and as clear here as it had been below the balcony at Bourzi. As I floated, I thought dreamily, "I must tell Darn to write down in her helpful hints to travelers and underline it, *always* bring a bathing suit to Greece."

Rounding the big curve on our way back to the hotel, I stopped at a sight that for all time will epitomize for me my own conception of ancient Greece. An army of ants was moving across our path, thousands of them, in a solid formation six inches wide, and in length extending beyond either extremity of the road. They were building or moving a colony. Each member of that tremendous army carried something, or a portion of a burden shared by eight or more. I squatted on my haunches to watch, and called Sophy and Luz to see. "This," I said, "is Greece in the making. There goes the stadium at Epidaurus, the city of Mycenae, the summit at Delphi."

It is, perhaps a curious way to think of Greece by way of an army of ants crossing a road at seven on a May morning over the Bay of Nauplia. I think of it often.

We left immediately after an early breakfast, regretting we were not staying on for several days; but there were other plans afoot. We were back in Athens in time for a late lunch although we dallied on the way, at Mistra and Tiryns. We dallied longer at Argos. A further point of congeniality among us, we had already discovered, was our immediate response to the picturesque sight, however trivial. Certainly Mistra must be visited. The city reached its full flowering in the Byzantine period and happily the evidence of this has been well preserved. This is the place of the great frescoes of which much has been written by scholars, and that we who are not scholars found superb. The road to it is a terror.

Curiously, although the ruins of Tiryns are better preserved than those at Mycenae, to us they were nowhere near so dramatic.

We did not stop in Argos because of ruins to be seen there. We stopped, for one reason, because the car could not push through the press of traffic on the narrow street, and for an even better reason, that this was the day of the wool market. We could not congratulate ourselves on a precision of schedule that had brought us at midday, on Saturday, into the center of a market town. We could only be delighted such a happy accident had taken place.

Luz was out of the car on the instant Marino, lifting his hands from the wheel, had waved them in the air to indicate the futility of attempting further progress.

Women and men, most of them in bright-colored peasant dress, stood beside or sat on mounds of coarse wool. These mounds were dotted along the curb, and over the village square. Each mound was the place of business for the owner who stood by. Prospective buyers moved from one to another and the owners would extend a fistful of wool to the visitor, inviting him to feel its texture. When a purchase was made, the seller would help hoist the heavy load onto the shoulders of the purchaser and start him on his way. Several priests were buying. I saw one ride away on a bicycle, a bag of wool over his shoulder, a jug of wine tied to the handlebars. Donkeys that had evidently been the carriers of the wool wandered up and down the street, lackadaisically tended by small children. All the shops were filled with customers; business was splendid. It was evident on market day there would be no shop doors closed from noon until five.

Before we drove on, Marino led us to one of the little shops and showed us there a massive, shaggy coat of coarse black wool. When he pointed from this to the mounds, we understood this was the kind of garment most frequently made. He made us understand, too, that in addition to its warmth, it shed water, essential to shepherds up in the mountains.

Marino had bought us a bag of oranges; he had also secured helpers to keep a passage clear for us. As we drove off, Darn, Sophy and I were already peeling the succulent fruit, Sophy murmuring happily but somewhat inaudibly that however much Florida and California competed, Greek oranges were sweeter and juicier than the product of either of those states. Luz did not eat one though we reminded her breakfast had been early and lunch would be late. She was loading her camera, singing happily to herself as she worked.

Mr. Papastratos gave a party for us on Saturday night at a taverna called Bukaresti in the Plaka. Dinner was at half past ten; we were thankful lunch had been so late. The Bukaresti is a delightful open-air taverna, with delicious food and musicians who move among the customers. The occupants of each table at which they stopped sang the songs they played. When they had made a tour of the garden the musicians settled in one corner of the dance floor and the dancing began. There was very little of the sort to which we are accustomed at home, but a number of the circle dances we had seen done on the *Queen Frederica.* We joined these along with the other members of our dinner party. When there were not other dancers on the floor, men rose singly from various tables and executed solo dances, each individual preoccupied with his own intricate steps. This occurred a number of times when the circle dances were not going on. The men were not rowdy, and certainly not showing off. They simply liked to do steps alone. No one in the taverna became intoxicated. There was only an overall air of gaiety and general participation. We had a thoroughly delightful time that lasted until half past two.

Sunday was very pleasant but not a day of rest. We went out early to pay our respects to some of the landmarks in Athens with which we had become, by now, on familiar terms. Each of us, we discovered, had arrived at this familiarity by the same route. This was to pay a visit to one or another of these places in the course of any walk or errand to be done. Since we were making Athens our base for a month, we had not been obliged to include everything in a single "grand tour." Separately each of us had visited again and again the Archeological Museum and the Benaki, as well as the outdoor landmarks. In addition to the beauty of the displays, there is a particular fascination in the Benaki Museum. This was a private collection. Seeing it is a little like going through a house one has rented furnished, and guessing from the books and furnishings the personality of the owner.

I sat a long time, one day, on the Areopagus. That is the wide, flat-tabled rock halfway between the Acropolis and the city, where once the Supreme Court of Athens sat. It is also the rock on which St. Paul stood when he preached to the Athenians.

I found the Agora less inspiring than the flat rock. I knew the Agora was the market place of ancient Athens. I knew its restoration had been a major project of the American School for Classical Studies over a number of years. Some of my college friends have made brilliant contributions to this work. The restoration necessitated the destruction of the old Turkish quarter. Many people who knew and loved that picturesque section, and are not archeologists, deplore its obliteration. To other sightseers this restoration provides a vivid recreation of antiquity. One point of view I am sure is common to all tourists to the Agora, that the time for visiting it should be the early morning, or the very late afternoon. The sun on that exposed flat area makes other hours intolerable.

The theater of Dionysus, each time I visited it, was even more bristling with restoration work and workers than the Agora, but this was for a specific purpose. A music festival was to be held there later in the summer inaugurated by Dimitri Mitropoulos, coming home from America for the event. The theater is on the slope of the Acropolis. It seated fifteen thousand and will seat that number again. Those early audiences saw the plays of Sophocles, Euripides, Aristophanes, Aeschylus and other dramatists. Like the theater in Epidaurus, this one has a front row of special and imposing seats, obviously for the important personages in the audience. The seats are of stone but broad, with wide arms, the ones of the theater of Dionysus even more elaborately carved than those of Epidaurus, because they include the title of the personage for whom each seat was reserved.

Theseum is the best preserved of any temple I saw in Greece. It was built in the fifth century B.C. as a shrine to Hephaestus, the God of Fire.

On that Sunday morning I do not know where the others went, but I visited the temple of Olympian Zeus and the nearby arch of the Emperor Hadrian. By agreement, however, we were all back at the hotel and on our roof to see the changing of the guard at eleven o'clock. It changes in front of the House of Parliament on Constitution Square every Sunday. Each week a different branch of the armed services takes over the duty. This was the Sunday for the Evzones, the Royal Guards. They are the soldiers so widely photographed because of their picturesque costumes. The uniform comprises an embroidered white tunic, a sharply flaring ballet skirt, tight-fitting white trousers that look like men's old-fashioned under-drawers except these are bound to the legs by narrow strips of black, wound around from ankle to thigh. The cap is tasseled at the peaked end and the shoes have bright red pompons on the toes.

When the sound of the band heralded the approach of this color-

ΔΦΛ
Vasiliu

ful group, Luz steadied her camera on the balcony rail. As the troop, rounding the corner, marched into sight toward us, she pressed the button. There was no answering click. She restored the camera to its case and left the balcony. She told us later this was a fault that had developed in the back-winding knob when she relieved the film from its bucket, and she was going to try a Plus X after her Tri X. I congratulated myself my camera did not require me to know what she was talking about.

We drove to Kephissia for lunch, at the house of Mr. and Mrs. Pothamianos. Kephissia is a charming and fashionable suburb, fourteen kilometers out of Athens. It is in the hills and therefore cool, which is the reason Athenians prefer it to a house by the sea. We saw one or two restaurants that looked delightful. I think lunch or dinner there would make a pleasant excursion. Our fellow luncheon guests were charming, cosmopolitan, widely traveled, warm and hospitable. With the exception of the four Americans, all the guests spoke, easily, several languages. Had I not visited hospitals, rehabilitation centers and the like, I would not have had an inkling the beautifully dressed, charmingly gay women at the party worked every day but Sunday, and for more hours a day than our unions would permit.

The youngest of the Pothamianos' three children, a little girl of twelve or so spoke to the guests as we arrived. She lunched with her governess at a table in the garden beyond the terrace on which the party was seated. I had learned from another friend in Athens the story of the birth of that little girl. She was born in the days of the terrible Communist uprising when Constitution Square in Athens was a battlefield, and the Pothamianoses lived just off the Square. We four Americans were the only guests who had not participated in any of the horrors the rest of them had shared. A stranger would not have been able to isolate us by virtue of any greater gaiety, or absence of bitterness or self-pity. The little girl in the garden has a recent as well as an ancient heritage of which to be proud.

Chapter Thirteen

SUNIUM, that is also spelled Sounion, is sixty-four kilometers from Athens. We drove there on the morning after the Pothamianos luncheon. I had admitted to my table companions at the party the tremulous mousse of cowardice to which I am reduced on a mountain road. My hearers had been astonished. It had not occurred to any of them as Greeks to consider a mountain road different from any other. When I told them we were driving to Sunium the following day, they brightened. Now there was a road, they assured me, that could not cause me any vertigo nor the slightest apprehension. It ran along the sea itself.

So it does. It runs right along the sea at a height of a thousand feet or more, with not so much as a guard rail of kindling wood between its outer edge and the drop below, but I said firmly to my companions, "There is no use crying over curving roads, and if you want to see Greece you have to look beyond them."

I took my hands from my eyes and sat on them; I wanted to see Greece. I affirm again as I affirmed on that road to Sunium, though seeing Greece requires a stout heart, strong ankles, sound lungs and a steady head, the reward is so abundant as to overflow and sink out of sight these requirements. They total a very modest price of admission.

At Sunium—on a hilltop of course—twelve, perhaps one or two more or less, Doric columns still stand. They are from the temple of Poseidon which was built in the fifth century B.C. They look down on the Aegean Sea. It may be because the sea there is preposterously blue, or that the marble of these columns is not like the marble of other temples, that makes them seem as white as new snow. To stand at a little distance behind them and to look between any two of them at the sea below can make the senses reel from the beauty, as giddily, I think, as my head reels at the edge of a mountain road. I am provoked with writers who belittle this scene. To the four of us it was so beautiful as very nearly to make us weep. We were unanimously indignant, too, at the defacement of the columns by signatures of visiting tourists. We were not appeased by learning that one of the signatures is Lord Byron's, or that a traveler there in the seventeenth century wrote of finding this defacement already begun.

We lunched at the tourist pavilion. It is at the foot of the hill on which the temple stands. Our table faced the sea and so we were not impatient, though the service is a little slow. In the other pavilions we had visited the same luncheon was served to everyone; there was no choice of dishes. Here the food is à la carte, and we did not think it quite such good quality as at others.

We went swimming after lunch off a beach just round a curve at the base of the hill on which Sunium stands. There was a taverna on the beach, little more than a shack. Some half-dozen men were seated at a table in front of it. We eyed them dubiously.

"Thugs," Darn pronounced succinctly.

Marino hunted out the proprietor and brought back an invitation to change inside the shack. The room to which we were allotted had an occupant, we discovered, a small child taking an afternoon nap on a bed in what was little more than a cubicle. There was, of course, no screen in the open window. Flies were crawling over the child. It was not a pretty picture. We withdrew from it and the room, explaining by pantomime we were afraid we might waken the sleeper.

Agreeing to this, Marino led us back to the beach. Pointing to a group of rocks a few yards away, he indicated this would be an admirable place in which to change.

We know now, because before we left Greece we had gone swimming at many beaches, in that country no bystander gives so much notice as a turn of the head to anyone who is getting in or out of a bathing suit. Perhaps the men outside the taverna, whom Darn identified as thugs, were steady churchgoers and dependable men, perhaps they were thugs. The only thing about them I can prove is they were totally indifferent to the sight of women dressing or undressing.

On the seventeenth of May at six in the afternoon we sailed from Piraeus for Chios. Marino had insisted on getting us to the boat by five. We had protested, but as usual he had been right. Though we had two cabins reserved and the tickets in hand for them, we had some difficulty proving our claims to the ticket collector. This was because he was distracted by the general confusion. So were we, but fascinated.

It would have been a pity to arrive just in time for the sailing and miss the hour's spectacle that preceded it. We secured excellent spectator seats. We watched passengers come on board with hand luggage I doubt the *Queen Mary* would have welcomed. We took on live chickens, one goat, a great many strings of fish, ditto cheese, and ditto garlic; large rolls of bedding, large tins of gasoline, large and small babies. I have never witnessed on a New York dock such dramatic farewells as those that took place when our passengers were torn away from their loved ones on the Piraeus wharf. What with livestock, the bedding and the heartbreaking farewells, I surmised we were carrying colonizers bound for a remote island. I found they were on their way to visit relatives by means of an excursion rate recently inaugurated, that was good for one week's absence.

When our little boat drew away from the dock the clamor of heartrending cries between dock and deck would have rendered inaudible a blast from the *Queen Frederica*. Therefore, of course, no one heard a cry from one individual; but happening to be looking toward the stern as we nosed out, I saw a woman standing up in a rowboat waving both arms excitedly and I saw that her mouth was open wide. I assumed she was calling our attention to her plight. Two men were rowing the boat with a fine flourish of oars but inconsiderable speed. Someone on the bridge must have caught sight of the tardy passenger, because our boat obligingly slowed, the rowers quickened, their passenger was transferred to us by two of our sailors, who lifted her up with a powerful swing and a firm grasp on her arms and buttocks. Her considerable baggage was heaved after her. Our ship resumed speed.

On our arrival we had gone with our porter to see our bags stowed in the proper staterooms and had realized at first glance they were strikingly unlike the de luxe accommodations the travelers' agency had promised us. Sophy had explained the discrepancy, muttering glumly as we went back on deck, "Some friends have got into the act again. They must have asked the president of this line to be sure we had the best cabins."

Our departure accomplished, we were preparing to return to our cabins when Darn stopped us and pointed across the water. We were at the moment passing a dock other than the one from which we had left. Moored there was a boat that bore the name *Kanaris*. That was the boat on which we had been booked to travel to Chios. What we were on we had not the faintest idea, but we discovered, racing around the deck, the name of our vessel on a life preserver. It was the *Karaiskakis*, a name we had not heretofore heard mentioned. This discovery posed the problem of where we were going, and also how we would find this out.

Darn, of course, was our only link of communication with Greece. The only sentence at her command, we knew, was "My friend is unable to eat anything with garlic or onion in it." We urged her to try some variations on this, and with her went in search of a ship's officer. We found one and though Darn disconcerted him somewhat by throwing out, in addition to the sentence, the words for prunes, oranges and please, she steadied after a minute or two, and remembered the word for ship. Then she got into her stride, begging me to keep quiet because under such urgency I was saying over and over, "*Thalassa*," which was the word for "the sea" when the *Anabasis* was written, but has not been in common usage since then. Inasmuch too, as what concerned us at the moment was not the sea but the boat we were on I was admittedly off the track.

Darn pointed back to the *Kanaris*, scarcely visible by now. Sophy, the executive and banker, displayed our tickets marked "Chios" on the *Kanaris*.

Communication was established but it was not a clear line. The officer was first offended that we seemed to be mistaking him for a ticket collector. When that cloud was dispersed, he was bewildered by our agitation. Did we not want to go to Chios? Certainly we wanted to go to Chios, that was what was troubling us. Evidently we were not on a boat bound for Chios. The officer with shoulder shrugging that very nearly covered his ears, and with palms violently extended toward us, wished by gestures to inquire why we should have any doubts, since our tickets said we were going to Chios. He suggested to us with eloquent pantomime we were foolish creatures to care about the name of the boat. What was written down on a ticket had nothing whatever to do with the actual boat that might be used. He was not associated with a company that had only one boat. He stretched his arms wide to encompass the fleet under his company's flag. Sometimes one was used, sometimes another. Who could tell?

"*We* can tell," Luz said, as we started once more for our rooms, "if we arrive in Chios at half past six tomorrow morning."

We arrived in Chios the next morning but it was not at half past six. Sometime before four we were aroused by deafening blasts from the ship's whistle, a ringing of bells and the sound of feet running along the passageway outside our cabins. Since I always anticipate such contingencies when at sea, I said at once, "The ship is sinking and there's a mutiny."

An instant later there was a violent pounding on our door and the voice of our steward calling in confusing but loud English, "Up. Up. Chios by half one hour."

In twenty minutes we were dressed and on deck, though it had taken forceful persuasion on the part of my companions to induce me to wear the clothes I had taken off at bedtime, instead of the life jacket I had got into over my nightgown on hearing the steward's message.

"He's been told to say that," I had declared, "to avoid a panic."

Even in our clothes we were not subjects for a picture of the well-dressed woman. Each of us had seized whatever garment was nearest at hand, no matter whose. We were unwashed, uncombed, and their hats and my veil over our unmade coiffures were rakishly askew. When we burst on deck, we saw we were on a calm sea and within close sight of a harbor.

The whistles and bells had not stopped their lively antiphony. It was almost impossible over their noise to hear a human voice. I saw the ship's officer we had interrogated the evening before. I shouted at him. He saw us and did his best to elude us, but we cornered him.

In such an emergency, Darn understandably could not even think of the word for prunes. We all begged him in English at the tops of our lungs, to tell us what in Heaven's name was going on. By the patient way he shook his head and the discouraged downward shrug of his shoulders, he conveyed he considered us as quixotic as he had thought us the night before.

"Chios," he said, in the tone a parent uses when saying to a child, "I've already told you twenty times."

"But why Chios now?" we wanted to know. And each with a simultaneous inspiration pulled up a sleeve and tapped her watch at the half past six mark.

The officer pointed upward. I thought he was calling on God, but we decided later he was indicating the authority of the captain. He conveyed by subsequent gestures that the captain was an impatient man, the sea was calm, we had made good time. The impatient man saw no reason to dawdle, just because a schedule marked an arrival at half past six. The bells and whistles were giving notice of this change of plans to the inhabitants of Chios.

We released the officer and went to the deck rail to watch. We were close enough now to see, in the faint daylight before sunrise, people assembling on the dock, arriving there on the run. As we coasted in to our landing, the whistles and bells stopped abruptly and the sudden silence was quite as startling as the cacophony had been when it roused us. I picked out two men in a sort of working uniform looking up and along our deck as if searching for someone.

I said to the others, "They must have been sent by George Livanos' uncle to fetch our luggage."

I had memorized the name of George's uncle and I called it loudly in the direction of the two workmen. "From Mr. Fafalios?" And I repeated, "From Mr. Fafalios?"

The second time I called it, a distinguished-looking gentleman a few feet away from the pair to which I was directing my voice raised his head sharply, looked in our direction, waved his hand and said, "Fafalios. Here."

Luz was reproachful. "It's not a good beginning," she told me. "He thinks you took one of those cutthroats to be our host."

The two cutthroats were porters Mr. Fafalios had engaged. He brought them on board in his wake and a delegation as well. We left the deck and met them at the head of the gangplank. To our surprise Mr. Fafalios, instead of conducting us down the gangplank, indicated we would all move into the lounge, except for the porters, whom he dispatched after learning the numbers of our cabins. He ordered the steward to place chairs in the lounge in a circle and we all sat down. We numbered nine. The visitors included four men and one woman.

Vasiliu

Mr. Fafalios bowed to the woman and she spoke. "I am Mrs. Cardamitsi," she said. "I work with the English during the war so I am an interpreter. Now I introduce us. This is Mr. Contelakis, publisher of our newspaper."

We bowed.

"This is Mr. Papantchakis, head of tourism."

We bowed.

"This is Mr. Nico Minadakis. He will be your interpreter while you are here."

We bowed.

Mr. Minadakis said, "I, too, am with the English through the war. I have many English friends. We will have a jolly time."

Mr. Minadakis was short and chubby. He had a number of gold teeth and displayed them frequently. He carried in one hand a pair of black kid gloves. I never saw him without them, even on a day we went swimming. I never saw him put them on. Darn reported some days later she had managed to get a good look at them and could swear they never had been worn.

Mrs. Cardamitsi took the lead again. "Now you will introduce yourselves, please," she requested, "and give short biography. I will translate for our newspaper. We will be very interested."

We were surprised and skeptical, but Darn led off.

When Sophy's turn came she captivated her audience by adding to her dossier an impromptu and somewhat emotional speech about Greeks, Americans and brotherhood.

We left the ship immediately after this speech. It had seemed to call for a general rising and I was profoundly grateful. I had no confidence there would be any more warnings of the captain's departure than he chose to give.

We stepped from the gangplank onto a broad thoroughfare that was both street and quay. It was paved with cobblestones and there were houses and a hotel on its inland side. The porters carried our luggage in two enormous mounds, each piled on a wheelbarrow. We were ushered into a large black, old-fashioned limousine with folding seats that enabled all of us to be accommodated somewhat tightly. Our destination was only a few blocks away, we could easily have walked, but evidently our arrival was to be something of a ceremony.

The house was beautiful, with a tall façade and double circular staircase leading up to it, all of marble. The house was set some distance back from the street, and separated from it by a high iron fence. As we came up the steps, the double front doors opened and a woman stepped out across the threshold. She was flanked on either side by a little maid, the maids looking the more diminutive because the door itself was by the American pattern excessively high. The woman was tall and very handsome. She was, as I had guessed, Mme. Fafalios.

When we had shaken hands all around she nodded to the maids. They stepped forward to each of us in turn. One carried a tray that held glass saucers, one for each member of the company. In each saucer was a piece of candied fruit about the size of a plum embedded in a thick syrup. A little spoon, not much larger than an after-dinner coffee spoon was in each saucer, its bowl in the syrup. On the tray the other maid carried were glasses, one for each person.

I know that in the course of a lifetime every individual faces obstacles that seem insurmountable. To as many as I can reach I send this word of comfort, "Whatever is confronting you it is not, I am sure, a candied fruit and a glass of ice water at a quarter to five in the morning." This is a Greek ceremony of welcome. The ceremony includes spooning up the blob of fruit, dipping it into the glass, eating it at one mouthful off the tiny spoon, and then drinking the sweetened, cold water. To face it is hard. To down it is harder. But what is hardest of all is to keep it down.

While my digestive tide was rising and falling with unnatural rapidity, I was asked with the others to make a group for photographing. As the sun rose, our pictures were taken on the marble balcony at the head of the stairs outside the Fafalios house.

We were shown to our rooms immediately after, with the promise our interpreter, Mr. Minadakis, would return later for a morning's excursion.

Our rooms occupied a wing on the first floor. They were large, high-ceilinged and, from a sort of crown in each ceiling, a cloud of mosquito netting billowed over and around every bed. We had the luxury, also, of two bathrooms, each with enormous tub and plenty of hot water. We bathed and then crawled into bed. This last was not an easy process. It involved picking up an edge of the mosquito netting and hunching under yard after yard of it, at the same time climbing onto a bed that was exceptionally high. During the entire week at Chios I never once completed this maneuver without discovering at the moment of my tired arrival on the pillow I had left on the bed table outside the netting the object I had intended to take in with me, hot-water bottle, glasses, book, Kleenex, whatever. Each time I had to make the decision of the relative importance of securing the objects and not diving under the yardage that separated me from them.

We had all of us slept when we were called to breakfast. We were ravenously hungry. The family had long since finished their meal. When Mme. Fafalios had seen us to the table she excused herself. We were thankful for this a minute or two later when we took stock of what was before us. The sight was something of a shock and we would not have wanted our hostess to be aware of this. At each end of the table was a basket of fruit, beautiful and luscious to the sight and taste. There were large pitchers of tea, smaller ones of hot milk. There was a basket containing hunks of what we identified as French bread, toasted. The shock was in the double row of dishes that stretched down the center of the table, from the basket of fruit at one end to the corresponding one at the other. These dishes contained almost every variety of French pastry I have encountered in all the dessert trays that have been wheeled to my table at restaurants.

We held a conference. There was no need, we decided, for all of us to challenge our digestion. One digestion, one victim, would be sufficient. We drew lots. Darn won, or lost, according to the point of view. With admiration and apprehension we watched her down the greater part of a chocolate *éclair*, and all of a *mille feuilles*. When Mme. Fafalios returning, was dismayed we had eaten so little, Luz, Sophy and I perjured ourselves by assuring her we had divided the sweets among us, not allowing ourselves to eat more though we had been mightily tempted, because of our figures. Darn did not join this perjury. She held her lips tight together and stared straight ahead of her. After I had persuaded her to take a second cup of tea, strong, and without sugar or milk, she told us she felt all right again as long as no one mentioned anything to do with sweets.

Shortly after breakfast our interpreter called for us with a car and took us on a tour of the town. We started at the library, where the director showed us its treasures.

The church is next door. We paused for some time in the outer courtyard to see the extraordinary mosaic that covers the whole of it like a carpet. This was the first of many we were to see in Greece. They are done with pebbles in intricate and effective designs. Sometimes they are in color; these were black and white. The overall effect was stunning. The church itself is of no particular distinction, but we learned something from the icons none of us had known before. There were many of them in varying sizes, but a number of these were silver-coated in a kind of patchwork. Darn, the questioner, asked if this was an evidence of vandalism.

Honeybunch was shocked. This is the name we had already bestowed, privately, on our interpreter, partly because we found his name impossible to remember, but more particularly because of his dimpled roundness and honeyed smile that he turned on almost constantly. Unless we were funnier than we had any idea of, this must have been for the purpose of allowing us to bask in the rays of gold his smile disclosed. He even managed to smile when he was shocked at Darn's question.

"Oh, no, oh no, oh no," he said insistently. "There is no vandalism. This is silver growing, not being taken away."

He explained further that each patch was a fulfillment of a vow, or an expression of gratitude for prayers answered, the suppliant providing as much silver as he could afford. The hands and the head seemed always the first to be adorned.

Leaving the church we retraced our way somewhat in order to drive along the coast. Not far beyond the dock where we had landed we had our first glimpse of Greek windmills. They make a lovely silhouette on a flat landscape with the sea beyond them. The part of a Greek windmill that turns is made in sections, as a pie is cut. Each of these sections is a shaft to which cloth is attached like a sail. When the mill is not working each sail is furled around its standard, but when the mill is revolving the sails, unfurled, billow full. I have seen balloon jibs puffed out, but to see a full circle of them puffed to their utmost, and revolving at the same time, provokes a cry of pleasure. At least that is what the sight of the windmills provoked from the four of us. We wanted to see them more closely, we said. That was a mistake, because these particular windmills are placed alongside a tannery. I do not believe any of us could have stayed long in that neighborhood, but when Darn murmured faintly, "I cannot take a chocolate *éclair* at seven and a tannery at nine," we made for the car on the double and drove off rapidly.

We continued along the coast and looked across the water at Turkey, so close I made the mistake of saying, "One could swim to it."

Since my companions knew I can swim only fifty strokes at a time, and that only if I count them, and Honeybunch volunteered the information the distance was actually seven miles, my innocent observation was answered by derisive hoots.

Whenever in Greece I thought a road was improving, it immediately took a turn for the hills. While I was still looking at Turkey and being told exactly where Smyrna was, I heard the car go into second gear. I instantly transferred apprehensive attention to the road ahead and saw we were winding up again.

I did not go with the others all the way to the top of whatever the car was climbing. When I learned our objective was a view, I was not interested in achieving it. My breath is quickened, but not by pleasure at the sight of a panorama that spreads around me and lies far below me. I prefer charm to grandeur. When I heard Honeybunch say we would pass close by Homer's Stone, my breath was quickened by pleasure and a tug of excitement.

I left the car and walked back a short distance along the road until I came to a path Honeybunch had told me I would find. It is not difficult to discover. I climbed up through a glade where the ground was patched with pieces of sunlight. To walk through a woods in Greece is in itself an unusual experience. Invaders down through the ages have very nearly stripped the country of its forests. To walk through a woods and emerge at the base of a very large, flat rock, where pupils might have sat and listened to Homer speak, is an experience of a lifetime, certainly of my lifetime.

The path narrowed and deepened here. Its first depression, I like to think, was made by those pupils. I followed it to the rock itself and sat down. I faced and looked up at a smaller stone, hollowed to a shape like a bath chair. They say Homer sat there when he taught. I know that seven cities claim his birth, Smyrna, Rhodes, Colophon, Salamis, Argos, Athens and Chios. I know there are scholars who doubt his existence as a person at all. But if there was a Homer, and if that Homer lived and taught in Chios, then one day sitting on the stone at which I was looking, he said aloud to listeners sitting on the rock where I was sitting, their faces upturned like mine, "I sing of the wrath of a god."

I heard another voice that morning, too, of course; Mother's voice, telling me the story of the *Iliad* when I was very small, and later, when I knew a little of the language, reading it aloud in Homer's language. I heard, too, her own refrain that had always been our own Greek chorus to Homer's poem. "When you and I are in Greece . . ."

Indiana folk call a long and pleasant conversation "a lovely visit." That sunny morning in Chios, we three had a lovely visit, Homer, Mother and I.

The car was waiting when I returned to the road. There was time to visit the hospital, Honeybunch said, before lunch. He wanted us particularly to see it, because a whole new wing not quite completed had been given by my friends, the Livanoses. We learned from the head nurse the American Red Cross has also made generous contributions.

The hospital is not only an excellent working plant with top-quality equipment, it is also a delightful place; in itself good therapy. Great attention has been paid to gardens that lie between the entrance gateway and the buildings. On the other side the rooms look out across the water.

On the way home Honeybunch told us the hospital and the schools on Chios were the first ones established under Turkish occupations. The Turks, he said, had not been in favor of hospitals. According to their belief at the time, illness was the result of wrongdoing and to alleviate it was to become a party to evil. They had not wanted to sponsor education since that might bring about rebellion. When individual Greeks living abroad had sent back word they would finance such institutions and furthermore pay handsomely for permission to establish them, the Turks decided the benefit from such payment would counteract the possible harm from the institutions themselves.

This was the same thread in the Greek pattern the Captain of the *Queen Frederica* had shown us, this passionate national feeling of Greeks in whatever part of the world they live. I had begun to be aware in Athens of how strong this thread is. What I saw in Chios confirmed my impression; things I came upon later corroborated it. I cannot back my impression by any authoritative knowledge, but what I saw and heard gave me this picture of the Greeks at home and abroad: That under the long domination of the Turks, Greeks were unable to become prosperous. Therefore, wherever possible a child of promise in a family would be sent to relatives dwelling in another part of the world. The obligation on both the relatives and the recruits was to earn money in order to help the homeland. Therefore, fortunes are not made in Greece, but Greece receives benefits from those made elsewhere: libraries, schools, hospitals, home industries, youth centers. The list is the same as that for community services anywhere, but with this difference. The community pays what it can for the upkeep, the establishment itself is by private donation.

Before lunch we gathered on a sun porch behind the dining room. A young boy was waiting there, handsome, shy but with a quick smile. He looked to be about twelve years old. Mme. Fafalios explained he was Nico, their youngest son, the only one at home. The two older sons had been out of Greece for several years, receiving their education and training abroad, preparatory to taking their place in the family business. They probably would never return to Greece to live. Mme. Fafalios explained this simply, matter of factly, but her face lengthened into an expression of hopelessness, and when she had finished talking, she suddenly hugged little Nico with such violence it was as though at that instant someone were trying to take him away from her. We were served Ouzo with a glass of cold water on the side to dilute the Ouzo if it were preferable that way, and it was, for me. We were offered hors d'oeuvres too, of olives, little squares of smoked lobster and roe, slender strips of cold tongue. We were hungry, the morning had been long and we had been active over the greater part of it. We ate olives, roe and tongue. This was a mistake, but we had not foreseen, in spite of the amplitude of our breakfast, what lunch would comprise. It began with a wonderful lemon soup that is a Greek *specialité*. After that we had roast lamb, fresh peas, potatoes, lettuce and cucumbers, and for dessert a cheese that is a *specialité* of Chios, in a mound as large as a melon and not unlike in appearance angel-food cake. Mr. Fafalios cut it in slices the size in which an angel-food cake is divided. With this we were served honey and were instructed to spread it over the cheese. The honey was from Mt. Hymettus and delicious. The last course was of oranges and Jap apples.

Chapter Fourteen

HONEYBUNCH left after lunch but promised to return later for more sightseeing. We, in turn, urged him not to feel obligated to hurry. The only thing each of us wanted to see at that moment was her own bed.

We found our beds opened for occupancy, the mosquito netting tucked in around each one, nightgowns laid out and the wooden shutters at each window tightly closed. In a Greek house you do not drop down on a couch after lunch for a spot of reading and a little doze; you observe a siesta by undressing for it and sleeping through it. Darn and I observed it properly, but at some time while we slept Luz and Sophy rose, took their bathing suits and went for a swim. They were away when Darn and I wakened, and we resented this bitterly with reason, because they were not on hand to share the manner of our awakening.

We were aroused by a tapping on each bedroom door. When Darn and I had answered, the two little maids who had greeted us in the morning came first into my room. Darn stumbled in sleepily at that instant. I never saw a look of benign drowsiness fade so rapidly as I saw it wiped from her face when her eyes widened and met mine across the trays the maids carried. On them were the saucers, spoons and glasses we had seen at sunrise. They held the same kind of refreshment, the candied fruit in its puddle of syrup, cold water in the glasses.

We entreated the maids by urgent gestures to leave the extra dishes and glasses; we would make sure our friends received them on their return. To our disappointment the maids indicated vividly this would not do, the proper hour for this delicacy would have passed and furthermore the water would not be cold enough. They removed the dishes and glasses, ours too, but not until they had supervised our consumption of their contents.

Luz and Sophy returned and soon after them Honeybunch arrived as he had promised. He held his black gloves creased in one hand and said anxiously between smiles he was afraid he might have kept us waiting. He had become engrossed in a philosophic discussion with a friend, he explained, and had been foolishly oblivious to the passage of time. With our assurance we had not been pining on the doorstep until he should have arrived, the tempo of his smiles accelerated.

He directed the chauffeur to drive us on a route opposite the one we had taken in the morning. This is the road through the part of Chios that makes that island unlike any other in the Aegean. It is the Campos, a name given the residential district that is a little away from the town itself. In this district and beyond are the lemon groves and the mastic for which the island was famous. The lemon groves are so extensive it is said when the wind is offshore the scent from the lemon blossoms can be identified five or six miles out at sea. The guidebook published in Chios and written in French is itself a bouquet of flowery language. It describes this scent over the ocean of the lemon-tree blossoms as creating "*une mer embaumée.*"

The mastic tree is a species of evergreen, its resin, yellowish in color, was gold for the inhabitants of Chios over a long period of prosperity that it created. The resin was used in making varnishes, in cements of the sort used in attaching tiles to a surface. It flavored various liqueurs, and was itself in liquid form a favorite drink in any part of the world where Greeks lived. But its best-known use was as an early form of chewing gum, particularly enjoyed by Turkish ladies. Only the gum from the mastic tree on the southern part of the Island of Chios would satisfy the delicate tastes of the exquisite creatures who formed the Sultan's harem, and the aristocracy of the Turkish empire.

Osbert Lancaster in his book *Classical Landscape,* a volume that should be in the traveling equipment of any tourist to Greece, calls the Campos in Chios the residential section, but the official guidebook, the one written in French, designates it as the whole of the immense plain as well, where the lemon groves are planted.

If it is the entire area that is the Campos (and that is sometimes spelled Cambos) then the mastic trees and the residential section make it unlike other places. If the Campos denotes exclusively the residential section, then the distinguishing mark is that the traveler through it can see nothing of it because of walls. The roads are narrow, the walls rise high above a car top; they are of stone, and they extend for miles. Once in a very great while, there is a wrought-iron gate that can be peered through. The sight within is magnificent, a tall house that is built on a series of terraces and, beyond, gardens of such splendor as to make an American gardener go home and tear up by the roots, in despair, her meager plantings. Most of these magnificent places are, alas, untenanted now, their owners living abroad. They had been built originally by the Turks, with the high walls, of course, to insure that the wives and daughters of the household should have protective isolation from the inquisitive eyes of other Turks. Some of these houses date back to the fourteenth century. When the Turks were finally ousted, the Greeks as they became prosperous took them over. The Greeks at Chios became very prosperous, not so much from their fruit groves and mastic trees as from the ships they built. Chios is the home of most of the shipbuilders whose names have become famous throughout the world.

To our surprise and pleasure we stopped at one of these estates. The entrance was a massive solid door of iron, black but studded with knobs of brass. In the center there was a large coat of arms, also in highly polished brass. The door itself was certainly eighteen to twenty feet high. The signal for visitors was a sizable metal circle to the right of the door, actually a wreath of bells. When Honeybunch pulled a cord that hung below it, all the bells were set in motion, and the wheel revolved. Within a minute or two the great doors were pulled open by a man in working clothes who identified himself as superintendent of the estate and requested to know our identity. This accomplished, he stepped back and waved us ahead of him to such a sight as I had thought was to be found only in illustrations to a child's book of fairy tales. We thought we were visitors by special intercession of Mr. Fafalios and Honeybunch. We learned this was not so. Visitors are welcome if they will anticipate their arrival by a note to the owner, who is Mr. Phillip Argenti, at Chios. Permission is readily given and if the owner is not in residence his superintendent will receive the visitors. Mr. Argenti, we were told, lives part of the year in England, and the rest at Chios. He has written authoritatively of the island in books, *Folklore of Chios, Costumes of Chios* and others whose titles I did not learn. The restoration to its original form of his place in Chios is a work in which he has been engaged for many years.

From the entrance gate we stepped into a courtyard. The pavement of this was made of small round pebbles such as we had seen at the church, except that here was an even more ornate design. In the center of the courtyard there was a large square of marble that enclosed a sunken pool and also a water wheel. The pool carried on its face a coat of arms. In the distance beyond were growing, much of it in bloom, wisteria, rose geraniums, roses, oleanders and farther off we identified, by the shiny dark leaves rippling in the breeze that is always present a vast grove of orange trees.

As we walked along the garden paths we came upon another marble reservoir, in its center a tremendous wheel, about the size that operates a mill in a stream. This one, the superintendent told us, regulates the irrigation of the garden. Nearby there was a small building; the exterior of this was almost solidly covered with Byzantine designs geometric in form. Outside, there was a square marked off by marble benches. In the center of this square was a star of marble inlaid in the ground. The superintendent told us the purpose of this square originally had been for family conclaves; the women sat on a bench on one side, the men on the other. The conclaves were held when there were marriages to be arranged, wills or other important family matters to be discussed. This meeting place away from the house was in order that such intimacies might be talked of freely, far from the ears of servants. This building and square are now as they had been in the fourteenth century.

We walked by a bathhouse of typical Turkish design, to one side of a large marble pool. We stood on a terrace looking down on a rose garden on one side and beyond it another filled with tulips, stock, anemone, and everywhere borders of daisies. Gardenias, too, were in bloom. Before we left we were given bouquets of these and roses.

Honeybunch's sister was at the house when we returned; Honeybunch, introducing her, explained they had both been invited to dinner. Sophy, who has a tendency to be carried away by a suggestion of a party, proposed we be hostesses at cocktails before dinner. While the rest of us went to our rooms to dress, she hunted out Mme. Fafalios to extend the invitations. She reported back to us that the Fafalioses occupied an apartment on the ground floor of the house. Our suite and other rooms we had not seen were not, as we had supposed, on the first floor, but by virtue of the marble staircase that led up to the entrance actually an upper story. The house proper, therefore, was ours. The Fafalioses would join us only for meals. Explaining this, Sophy said, Mme. Fafalios had revealed she spoke French very well, though she knew only a few words of English. In the presence of Honeybunch she had been too shy to expose this knowledge. She had said further she and her husband would be delighted to be our guests at cocktails.

This time Sophy had been carried much too far away. As a party it was moderately successful, but the cocktails were a lamentable failure. Honeybunch took it upon himself to order one of the little maids, whose name we learned was Poppy, to bring him some mint from the garden. He explained meticulously to Sophy this, he hoped, might cover the taste of the drink. Mr. Fafalios surreptitiously requested something from the other maid. A few minutes later she returned with a bowl of sugar. Mr. and Mrs. Fafalios divided the entire contents into their Tom Collinses.

The party took place on a broad terrace to which the wide center hall opened. It provided a beautiful place from which to watch the sunset glow on the water, and, as darkness came on, the lights sprinkled across the way in Turkey. We saw a large boat come into view. As it drew nearer, the two maids left the terrace and hurriedly went into the house. A minute or two later, as the boat passed abreast of us, all the lights behind us in the house suddenly went off and came on again, a number of times in rapid sequence. Simultaneously the boat's whistle blew vigorously, startling me into spilling a good portion of my drink. Mme. Fafalios laughed at me and forgot her shyness. She explained the boat passing us was the one on which we had arrived that morning. It had visited several other islands during the day, and was now on the return trip to Athens. The captain was saluting this house because it held visitors he had brought. The house lights were flashed as a return of his courtesy.

I said aloud what a charming exchange this was, but thought to myself I would have been more appreciative had the captain been less eager to deliver these visitors. I found it hard to believe it the same boat and this the same day that had brought our arrival at half past four. Immediately after the passage of our boat we saw a string of lights moving across the water away from us. They looked to be powerful and yet at the same time shrouded though the night was clear. Our American group pointed to them almost simultaneously, and Honeybunch explained they were lights on a string of fishing dories being towed out by a mother boat. The reason the lights looked misty was that though they were very powerful acetylene lamps, each was installed face down over the stern of the boat that carried it. The purpose of this was to attract the fish. As they moved farther from us they looked like giant fireflies bobbing just over the surface of the water.

Mrs. Cardamitsi, the lady interpreter we had met on the boat many hours before, arrived as we were going in to dinner at about half past nine. She apologized for her tardiness; we had not known she was expected. She explained she had been at a pinochle party and had she left earlier she would have been out three drachmas. She had stayed on, of course, and had made up her loss and a little over. She was in high spirits.

Mme. Fafalios said, as she seated us, we were about to have the light meal of the day; for them the midday meal was the dinner. I would not have clasisfied what we ate as a light supper. We began with cold lobster and hearts of artichokes, served with a sauce made from the lobster roe. The next course was a red fish, peculiar to that part of the world. It is like a mullet but very large and in taste one of the sweetest and most delicate I have ever eaten. The whole fish on a platter, surrounded by a ring of cucumbers, was set down in front of Mr. Fafalios.

Mme. Fafalios had seated me on one side of him and, in response to a vigorously nodded indication from him, Sophy was on his other side. During the day we had seen him only on our arrival and at lunch. He had spoken very little, explaining apologetically his English was bad; but now at dinner he made a little speech. Though the English was faulty the meaning was clear: that as head of the family he had the authority and the privilege either of taking to himself the choicest delicacy set on the table, or of bestowing it as he wished. This evening he chose to bestow it as a mark of welcome to a guest.

The four Americans made little humming noises of pleasure and watched. Mr. Fafalios picked up a serving knife and fork, leaned forward and with a dexterous flip of the knife extracted each eye from the fish, scooped them up with the fork, and deposited them on Sophy's plate.

Nature has favored Sophy with what is commonly recognized as a peaches-and-cream complexion. Looking at her across from me, I saw the peaches fade away and the cream disappear under a green overlay, not unlike mold. I saw her eyes bulge, too, as she looked at those on the plate in front of her. After a pause no one had filled with talk, Sophy lifted her head and spoke; at first with some difficulty because she seemed to find it necessary to swallow a number of times. When this spasm had passed she swept into a flood of oratory that of itself qualified her for a high diplomatic post anywhere in the world. She spoke of the symbols of hospitality and friendship peculiar to each country, and how a tangible expression of these good feelings made for a solidarity of friendship. Then, she said, the recipient of such expression must be permitted to reciprocate. Since she had with her no corresponding American symbol of friendship, she begged to be allowed for one moment to take the place of Mr. Fafalios and bestow on him the evidence of friendliness she and her companions felt for this country and this house. Scooping up the two eyes, she placed them on Mr. Fafalios' plate.

The speech was received with a round of applause and a startlingly loud "Hear, hear" from Honeybunch. Mr. Fafalios accepted happily the return of the fish eyes with a bow to Sophy and confirmed his acceptance by eating them at once, one after the other, first extending one on a fork almost directly under Sophy's nose, to indicate he was sharing them with her. She did not flinch, she did not even turn her head, she only slewed her eyes away from the dainty morsels.

After a few moments the green mold receded, the peaches and cream returned. She even ate her portion of fish and the courses that followed, cheese with honey, and after that oranges and Jap apples. We had coffee after supper in the sunroom. It was Turkish, thick and syrupy.

Another guest came in for coffee and the evening. She was Mrs. Frangaki. She taught English in the school in which Nico was a pupil. She spoke the language well and told us the study of English was begun in the earliest grades. Hearing this I groaned inwardly at the backwardness of our American curriculum.

Honeybunch volunteered to sing for our entertainment a popular song of Chios, though Mrs. Cardamitsi remarked audibly she did not consider his voice one we would enjoy hearing. When he had finished he bowed a number of times. Unfortunately the bows were not in response to any applause, but he seemed not to notice this discrepancy, and we hastily made up for it by clapping the bows. This not only satisfied him, it inspired him to further effort. Over her protests he ordered his sister to join him in a native dance. They did the dance very well to the accompaniment of a somewhat reluctant rendering of the necessary song by the other Greeks. To our dismay we were requested by Honeybunch to provide, in return, a number of some sort, a request echoed strongly by the others.

Darn was the one who suggested and insisted on the selection. Honesty forces me to record, though I blush with shame as I set down, that we four middle-aged women rose to our feet and sang, quaveringly but in parts, our college song that happens to be in Greek. I think the selection mystified our audience. They knew it wasn't English but I'm sure they had not the slightest idea it was in Greek. Nevertheless, they applauded roundly. I have seldom found people anywhere with such beautiful manners as the Greeks.

To forestall further performances from anyone I suggested I teach the group to play Scrabble. My suggestion brought precisely the results I had anticipated, murderous looks from my friends and an immediate rise to their feet of our guests with murmurs of how much later it was than they had realized, and how tired we must be after such a long day.

Once inside our rooms my friends had the grace to congratulate me on this ruse. Darn and I, before parting for the night, exchanged an extra handshake of mutual congratulation that in judgment for escaping the afternoon sweetmeat Sophy had very nearly received a comeuppance from the eyes of a fish.

Each day that followed repeated the pattern of the first. We made only one change in it. Finding the Fafalioses had requested the services of Honeybunch as a constant companion, we persuaded them we did not need such persistent attendance. Though we appreciated his kindness in giving up so much of his time, we had found when he was there Mr. and Mrs. Fafalios became self-conscious about their language difficulties and spoke very little, but in his absence they were less restrained, and we found them thoroughly delightful.

We learned, too, that Honeybunch was at home on one of his rare vacations from a job he had occupied since the end of the war on the Gold Coast, and we were distressed to take so much of his time away from his own family. The fact that he was willing to divert so many of his precious hours to making our stay pleasant and rewarding to us was only one other instance of what we had experienced everywhere we had been in the country, that to a Greek no thought of personal inconvenience is involved when he sets out to make a traveler feel welcome in his country.

Alone we explored the town, wandering up and down its narrow winding roads. We frequently encountered a group of old men playing cards. Since there are no sidewalks the residents, in order to be outdoors, sit in the street on chairs, generally tilted back against the front of the house. Ours was one of the few in the town that was separated by a fence. Wherever we went we were objects of curiosity of course. We had been told we were the only Americans on the island, and its inhabitants had been told we were there. People looked at us but did not stare; wherever we went we received some mark of courtesy. Buying stationery in a shop I was presented by its proprietor with a set of picture postcards depicting views of the island.

With Honeybunch or Mr. Fafalios we paid formal calls on the Mayor and other dignitaries of the town. At each call we were served Turkish coffee and that sugared fruit with cold, sweetened water as a chaser.

We grew used to seeing men, as they passed us on the street, or sat in a café, running between their fingers a string of beads. We had seen this first in Athens, and called one another's attention to it, deciding this was a form of prayer, probably a holdover from Turkish Mohammedanism. We learned we were entirely wrong in thinking it had anything to do with religion, though we were right that the custom had originated during the Turkish occupation. The beads are known as laziness beads, or sometimes, nervous beads. Very few women but almost all the men in Greece carry them in their pockets and use them frequently. The string is not long enough to form a necklace yet a little longer than a bracelet. Mr. Papastratos, we had noticed the day we had met him, was running such a string through the fingers of one hand almost all the time he was talking to us. When we had become not quite such strangers to one another I had ventured to ask about this habit and learned from him it had no religious significance. He told me, too, these beads, always amber, are sometimes very valuable, their owners taking pride in their intrinsic worth and beauty. Mr. Papastratos had also revealed with candor that Greeks tend to have a highly nervous temperament, and this habit of the beads is soothing.

"I myself," he said, "am able to keep my smoking to a minimum by using the beads. If I did not have them I would smoke to excess."

One morning at six, we walked down to the quay to see fishermen spread and mend their nets after the night's catch. It was a beautiful sight in the early morning. The quay that is also the main street is cobblestoned and wide as a boulevard. In those early-morning hours no traffic is permitted along it. The nets are spread over its length and almost its entire width, allowing only passageway at either side for pedestrians.

As we skirted the nets walking along one of these edges we stopped frequently to watch the men, who sat crosslegged while they mended. They held off the ground that portion on which they were working by slipping it between two toes. When they had finished mending one place they searched for another break by running the net rapidly through their toes, not touching it with their hands. Each man worked separately, covering a considerable area, so that these seated figures were spaced irregularly. They wore bright-colored caps with long peaks ending in a tassel over the shoulder. The nets were a rich brown. Looking from one end to the far extreme of the quay, the figures looked like irregularly planted shrubs with bright tops growing out of rich soil.

One day we visited Nico's school, where the children put on a program of dances executed with astonishingly accurate rhythm. But Nico, at the sight of us, became too shy to take part and was, understandably, reluctant so much as to acknowledge our presence.

From the school we went across the road to the orphanage, and bought there some of the exquisite hand-woven and embroidered linens the older girls had made.

Driving home from these visits, I asked Honeybunch to stop at a hotel I had passed several times on the quay. I wanted to learn about its accommodations in the event other travelers might wish to visit this usually untoured island. I found the Hotel Pelineon spotlessly clean. A single room is thirty-three drachmas a night (about $1.25), forty-nine for a double. All the meals are à la carte. Each room that looks out on the harbor front has its own little balcony, and every room its own washbasin with hot water twenty-four hours a day; also there is a large bath on each floor.

Apart from the delightful and unusual experience we had of living in a Greek house, with members of its household, an excursion to Chios is rewarding to the tourist. If he did not stay overnight in this little hotel, he could arrive on the boat from Piraeus at whatever hour the captain selected, and return that evening by the same boat. During the day he could visit the villages of Pyrghi and Mesta, the monastery of Nea Moni, and in addition the interesting excavations that are going on at Emporio. This part of the island achieved distinction in the early Bronze Age. It was from here the four bronze horses were taken that now are identified with Venice, those magnificent figures above the entrance to St. Mark's. The monastery of Nea Moni contains mosaics as fine as are to be found anywhere. It is scarcely necessary to add, I think, that the monastery can be reached by climbing on foot or on the back of a donkey, after a car has gone as far as the road permits. These methods of transportation can be arranged by the proprietor of the little hotel.

Pyrghi is a drive of about an hour and a half from the harbor of Chios. Mesta is half an hour further. Pyrghi is a village dating from around A.D. 1000 with very little change in character since that period, either physically or in the inhabitants' way of living. It was untouched by the devastating earthquake of 1881, therefore with no need for physical rebuilding it continued in its original habits. The Mayor of Chios is not happy about this. When the town is mentioned he squirms a little and speaks of it half apologetically, half irritably. "It will be changed," he says. It is not a model town according to standards of cleanliness but it is a reproduction, since it is a continuation, of the way of living in the Middle Ages. It numbers three thousand human beings and six thousand animals within its walls. The evidence of these animals is everywhere. Luz had to wade through muck in order to photograph the exterior of the church, but the church is twelfth-century Byzantine, with interwoven pattern of stone and tile, the exterior ornamented with rosettes in ceramics.

Like the other towns of its day, Pyrghi is within two walls, an outer and an inner. These, of course, were for protection, particularly from pirates who, they told us, were Arabs. Apart from the loot they might secure, these invaders had a personal mission to accomplish. Killing a Christian, man, woman or child, insured special consideration in Heaven. To defeat the accomplishment of this mission the villagers built watch towers on the highest spots outside the town and placed in them lookouts. When one of these saw a ship approaching, he lighted a bonfire, and the village below, warned, made its preparations for defense. The streets are very narrow, the houses open directly onto them. As we walked we could look through open doorways and see the walls decorated with symbols of the Crusade and Byzantine patterns, such as decorated the exteriors. The houses are, for the most part, two stories, each with its balcony; in some of these ovens project from the second floor. The inhabitants were all in native costume, not very clean, but picturesque. We were of course surrounded and followed by them with polite curiosity. The women indicated shyly they would like to feel the material of our dresses. Sophy, who has a strong sense of social responsibility, not only gave ready consent, but volunteered to demonstrate the particular features of her costume. She took off her skirt and revealed matching shorts beneath. Honeybunch blushed at this striptease and transferred his black gloves nervously from one hand to the other several times. The villagers were appreciative and enthusiastic, and said to one another, as Honeybunch translated, this is what they should adopt for working in the fields. They were pleased, too, with Darn's skirt when she showed them it was divided, enabling her, should the occasion arise, to ride a donkey astride. If visitors at Pyrghi next season find the women no longer wearing their native costumes, they can place the responsibility of this innovation, after nine hundred and more years of conforming, among Darn, Sophy, and Abercrombie & Fitch.

It is not possible to drive quickly the distance between Pyrghi and Mesta. There is heavy traffic of cows and donkeys, none of them accustomed to automobiles. As we left Pyrghi, we passed a number of round threshing floors, each one walled and each one, Honeybunch explained, the possession of a family.

Mesta is medieval, untouched by time, but cleaner than Pyrghi. The two villages are unlike anything else we saw in Greece. At Mesta we left the car outside the walls and went through one of the two entrance gates down a long dark tunnel, emerging into a narrow

EK
Vasiliu

street of the village proper. As we walked along it we could very nearly touch with our fingertips the walls on either side.

A gentleman came hurrying to meet us. He introduced himself. He was Mr. Zervudis, he said, a friend of Mr. Fafalios, who had sent word we were coming. Seeing our car draw up outside the wall, a woman whose house was close by had surmised we were the expected visitors and had run ahead to tell Mr. Zervudis. The woman, breathing heavily, stood behind him as he explained this to Honeybunch. Mr. Zervudis himself was a little out of breath. Evidently they had not wanted us to step inside the village proper without an official welcome, and this, we knew, would include the inevitable ceremony of hospitality.

We followed our host to his house. The walking was not easy, even though we were wearing our rubber-soled shoes. The streets are paved with small, very rough stones, and used only by pedestrians; not so much as a donkey cart comes inside the walls. The living quarters of the Zervudis house are on the second-floor level. Mr. Zervudis explained this arrangement. The animals are kept on the first floor; the upper level has more light. Mrs. Zervudis met us at the door. She was charming. She shook hands all around and then led us immediately to a large table covered with an embroidered cloth, but over this was spread a transparent material to protect the embroidered centerpiece beneath. There we were served the inevitable dish of candied sweet, the glass of water and the cup of Turkish coffee. But by this time we had become digestively so acclimatized we were able to down the refreshment without so much as one subsequent upward threat. Mme. Zervudis also put on the table almonds and a variety of little cakes.

Mr. Zervudis was apparently the leading citizen of the town. He told us he had at one time traveled for six months in the United States, but had forgotten the little English he had learned on that trip. He asked Honeybunch to apologize to us for this lapse.

Mme. Zervudis was reluctant to let us go when we had warily and by easy stages suggested our departure. I think she saw few people from other places, was herself of a superior background to the village inhabitants, and therefore lonely in this restricted environment. Nevertheless she did not accompany us on our tour, but said her good-bys at the door.

The runner who had apprised them of our coming had not joined us in the house. She had evidently sped on to give the word around the village of the arrival of strangers. When we came out of the house, we found a great part of the citizenry assembled in the little street, men, women and children, all smiling, all evincing friendly curiosity.

Almost all the men wore full-sleeved blouses and homespun aprons over their trousers. The women were in native Greek costumes, but wore on their heads a kind of kerchief we had not seen before. This had a stiff edge over the forehead like a visor, a practical arrangement as well as picturesque. It provided a shade for the eyes when the women were working in the field.

We visited the church, finding it the same period as the one in Pyrghi, except that a small addition had been made in the eighteenth century. When this was done the original paintings, we were told, had been covered over. Now there is restoration work going on, and the plaster is being removed.

On our way back to the car we paused at a house of one of the women in the group that had accompanied us. She wished us to take to a friend in Chios a package she had prepared on learning of our coming. She gave us, in addition, a large bag of almonds to show her gratitude to us for performing this errand. We were stopped once more, this time at the gate, by a very old woman. She wanted to know if by any chance we spoke French. When she learned we did she moved quickly from one to the other holding a hand in both of hers. She had spoken French, she said, when she had lived in Cairo forty years ago, and was hungry for the sound of it again. She urged us to come to her house for lunch. She had a fresh-caught red mullet. Regretfully we told her we were expected back at Chios. She begged us then to come into her house, so that she might welcome us. We knew what that meant, and endeavored to sound regretful when we told her we must leave.

Departures themselves are not easily achieved in Greece, but reasons for them are even more difficult to come by. To say one will be late for an engagement will not serve; it will not even have any meaning. We did leave at last. Our departure was, in the opinion of four Americans, a triumph in diplomacy and perseverance.

That evening we were entertained at the Chios Beach Club, because it was Mr. Fafalios' name day. The club is close by the house and so we walked. The night was warm and the moon was bright Tables at the club were placed around a raised platform for dancing and the order of dances was much the same as we had found a the taverna in Athens, with one alarming exception. When indi viduals were inspired by the music to quit their tables and do solo dances, the other guests expressed approval and encouragement b throwing their wine glasses to the platform at the feet of the dancers This provoked hilarity all around, the ringside spectators pounding on the floor with their feet, clapping their hands when they were not slinging glasses. The dancers laughed as they leapt and turned endeavoring to avoid the pieces of glass that flew up as goblet splintered on the floor.

Our table was close to the edge of the platform. We dodged frequently as fragments came our way. When the dance wa over I looked closely at those performers who passed close to ou table. Not one of them was bleeding. A waiter swept up the glitterin debris from the floor and handed around a fresh supply of win glasses.

We went back to Athens the following night. We were a littl heavy of heart to leave the friends we had made. We were even heavier by poundage because of the food we had eaten. There wa dieting ahead of us but beautiful memories to sustain us: of a leg of baby lamb spread with chopped sage and lemon juice, wrapped in parchment paper with butter on top of that, and roasted *trè doucement* for an hour and a half, of lobster, hot and cold, with mustard sauce, of lemon soup and fish soup, cold zuchini that had been peeled whole, cooked lightly and then marinated, of tidbit of orange peel rolled and held together with a toothpick. Dan wrote down how to make this, but I doubt the flavor will b quite the same, when, nibbling it, I am not looking out over th Aegean at fishing boats with lights turned down into the water However, I know that to cook it, I must put the slivers in boilin water for an hour, then take them out, drain them for half an hour, and cook them forty-five minutes longer in a sugar syrup. And oh, the fish; the *kalamari*, big, served cold and stuffed with rice tomatoes and raisins; the *kalamarakia*, so tiny eating them is lik eating a dish of crisp, sweet rice; the *maiatiko* that comes in May and is served grilled; the *psipoura,* something like a sole only a little thicker, and always the *barbouni,* the red mullets. When I think of Chios, I shall remember these as well as mosaics in a monastery and medieval villages.

Mr. and Mrs. Fafalios and Nico took us to the dock. This time we walked from the house, porters trundling our baggage in hand carts. Other friends were waiting there to say good-by and present us with bouquets of flowers. We were happy to learn the ceremony of leave-taking is confined to bouquets; it does not include candied fruit and a glass of cold water.

As we passed the place that had been our own for a week, our boat whistle blew, the lights of the house flashed on and off, and from the terrace on which we had sat every evening before dinner, two little maids waved a white tablecloth over the railing toward us.

At dinner our steward told us, breathlessly, we had a distinguished passenger on board, no less than a Greek general. As we were coming into Piraeus the next morning I saw him flanked by lesser officers. A delegation of men on the quay in uniform was obviously a reception committee. The general surveyed them and the approaching scene with impassive austerity. I happened to walk behind him as I left the deck to collect my belongings. He was holding his hands behind his back and running rapidly between them a string of nervous beads.

Chapter Fifteen

KOULA, my chambermaid at the King George, welcomed us all back with warmth and eagerness, rushing from one room to another to help unpack, bringing us trays of breakfast to supplement the daylight snack we had had on the boat.

I walked into Darn's room and arrested her unpacking. "I'm going to bring Koula to America," I said.

Darn brushed me aside. "I've already written it down," she told me.

I paid no attention. "She's a product of the war," I continued, "no education, not enough food, shares one bed in one room in Athens with a brother and sister. They sleep in shifts. And look at the way she has learned English, for instance, with no Berlitz professor like you, either."

"Do you want me to write that down, too?" Darn asked.

I returned to my room and resumed my unpacking.

The day was scarcely long enough for the accomplishment of all the missions on Darn's "Things to Be Done" list. Fortunately all of us did not have to do all of them, but there could be no postponements, because we were leaving that night on the *Semiramis* for a week's cruise among the Aegean islands.

Darn had a fitting, Luz had her camera checked. We all had a hairwash. This was a mistake on my part. I shall not again entrust long hair to a Greek coiffeur, even though he assures me by pantomime, as this one assured me, he can handle hair that sweeps the ground like a train. I thought for a time I would have to leave the shop either with my hair shaved off, or with a hairbrush wrapped up in it.

I paid a visit to the post office with Marino and a notice that galley proofs from my publisher were waiting me there. At the end of an hour, I would have been glad to make the Greek Government a present of the opus I had come to secure. Publishers mail their products in a cardboard container that is stuffed with shredded paper. Greek officials take a sharply suspicious view of this. After I had signed ten or a dozen affidavits that asserted I have not the slightest idea what, the little band of officials gathered for this transaction was still not satisfied. Marino was obviously not happy either. Though he had shaken hands with me and patted me on the shoulder several times to demonstrate to the authorities, I suppose, I was a trustworthy character, he had broken out in a fine dew on forehead and palms that necessitated an almost constant mopping over with his handkerchief. But when I pushed the package back at them, shrugging my shoulders and indicating I didn't give a damn, the official group became even more lowering and Marino more violently be-dewed.

I know now that to relinquish anything questioned by authority gives rise to a far graver doubt of the validity of both the possession and possessor than a fight for it, no matter how time-consuming that is for everybody. I finally discovered the roots of their suspicion were in the shredded-paper packing. I promptly offered this to them. I watched five men first endeavor to discover something written on each shred, and then tear the strips of paper to even smaller bits until they had created a mound of confetti on the counter top. It took time but it pleased them. The pages of the manuscript were not of the slightest interest to them. Illogically I found myself irritated by this indifference. As we waited for the elevator, Marino explained the reason for their distrust. People sometimes send nylon stockings and conceal them cleverly in the hope of avoiding duty to be paid by the recipient. Marino's pantomime was not adequate to explain to me how nylon stockings could be concealed in shredded paper.

The elevator itself in the Greek post office was for me more a hazard than my manuscript under suspicion. I had never before seen this kind of carriage. Marino told me it is fairly common in Greece. If I encounter one again I shall be both nimble and serene. I consider the machinery both ingenious and practical. These elevators are a series of open-faced boxes that run on a belt. One set of these is for the ascending elevators, another for the descending chain. The expectant passenger stands poised for a quick step. A box may pass with several passengers inside. He waits for the next. If this is empty, or at least not too filled, he steps in quickly, and then prepares himself to step off as quickly when he approaches the level of the floor at which he is disembarking.

By late afternoon, we were repacked, our errands done, our favorite sights revisited. Once more we took the road to Piraeus.

Boarding the *Semiramis* we saw immediately, at the head of the gangplank, young George Pothamianos, the son of Mr. Pothamianos and La Belle Hélène who had been so kind to us. We knew the *Semiramis*, though chartered for cruises by the government, actually was one of the ships of the Pothamianos Line; Mr. Pothamianos had helped us secure accommodations for this trip shortly after our arrival in Athens. We had not been dilatory; it was simply that in America we had not known the cruise was available.

We had not imagined friendship and a sense of hospitality would go so far as to prompt sending along the son of the house to insure our comfort and enjoyment. Over our protests at this discovery, young George, a handsome, charming man, about thirty, insisted that as a member of the family firm it was part of his job to go occasionally on these cruises to make sure everything was up to standard; that it was also in the way of a vacation.

He had reason to report to his firm a well-conducted cruise. It lasts for five days and includes a visit to the islands of Milos, Santorini, Crete, Rhodes, Delos, Mykonos and back to Piraeus. The boat leaves on Monday and returns on Saturday. Bearing in mind the Greeks' whimsical approach to any hour of the day or night, a traveler should make careful check of the scheduled time for departure.

We went to bed immediately after dinner, in case this Captain, like the Master of the Chios, was subject to whims. We were up at daybreak, in the nick of time, and on schedule, to watch our entrance into the harbor of Milos. It is a sight not to be slept through. The harbor is as round as a teacup, the mountains rise all around it. Looking back, within a few moments of entering, we could scarcely see how we had got there. Most of this region, we learned, is of volcanic origin. Without knowing this we had said to one another the harbor looked like a crater. I had seen deep-blue water in other parts of the Aegean, but by comparison with the depth of color here, the other was as aquamarine to sapphire.

We were reluctant to go below at half past six for breakfast. I was even more reluctant to leave the ship itself when, called to disembark,

I discovered our only means of exit was in one of a string of tiny launches that bobbed about on the surface of the water, hideously far below us. "Lunches," George Pothamianos called them, but it was not my idea of any sort of refreshment. We were connected to the first of these by another of those fairy ladders, such as had waved between the *Queen Frederica* and the dock at Piraeus, open on either side and nothing to grasp but a rope attached in scallops to slender fragile props set at intervals down each side of the stairway.

I made the descent, but halfway down I paused, shutting my eyes, and thought wistfully of the cornfields of my native Indiana that can be seen from a flat road, and no water anywhere.

No sooner were we on land, safely, to my surprise, than we were hustled into small and ancient buses. From there, as I might have known, we drove up a mountain road. We did not slow down for the curves; had we even paused, those ancient vehicles, I think, would have coasted all the way back down again; or, as I predicted frequently to my companions, hurtled backward over the edge. We stopped at the top and held our positions there, because each driver wedged his vehicle between a stone wall and a small ditch.

No sooner had we got out than we were led on foot by the ship's guide down a precipitous and rocky path, on the other side of the mountain. This brought us to the beautiful ruins of a theater built of marble in the second century. At one time, the guide told us, it had seated some fourteen thousand people, but there are only a few rows left untouched. Over the centuries, he said, the rest had been carted away for use as building materials.

Whenever I think of this theater, I shall remember a peasant woman there. I had wandered a little distance away from the sight-seeing group when I saw her. She was standing below me on the mountainside, outlined sharply against the wide landscape beyond. She was tall, slender, dressed in black even to the kerchief tied around her head. Her profile was the Athene's on a Greek coin. She held in her arms a baby lamb, its head nuzzled under her chin. She smiled a little when our eyes met and inclined her head with Olympian dignity.

When we returned from the theater to the path by which we had come, we found it blocked by donkeys and little boys attending them. We had not seen them in the village at the head of the path; evidently they are kept out of sight, because the way down is too steep for riding. I promptly announced my decision to mount one. The mounting was nowhere near so prompt as the decision. Standing, I could very nearly have put one foot over the little beast's back, but this seating arrangement was not approved by the donkey boys. They indicated vehemently I must ride side-saddle, on what was not a saddle at all but a strip of wooden slats. The only way to arrive at a sitting position is by backing up to the animal. With a boy at either elbow shouting "Hup," I did this, but the boys "hupped" so vigorously, I very nearly went clean over the creature with my feet where my seat should have been. The boys, however, with the vigor that had elevated me, pulled me back and settled me on top. When I was upright on the row of fencing that passes for a saddle, my friends and a number of the ship's passengers who were strangers to me cheered. Staying on top the lattice work is not so easy, either, I very soon discovered, because there is nothing to which one can cling, except what one is sitting on, and that rolls a little back and forth. However, I enjoyed the ride and even more the astonishment of my friends that I, of all the group, should have been the first to venture this.

As we waited in our little bus for the others to be filled, Darn leaned out a window and held a conversation of sorts with a woman who stood a few feet away from us, at the gate to her cottage. Darn indicated flowers growing in the garden behind the woman, and called them by name "luluthia," which the woman recognized. She smiled happily, nodded her head a number of times in vigorous corroboration and ran from the gate into the house. Darn, turning back to the rest of us, said regretfully, "I must have embarrassed her."

A few minutes later we heard a strong knocking on the outside of the window nearest Darn, and looking out saw the woman holding up to her an exquisite bouquet. Not embarrassment, we agreed, just characteristic Greek generosity and hospitality.

Ours was the head bus in the line, and so when we had skipped around the curves and bounced all the way down the mountain, we were the first to reach the dock. There were a few little stores along the quay. Most of them carried ship and fishing supplies, but Luz and I, exploring, found one that included in its merchandise large straw hats. Seeing them, we knew at once they were exactly what we needed for the island sightseeing, because we had been told there would be no concession to the strong sun by way of a siesta. A hat heavier than our cotton caps would be our only shelter from it. We tried a number on for size. I even found one that did not perch too high and too comically above my braids. The hats cost thirty-five cents apiece. While we were paying for them I saw on a shelf a bolt of twisted woolen cord in red and green, about half an inch thick. I pointed it out to Luz, insisting this would make an attractive headband for the hats that, as purchased, were a little bare. She was even more inventive. If we bought a sufficient length, she suggested, we could include strings to tie under our chins, in order to keep the hats on in the wind that was bound to prevail.

We communicated this idea, by gestures, to the proprietor of the store who had waited on us. I have seldom seen a man so astonished. He indicated this was his shop, he had purchased everything in it, he was ready to sell anything he had purchased, but never before had he received such an extraordinary request. Nevertheless, he took down the bolt, cut off the lengths we indicated, accepted payment for them and handed them over to us. When we had boarded the launch we happened to look back. He was still standing in the doorway and, in response to our waving, shook his head. It took us a little time to discover the reason for his perplexity. We learned it from George Pothamianos when he had the first sight of our hats and their trimming. He looked almost as astonished as the proprietor, and then laughed immoderately, we thought. We were wearing as headbands and chinstraps, he explained, Turkish cigarette lighters. It is a cord, or rope that can be set fire to at one end and burned sufficiently to light cigarette or pipe. This accomplished, it is snuffed out between the fingers. The average purchase of this at one time is about two, possibly three inches. Luz and I had each purchased two yards and a half.

We lunched on board the *Semiramis*. Darn had her notebook out, as usual, on the table beside her with the hope of writing down some new Greek words, or almost anything.

I volunteered some material. "Put down," I said, "that climbing these awful ladders to the ship from whatever is below is very little less horrifying than going down them. And don't forget to put down," I added, exultantly, "I was the first of us to ride a donkey."

Darn wrote a minute and then looked up. "I've written about the ladder," she said, "but one of the few things I do not need to set down in order to remember is you riding a donkey."

Actually, this day we were not out in the midday sun. We could even have taken a siesta, but we were too interested in the scene around us, and also, Luz's camera was working. At four o'clock we came through a narrow passage like the one into Milos, but even narrower, and emerged into a crater harbor like the one at Milos, too, except that this is more dramatic by far. This is Santorini; it is also called Thera. All around the cup in which we lay, walls of rust-red rock rose almost perpendicularly above our heads. Around the rim of these we saw a frill of shining white. That frill is the town of Santorini. I have never seen in any landscape such a sharp division by nature of color, the deep-blue water, the red rocks and the shining white of the town. The sight was so amazing we were reluctant to leave the deck, even to land and reach the town itself. The thought of the swaying ladder waiting for me below contributed to my reluctance.

Luz, Sophy and I took pictures extravagantly, though Luz moaned as she snapped that here of all places she had black-and-white film.

Sophy, folding up her camera, said she thought she'd take a few turns around the deck to get some fresh air before we went ashore. Luz paused in her photography to look with some bewilderment at Sophy.

I explained. "You have to know Philadelphians," I said, "to understand that. A Philadelphian does not absorb fresh air while he is doing something else. He has to go on a special mission for it. He can motor all day, but before he goes to bed, he must go out again to 'get' some fresh air. He plucks it like mint or edelweiss."

A young man standing near us overheard this conversation. He came closer and asked Sophy shyly, "I beg your pardon, but are you from Philadelphia?"

Sophy, a little discomfited, admitted she was.

The young man spoke with a rush. "Do you mind if I ask you this?" he began. "I know it's tiresome to say 'Do you happen to know so-and-so's,' but this Philadelphian was so nice to me. I went with her from Paris to Germany to the wedding of her niece, and in the end I was calling her aunt, too."

He went on a little breathlessly, telling the story of the trip, and his association with these people. "So you see," he wound up, "I couldn't help asking you when I heard you were from Philadelphia, because I think of Aunt E. as practically my own family."

Sophy smiled. "She's part of *my* family," she said. "She's my sister-in-law."

For the remainder of the cruise and his holiday from the government job he was holding in Turkey, John Peabody was a member of our group.

The ladder was no steadier than it had been in the morning. The boats were less steady. These were not "lunches"; they were rowboats. "Silly things," I thought glumly, as I sweated on the ladder above them, "making curtsies to me."

At the very moment I reached the bottom step the evil little cockleshell at which my shaking foot was aiming curtsied out from under me and for a whole lifetime by emotional reckoning, I hung by my hands over the Aegean Sea. I do not believe I would have fallen into it, even if the dancing little poltergeist had not come back under me when it did. From the difficulty I had in loosening my grip on the ropes, I think my simian inheritance is strong and tenacious.

I was no sooner on shore than I was up on a donkey again, but this time I was not a Lone Ranger. All my group chose to ride and so did most of the other passengers.

The only way to reach the town—and the town itself is called Thera—is to climb some thousands of steps on foot or on donkey back. The steps are wide, three or four people can walk abreast, and two donkeys. They are shallow and deep, and the risers are of marble. A pedestrian takes three or four paces from one riser to the next, a donkey, two. The donkey boys in Santorini wish travelers to ride astride, and we obliged.

The attendant of my steed indicated to me succinctly but effectively another requirement. I had hoped to keep to myself the manner in which I had been apprised of the additional rule, but Luz was riding beside me. A few minutes after our ascent had begun, she looked at me curiously a minute or two and observed, "Aren't you riding awfully far forward? You look to me as though you were on the creature's neck."

I was a little piqued that she would think I did not know how to ride, but I explained, "My boy wants me to ride forward."

"How do you know?" Luz asked. "I didn't hear him say anything."

"He didn't have to," I told her. "He has just given me a vicious pinch."

For the rest of the time I rode considerably closer to my donkey's ears than to his tail.

The island of Santorini rose from the sea at around 200 B.C. It is about ten miles in length, and at its very top is the town Thera that had looked as we saw it from the *Semiramis* like a white ruffle. Thera is white, but because of the date at which I am setting this down, I must with a heavy heart write instead, Thera was a white town. This week newspaper headlines have reported an earthquake that has almost destroyed that shining crest on Santorini.

There were, as I must use the tense, no ruins in Thera. Its charm lay in the magnificence of the views from each turn of its narrow, winding cobblestoned streets. On the door of nearly every house was a knocker of identical Turkish pattern, a slim, feminine hand wearing a ring and enclosing a ball. I tried to buy one, but I was unsuccessful. However, when I pointed it out behind the head of an old gentleman sunning himself, I was immediately taken by him on a round of shops, including an ironmonger's. My volunteer guide was a picturesque figure dressed in closely wrapped white puttees, a full blouse and an overcoat of heavy, coarse grey wool, embroidered in vivid colors. He carried a gnarled stick and walked slowly but paid no attention to my urgent request that he not take so much trouble. We gathered quite a crowd of followers before we had finished our rounds, and when I had rejoined my companions, each member of my local band shook hands with my original group, including John Peabody. One laggard catching up with us presented me with a bunch of flowers.

We made the down trip on foot. It was a happy decision. Other passengers went by on donkeys, the passengers grimacing as if they were biting into a lemon each time the donkey descended from one level to the next, because the beast did it by a four-footed jump.

I called to one rider, "How is it?"

His answer between clenched teeth was, "*Très incomfortable.*"

The *Semiramis* does not leave Santorini until after midnight, I do not know why, but it provided an opportunity for those who wanted to have a longer time in Thera to dine there at the taverna. A luxury hotel was under construction but was not as yet open. Indomitable as the Greeks are, they will rebuild, I feel sure, whatever the earthquake has damaged.

Before we went to bed that night we sat on deck a long time, not with a purpose like Sophy's, for grasping some fresh air, but for a last look. There was a new moon in the sky and the tiny lights of Thera were like basting-threads around the collar of Santorini.

We were at Crete early the next morning, and I repeat with feeling, we were *at* Crete. The *Semiramis* tied up to a solid motionless dock. I could have spent a happy hour, I think, repeating my exit from the ship for the pleasure of setting foot from gangplank to solid ground, but buses were waiting for us on the quay and we set off immediately after our six-thirty breakfast.

We were bound for Knossos and the palace there of Minos. A pox on those scholars who deplore the reproduction that has been effected in addition to the restorations in the palace of the great King Minos. These reproductions allow a traveler, no matter how meager his archeological background, to see vividly before him the way of life in its luxurious heyday around 1500 B.C. The palace is four stories high with winding corridors, bathrooms, running water to drink carried along hollowed-out stone from room to room, dressing rooms and separate apartments for the women, the king's council chamber, and in the Great Hall, his alabaster throne. On the walls, to the traveler's delight and the scholar's dismay, are the reproductions of the great murals. The originals are close by in the museum, but here in their original settings are strangely beautiful wasp-waisted figures, those of the men as slender as the women, the women in costumes and coiffures startlingly close to today's fashion, the men red-skinned to show their prowess in the outdoor world of sport, the women fair-skinned to indicate their aristocracy.

It was not hard to find the mural I looked for. This is the one of which copies are so frequently and widely seen, of the three young men and a bull, one athlete holding the horns of the leaping animal on whose back a second young man is performing like a circus rider. At the tail, a third athlete is poised for a leap to join or replace the performer.

Luz pointed out on one of the murals a detail of particular familiarity to her. It was a sea urchin. She still carried on the sole of her foot a faint imprint of the one at Bourzi.

In a cathedral a tourist can express his gratitude to its existence by dropping a contribution into a box for the poor. As we left the palace of Minos I wished for a box into which I might drop some expression of gratitude to Sir Arthur Evans for the transformation of King Minos and his court from a legend to a magnificent reality.

Whatever is legend and whatever the fact of the Minotaur to whom, annually, seven Athenian youths and seven maidens were sacrificed by order of King Minos, here is the labyrinth in which he dwelt and was found and killed by Theseus with the help of Ariadne, the daughter of Minos. The word "labyrinth" is a derivative of *labrys*, and that itself is the word for the double axe head. The double axe head, symbol of royal authority is imprinted, like a seal, on nearly every wall and object in the palace.

Buses took us back to Herakleion, where we had docked. It is the largest city on the island of Crete. This, too, is where the museum is located that houses the treasures from Knossos. Ours was a sequence I recommend to other travelers. Knossos first, in order to bring to the isolated pieces the background from which they were taken. I remember reading that, by the physical defect of acute nearsightedness, Sir Arthur Evans was able to see with clearer vision and in greater detail than other scholars the seals discovered at Knossos. It was by virtue of this defect the deciphering of their inscriptions was almost literally stumbled upon. I looked for, and found, some of these seals in cases. My more nearly normal vision than Sir Arthur's was just such a handicap as had impeded his associates. I could see nothing but a lumpy surface.

We lingered in the museum after other passengers from the ship had left at the heels of the ship's guide. I think they went on to Phaestus. Perhaps it is somewhat to our shame that we did not. Phaestus contains ruins of a Minoan city second to Knossos. I should have liked to see the great stairway of the palace, and other travelers would like as well the magnificent view that spreads below this mountaintop. We were filled to capacity by what we had seen. We did not want to have to tamp down that splendor in order to make room for more sights. Therefore after an hour or so longer at the museum we hired a taxi, returned to the ship, gathered up bathing things and were then driven to a little place called Tobruk, a few miles beyond Herakleion. The beach stretches for miles in either direction from this little spot, but we chose it because our driver indicated we would find bathhouses there. We found a taverna, and close by a row of bathhouses.

A charming young woman at the taverna led us to the bathhouses, indicating by shivering, however, we were a little ahead of the season. She apologized that the houses were being painted and therefore the doors had not as yet been hung; but she propped one up against each cubicle after she had seen us into it. We had not turned prudish but we were on the only sandy beach we had discovered in any part of Greece we had visited; not only had the others been pebbled so that it was essential to wear rubber shoes down to and even in the water, but those other beaches had been generously dotted with rock formations large enough to screen a swimmer putting on or taking off a bathing suit. We had discovered, appreciatively, the off-handedness of the Greeks toward this process; nevertheless, we were not inclined to put it to too vivid a test.

I doubt that I shall ever swim in such water again until I return to Tobruk. It was so soft it felt, we said, as if we were floating in folds of a fabric. It was warm but not tepid and so buoyant I flounced about like a dolphin.

We lunched at a taverna called Kharilaos midway between Tobruk and Herakleion. It is a charming spot with excellent food. We ate outdoors under a roof of plaited rushes and grapevines that made a soft light and nice patterns over the area beneath. At the end of the meal the proprietor asked Darn a question that she interpreted as a hope we had enjoyed our meal.

She replied enthusiastically for all of us, "Yes, yes, very much indeed, thank you."

The proprietor answered, "Then I shall get it immediately."

Darn understood and translated this, reluctantly. We waited in some anxiety. "It" turned out to be a bowl of small, dark cherries, smaller than any I know and sweeter. Before we left the proprietor showed us the trees from which they had been picked when we arrived in the hope we might request them. We stood at the doorway a few minutes to look, too, with pleasure at a row of windmills, silhouetted against the sea, their sails billowing as the wheels slowly revolved.

Back in Herakleion again, we let our taxi go and wandered on foot along narrow streets, pausing at my request at market stalls and shoe shops, because these are two of my favorite points of interest. Unlike Darn I do not seek shoes because the preceding pair has been a mistake. I hunt them and buy them because every pair I have purchased in Europe has been thoroughly pleasurable to me; not the elaborate ones with heels for stylish wear, but the peasant ones with almost no heel. I had bought a pair in Athens, another at Nauplia, a third in Chios, and I bought a fourth in Herakleion, of pale yellow leather. By the time I acquired these I had learned to ask unflinchingly for size thirty-seven. They cost a little over two dollars. The ones in Athens had been the most expensive, something over five. The ones from Nauplia cost eighty-five cents.

Old men we saw in the streets at Herakleion were the first we had encountered in Turkish costume or an adaptation of it, high boots, loose trousers that bagged in deep folds at the knee, and embroidered leggings. They did not wear coats. The shirt was a very full blouse and over this they wore a sleeveless vest, heavily embroidered.

From the market and shopping streets we moved on to see the

walls and the moat, mementos left by the Saracens in about 825. We had heard there were charming tavernas in Herakleion with good food. We were too tired to prove it, but other passengers to whom we talked next day reported this to be so, recommending particularly the Voyadzis. We dined on the boat and went almost immediately to bed.

Chapter Sixteen

THERE is a surprise at Rhodes for passengers of the *Semiramis*. On the day that island is visited breakfast is served at the luxurious hour of seven-thirty. For this particular cruiser, there is the added happy treat that the *Semiramis* pushes all the way up to a solid, unwavering dock.

Rhodes itself will be a surprise to the traveler who likes to see a place first and read about it afterward. That traveler by the time he reaches this island will have settled into the pattern of antiquity. He will be jolted out of it by the sight of this medieval town, not in ruins nor remnants, but the best preserved in this period throughout the whole Mediterranean basin. As a city it is, of course, very much older than the Middle Ages, but the Knights of Malta made it their own and very little of its antiquity remains.

I am not a traveler who looks first and reads afterward, and yet when traveling I am almost constantly in a state of surprise. It becomes embarrassingly and conspicuously evident to me on trips that my absorption quota and saturation point are both low. I had read about the Knights of Malta, but I did not know until I arrived at their stronghold they were also called the Knights of Rhodes, and the Knights or Hospitalers of St. John of Jerusalem, as well. I shall remember it now, I hope, because I have seen the beautiful building in which they cared for the sick, although visualizing it as a hospital, I shudder at the filth-infested place of agony it must have been. Long before we reached this building we had seen the deep moat and beautiful walls that surround the city and had walked through the ghetto. The ghetto is today an isolated section of the town, though happily now, by choice and with none of the barbaric associations that make one flinch today at the sound or sight of the word. There are pleasant streets, picturesque houses, a broad square with a fountain in its center, and pink-cheeked children playing around it.

The old hospital is now a museum. Two guides are provided by the *Semiramis*, one for those who speak English and another for those understanding French. At each place visited, the two groups form immediately out of hearing distance from each other. At the museum the English-speaking coterie assembled on the steps. That morning the lecture was particularly long and, I felt, somewhat rambling. I did learn that the dates of the use of the building as a hospital were 1405 to 1460, but that we would see in it now, as a museum, figures that dated to 500 B.C. I heard the guide say the reason so many statues were rescued from the sea was that the Romans had begun their looting at around 150 B.C., and many of the ships carrying the loot were sunk by the Turks.

By this time I had become restive and I moved away quietly. This was how I happened to be alone when I walked into a small room off the upper gallery. The walls were of rust stone, the only illumination a shaft of sunlight that slanted down from the one window there, across a figure so exquisite that at sight of it foolish tears for a moment blurred my vision. She is the Aphrodite or Venus of Rhodes, the loveliest Venus I have ever seen. I am not sure I do not count her the loveliest figure. I think no setting could become her better than the rough stone walls softened only by the sunlight. I would count it an impertinence to place her against a contrived and decorative background.

The museum holds other treasures. It is an interesting place to visit; it *must* be visited as long as Aphrodite lives there.

Leaving the museum we walked along the Street of the Knights. Peeking into courtyards along the way we saw jasmine hung over winding stairs that led to apartments above. Over nearly every doorway, as we pointed out to one another, was a magnificent coat of arms identifying the knight who had lived there. When we stepped into one courtyard to look with delight at its paved floor of tiny black and white pebbles, we learned from a young gentleman who descended at that moment from the characteristic winding staircase in the back this was the British Consulate. Even more interesting was the information that the Children's Pool of the UN in New York is paved in the same fashion as this courtyard, with pebbles gathered by children in Rhodes.

At the end of the street a little farther up we reached the palace of the Grand Master of the Knights of Malta. Structurally it is magnificent, but the heavy hand of Mussolini was laid upon its interior and the imprint of that hand is little short of disastrous. It is the appalling epitome of the quality attributed once to Lady Emma Hamilton, "So much taste and all of it so bad."

Our guide told me in recent years the Greeks have done a great deal to modify this garishness. I can only thank a merciful Providence I did not see it at its peak.

The palace did not hold the four of us long. I doubt the others outstayed us by any considerable period of time. We are not by our respective natures group minded. This is no virtue, it is simply our *modus operandi*. We like to explore for ourselves. Accordingly, with John Peabody, we found a taxi, drove about the city, fairly reeling with pleasure because there were trees and luxuriant green grass. The part of the mainland in Greece that we saw and the other islands we visited have the kind of beauty that is dramatic, breathtaking, but it is not a smiling landscape, and it is bare.

As we drove we began spontaneously to hum our little tune prompted by our pleasure, "We're off to see the wizard." At that instant I remembered a charming old gentleman who had called on us soon after our arrival in Athens. He was Mr. Nicholas G. Lély and his card read, too, "Envoy Extraordinary and Minister Plenipotentiary of Greece." During the call the Extraordinary Minister had said, "You will see much beauty and many wonderful things in Greece, but I venture to prophesy and to hope as well, that Rhodes is the place you will love. She has been my love for fifty years. I think that is permissible to me. She was given as a bride to Apollo, you know, but he left her and went away. So now she is mine."

We lunched at the Hotel des Roses. It is on the sea, has its own beach and delicious food. It is of de luxe quality and is not expensive. We were told two people in a double room with private bath pay ten dollars a day, and this includes all meals. Darn engaged a room. While we swam, she announced a little defensively, she proposed to lie in a hot tub and after that take a little siesta. She followed this program and was almost offensively smug over its superiority to ours.

In the late afternoon we took a taxi back to the *Semiramis*. Darn could not later remember what she had said to the driver of the taxi that resulted in his taking a sudden turn off the route he was following, the same one by which we had reached the hotel. He drove us through a section of the town we otherwise would not have seen, a section in which the streets were so narrow people sitting in the doorway of a house had to draw in their feet to allow us to pass. The street wound around just inside one of the outer walls. We looked through doorways into courtyards with flowers blooming everywhere.

At sunset I stood on the deck of our ship looking at the city we were leaving and thought ruefully that Byron's heart had been in better shape than mine was at the moment. At least he had asked the return of the whole of it from the maid of Athens. I was dropping bits of mine over a fair portion of Greece, but a sizable piece of it I put for safekeeping then and there in Rhodes, under the guardianship of the Aphrodite up on the hill in a stone room, dark now that the sun had gone.

We sailed from Apollo's bride to the place of his birth, the island of Delos. The legend is it was a floating island, but that when the time came for Leto, his mother, to bear her child, Zeus steadied the place and made it her sanctuary. There, like me, she gave birth to twins, Artemis and Apollo. I wonder if she was as surprised by this revelation as I had been when I learned of my accomplishment. Except for this bond, there is no further similarity between us. The place of her accouchement became a shrine to Apollo and one of the most famous in the ancient world. It would not have had such international significance had it remained only a place of worship, but it was also the birthplace of a political ideal and a way of life that provide today the only means by which the entire modern world can survive.

Delos was the seat of the Athenian League, the league that showed the way for the League of Nations and the United Nations. There was at the same time the Lacedaemonian League, but the pattern of this was not the one we have followed. The Spartans made theirs oligarchical in form, keeping Sparta the aristocratic head and her associates tributaries. The Athenian League was a league of democracy formed on equal rights, for mutual protection. The treasury of the Athenian League was at Delos where the member delegates met.

Vasiliu

I said all this to my friends at breakfast. We had not dropped anchor as yet and I was still unaware of the fact we were about to resume our earlier method of landing by way of small boats. Had I known this I would not have been so cheerfully talkative. I continued rehearsing aloud what I knew in advance about the place we were going to see. There was a conspicuous lack of responsiveness from my companions, but at least I was not interrupted save for an occasional muttered, "I know that," or "Oh, for Heaven's sake, please pass me a roll and eat your own, or something."

I am not easily downed. This quality of mine has been defined by others as lack of sensitiveness to my surroundings. I told my apathetic table mates that after the royal birth of the twin gods, no lesser ones were permitted. No child was allowed to be born on the island, and further, no one was permitted to die there. When I added there must have been a number of births and deaths just offshore in a boat, Darn asked me to spare them speculative details. I accommodated myself to this by picturing aloud what a sight it must have been for the inhabitants to watch the approach of ships coming on the annual pilgrimage to the shrine and the meetings of the league.

By the time I had finished the others were leaving the table and I had not as yet eaten my breakfast. My departure was, therefore, somewhat delayed. When I came on deck, after equipping myself in my cabin with straw hat, dark glasses, camera, canvas carryall and sweater, I found the others had gone on. I did not mind, but I minded extremely the sight of one little boat cavorting below that familiar wafting staircase, and me a solitary passenger.

My friends were waiting for me at the island, but I did not see them immediately. I was preoccupied as we reached the landing stage with getting myself onto it from the boat. I am not a leaper. I make a bridge by securing my hands to some part of the place on which I hope to land, keeping my feet in the boat. When the forward end is fast, I release the stern. After that I stand up. All of me was on the dock, and I was preparing to stand, when, lifting my head, I looked into the face of a bull, at not more than five feet distance from me. The last thing on earth I would have anticipated was a bull on a little dock in a far-off Greek island.

When the paralysis induced by the shock had eased a little, I began moving backward delicately. My mouth was open but I was unable to bring a sound from it. I think I would have kept on backing until water closed over my head had I not heard in the distance Luz's voice calling reassuringly, "He's Ferdinand's brother. Just move to one side. He's going on a boat."

This message convinced me a paralysis had also invaded my mind, that I should seem to be receiving a message that a bull was joining our cruise. Meantime, the bull had done nothing whatever. It continued standing exactly as it had been when I rose up in front of it. I continued moving, however, and would have backed off into the sea had not Luz come from behind the animal on a run and grabbed me with both hands as I wavered on the edge, one leg already out over the water.

A man appeared from behind the bull, gave it a slap on the rump that moved it to lumber from the dock onto a broad-beamed boat tied up there. Part of the rail was lowered like the side of a baby's crib, to permit passage. After that bull another one ambled on, then a cow, like a passenger in a subway rush, pushing to get ahead. Several donkeys followed without pushing, and after them a few pigs. I had not seen their boat when I landed from mine nor had I seen the animals other than the bull.

As Luz and I walked the length of the dock, her arm still through mine in support, we passed, of course, the Noah's ark, and saw a little knot of passengers gathered in the bow. We had to hurry to catch up with the rest of our party and the day was hot, so the others said. I was not aware of this as yet. Meeting a bull, I had discovered, is chilling to the system. In a very short time, however, I was aware of the heat and we continued to be conscious of it through our stay. There is not a tree on the island, but there is a considerable distance to cover and a good deal of climbing about to be done. Without rubber-soled shoes, dark glasses and a hat with a brim, a traveler would be acutely uncomfortable there.

When we reached the others they were dividing into the two language groups but the guides had not as yet begun their lecture. I took advantage of this to ask ours about the Noah's ark. The animals, he said, were brought over to this island to graze; it was considered to provide excellent pasturage. The boat that brought them was called a caïque, a type of sailboat most frequently found in the eastern Mediterranean. This one had an engine as well as sails. It carried passengers, too, as we had seen. They had come from Mykonos. Many tourists, he said, traveled this way. It was cheap and it also made possible a longer stay than a cruise permitted. The tourist pavilion on the island could accommodate a few overnight guests though it was not a large hotel.

The language groups were settled now. The stragglers who invariably fluttered back and forth had made up their minds which language to select that day. I joined my friends, who had seated themselves on a large marble block. The lecture began with the birth of the royal twins, and this included a considerable amount of obstetrical detail. I let my attention wander during this, thinking I would bring it back when I heard something more indigenous to Delos, but I delayed the return too long. What I heard when I picked up the thread was that the reason the body of John Wilkes Booth, the slayer of Abraham Lincoln, had never been found, was that it had been dissolved in lime. I listened after that and learned the ruins here are those of a rich community where money had been made entirely by trade. As the seat of a political league and a religious shrine, opportunities for commerce had been provided abundantly. I did not learn its association with Mr. Booth's interment.

When the lecture was finished we explored the ruins. They are of absorbing interest. The floors in the houses of the rich merchants are of exquisite mosaics. I stood looking down at one of these that had been placed there about the fifth century B.C. Hearing a noise overhead I looked up to see an airplane. I watched it a minute, smiling, and then looked down again.

It is not difficult to explore here the temples, the altars, as well as the houses; the terrain is fairly level. But the most dramatic sight of all on this island is the street of lions. This is an avenue that instead of being bordered by a row of trees is lined by a row of statues of heroic size, each one the duplicate of its neighbor: a massive lion standing erect, on a gigantic flat-topped pedestal, head high in the air. Some of these have broken and fallen, others remain intact. From them it is easy to visualize how the whole astonishing street had looked.

We were by now out in the midday sun, and the heat had become almost unbearable. We were glad to move into the museum. It provides more, however, than relief from the sun. Its collection is excellent, the sixth- and seventh-century statues unusually well preserved.

The pavilion is next door to the museum. We congratulated its proprietor on the location and ourselves on being in the shade. We heard people around us ordering Gazases, a drink we had not encountered before. We tried it and found it refreshing. Darn wrote it down on the list of Helpful Hints to Tourists. It is a bottled drink of carbonated lemonade, rather sharp than sweet.

The tour was over but our little group of four, and John Peabody, went by ourselves for another look at the street of lions that is down the hill, midway between the pavilion and the dock. There is, of course, always a hill.

As we turned back from the magnificent figures to resume our path to the dock, Sophy called sharply, "The boat's gone!"

Aghast we looked in the direction she pointed and could only corroborate her assertion. The *Semiramis* was not in sight. We held an idiotic conversation of "When did you last see her?" "When did *you*?" As though it were a pocketbook one of us had mislaid.

We broke into a run when this, naturally, had brought no helpful results, and as we scrambled and panted down the hill we called to one another breathlessly the impossibility that the other passengers could have got aboard so fast and left us behind. Our detour could certainly have occupied only a few minutes.

Darn wheezed accusingly, "You did take pictures though, Luz." We all knew she meant that when Luz takes pictures she takes also a considerable amount of time.

John, at the head of our little herd, topped the last hummock that separated us from the dock and called back, "They're all here."

We slowed down, endeavored to catch our breath, and at a dignified walk covered the distance in which we were visible to our associates. We were, of course, profoundly relieved to find them. Nevertheless, Sophy pointed out, they had not restored the *Semiramis*. I doubted she could have sunk silently, though this is a fate I habitually consider to be imminent for any ship on which I am traveling.

We were not, of course, the only ones concerned about its absence, though I was the only one who ventured the opinion aloud she might have slipped beneath the waters. The others were asking over and over the opinion of the guides, but they knew no more than we.

In the midst of our uneasiness and restless moving about the dock, someone shouted the approach of the little boats that had brought us from the *Semiramis*. We had no idea where they would take us, but suddenly we were eager to leave the island. The fascinating spot to visit had become a sinister place in which to stay, an island of ruins and no inhabitants save a little handful of people administering the museum and the pavilion that was far too small to accommodate all of us.

I whispered to Luz if I had to sleep in a street I would just as soon it were not the street of the lions.

We could learn nothing, of course, of where we were going, or why, from the boatman who rowed us, but after a considerably longer time than our arrival had occupied, we came around a point and saw on its far side the *Semiramis*.

As I stood up in our little boat I saw young George Pothamianos at the head of the fairy stairway. For the first and only time I made that ascent as though I were running up the stairs to my own front porch. This is proof of the effect curiosity can have on the nerves and legs.

I had been the last to leave the ship, but I headed the returning travelers. My companions were in the same boat and close behind me up the steps. We all talked at once, demanding of George what on earth had happened and why we were where we were.

He led us to the far side of the deck and pointed. "It's a yacht in trouble," he said. "It went on the rocks early this morning. Sent out for help. It's the rule of the sea, you know. We must help a ship in trouble. So we came over. Now we are trying to get a rope around her."

On the instant, Sophy, Luz, Darn and I looked at one another with a wild surmise. We spoke almost simultaneously. "It couldn't be." "It's not possible." "How ridiculous." "Luz, get your glasses."

Luz ran from the deck faster than she had scrambled down the hill at Delos. George and John Peabody, bewildered, looked from one to another of us.

I endeavored to explain our incoherence. "It's nothing," I said, "just an idiotic notion. Of all the yachts there are in the Aegean Sea, why we should think this particular one might be . . ."

Sophy interrupted. "Anyway," she added, "we don't even know when they were supposed to be taking the cruise."

Luz returned with the glasses, leaned against the rail and put them up to her eyes. By this time we were laughing at our own absurdity.

"My Lord," Luz said, and very nearly dropped the glasses from her hands.

I was next to her. I grabbed them, held them up and saw, clear and distinct on the deck of the foundered yacht, Grace Phillips, and beside her Neil, her husband. "There but for the grace of God," I said, and passed the glasses on to Sophy.

When we became coherent enough to explain the circumstances and the people that had so astonished us, George immediately volunteered to row over if we wished to send a note. We did and dispatched it. Through Luz's glasses we saw Grace watch him coming. receive the note, and read it, Neil looking over her shoulder. They broke into flamboyant gestures of astonishment and handclapping. We waited for some time but when George did not return we reluctantly left the deck and went to lunch.

While we were in the dining room a note from Grace was delivered to us, brought by a sailor from the Phillips' boat. After the first exclamation points of incredulity, the note included a list of telephone numbers and a request to deliver a report to these when we returned to Athens, if we had to move on and leave their boat still on the rocks. Our invitation to join us on the *Semiramis* was declined.

Grace wrote, "We must hold to the tradition that the captain goes down with his ship. We are not the captains and the ship doesn't seem to be going down, nevertheless, Neil and I think we'd better stick with whatever happens and our fellow passengers. So sorry you're not with us."

Reading this aloud, I looked up, passed from one to another of my friends a smirk of satisfaction that I was on a run-of-the-week kind of boat and not stuck on a rock in a luxury yacht.

We hurried on deck again and supervised the *Semiramis*' crew's endeavors to lasso the other vessel. When several tries proved unsuccessful and we were told by the sailors more than several times to get out of the way of the rope, we moved back a few yards. Almost immediately, though I will not believe it was because we were out of the way, the rope reached its mark, held, and pulled the yacht into deep water and safety. A few minutes later, the *Semiramis* resumed its course. An hour later the yacht was out of sight, but we were at anchor at Mykonos.

I had been told it is *the* white town, and that is no exaggeration. Santorini is white, but it is also high up with a deep blue sea as a base and the center distance filled with red cliffs. Mykonos is a seaside town, where houses, shops, hotels, even the streets themselves are whitewashed.

It has become a very popular summer resort. Artists go there to paint. Travelers returning almost break into poetry when they speak of it. Let them paint, let them poetize. They will not be joined by me in any activity at Mykonos. I am glad I visited it. I love the native-made things I bought there. I do not like all that unrelieved whiteness. I was profoundly thankful when the sun commenced to go down.

We wandered in and out of shops, buying presents for our dear ones at home; hand-woven pouch bags in bright colors, gayly striped hand-woven shirts to wear over a bathing suit, other oddments. At the end of the main street we saw a hotel that looked attractive. The Hotel Touriste Leto *is* an attractive hotel. We entered gratefully its charming cool interior and ordered tea. Sophy abandoned us. She was determined to find a place, she said, where she could swim, and we did not see her again until we were back on the *Semiramis*. The only person who came into the lounge while we were at tea there was Neil Phillips.

My walk of life has not led me around many Admirals, so I have no wide basis of comparison, but I have not seen an individual of any occupation closer to a boiling point of exasperation than this one-time Admiral in the United States Navy. His self-control did him and his training credit, yet he was a man sorely tried. We coaxed him to our table, persuaded him to take a cup of tea, and only then allowed him to tell us what troubled him. Luz asked if there were anything we could do to help.

That question uncorked the bottle, but without an explosion. What he needed, he began, was someone who could speak French and Greek. He had been told the wife of the proprietor of this hotel possessed such versatility. The reason he was in such urgent need of it was that he didn't know what had happened. The yacht had been chartered in his name. He must report the accident to its owner, and he, Admiral Neil Phillips, recently of the United States Navy, not only had not been awakened by it, but could not gather from captain or crew what it was that had caused them on a bright moonlight night, in a still sea, to pile up on rocks.

I thought to myself the barrier of language they had talked about so amusingly at Mr. Carter's cocktail party had suddenly raised its ugly height. I did not say this aloud. I asked instead if George Pothamianos had been of any help, since when we had left to go ashore he was still on the yacht. Neil told us then what George had done, adding had it not been for this they would not have dared risk pulling the boat off. It had been George's suggestion that he dive beneath the yacht, examine its hull, ascertain whether or not it was pierced by the rock. If it were not, then it could be slid off. Until we told him, Neil did not know George was the son of the owner of the shipping line that included the *Semiramis*. He had thought him simply a member of the crew. Now he understood, he said, why his own captain had put off in a rowboat like one possessed, at the approach of George, and had stayed barely within sight, rocking back and forth, holding his head in his hands, until the young man had departed.

"Of course," Neil said, "the old fellow recognized him and was ashamed. He had already conveyed to me he's afraid he will never be able to get another job. He spent a good part of the time crying."

We decided then it was no use asking George to try to talk with the captain under the circumstances. We found the wife of the proprietor instead, and learned the reports of her were true. Although she spoke no English she did speak both French and Greek. Every member of the yachting party spoke French, so there would be no difficulty now in learning what had occurred.

We parted on the dock. We took our launch back to the *Semiramis*, Neil hired another to carry him and his translator to the yacht. But what she translated we did not know. We sailed away, headed for Piraeus and the end of the cruise.

Chapter Seventeen

THE travel agency that printed circulars about the *Semiramis* cruises and a notice on the ship's bulletin board had said we would dock at 7:30 A.M. at Piraeus. We docked at 7. Some of the passengers were caught with their suitcases open but not our group. We had had our seasoning on the trip to Chios. We were prepared, we were not even surprised. Marino, waiting for us on the dock, said he had been told at the ship's office we would arrive at 6. That did not surprise us either.

However, a happy surprise was waiting for us at the King George. On the day we had arrived from Chios, set out on the cruise, and done a hundred things between, Sophy had had an inspiration to send a wire to Barbara,* an old friend in London, asking her to join us in Athens for a trip to Yugoslavia. There had not been time to receive an answer. As we walked along the corridor to our little cells a voice called out from a room farther down the hall, "Sophy, is that you? In Heaven's name tell me the word for orange marmalade."

We found Barbara sitting up in bed, eying with disfavor a plate of goat cheese on her breakfast tray. "I gave the maid," she said, "a magnificent performance of the necessity of marmalade for breakfast, and this is what I got."

Koula had heard our voices and came into the room on a run to welcome us. She was in time to hear Barbara's complaint and stopped dismayed. "Oh, madame, I am so sorry," she apologized. "I know the word marmalade but not what you were doing."

"She seemed a very intelligent girl," Barabara said reflectively, as Koula left the room.

I defended her intelligence warmly and added, "I'm going to bring her to America."

Darn promptly took her notebook out of her bag and began to

* *Forty Plus and Fancy Free.*

open it. "Would you like to know what else she's going to bring to America?" she inquired.

I forestalled that. Barbara had not as yet been introduced to Darn and Luz, and this provided a happy diversion from Darn's statistics.

Apart from the daily shoebag hour, the breakfast chat with Barbara was the only time awake that we took in slow measure until we were on a boat, five days later, bound for Dubrovnik.

No sooner had we separated from Barabara's room that morning than people and errands crowded in on us, accelerating our tempo and our pace to such an extent we were on the run a good part of the time with scarcely more than a passing nod to one another.

Alex Sherman and his wife Gina Bachauer had arrived from England. They gave a party for us at Gina's house a few miles out of Athens In Gina's childhood her family had spent the summers there. It was from that house the Germans had taken her father to prison and to which he was returned two years later, to die. With her husband she returns to it each summer, "like Antaeus," she says, to renew her strength by touching again her roots.

"The memories are here," she said, indicating the house and the garden where we sat, "happy and sad. But also, all around is Greek air and Greek light. I need them, too."

Alex, overhearing, interrupted, "It's an extraordinary thing, you know," he said, "about the air and light in Greece. It does something for you. You need to come back to it."

"Yes," I told him, "I know. I will."

The party in the garden was very gay. There was much discussion of the drama festival at Epidaurus to which many of the guests were going. They were dismayed and even more incredulous that we four should be leaving Greece at all, but particularly when there were in store the festival at Epidaurus and the wonderful musical events in the theater below the Acropolis. At one of these, Gina herself would play. We learned in the course of the evening how many times Gina would play during her holiday at home, a benefit concert for earthquake victims, another benefit for the Queen's charity. The list was long, her vacation was not, but she is a Greek. Therefore, as I had learned, spiritually or materially, she does not forget her country.

There were other parties, too. We were very gay those last few days, sad, too, because they were the last. When La Belle Hélène at a dinner at her house gave each of us an exquisite old coin so we would not forget Greece, I was so moved I made a speech. My friends told me later they would have been less embarrassed had I expressed myself in tears shed silently.

When we were not going to parties or to places we had first visited as sightseers that now were familiar and loved landmarks we must visit once more, we were doing the errands tabulated on Darn's list. Darn had fittings and bought shoes. We gathered up the bolts of raw silk that had been promised us by the old lady and were ready on the date she had specified. Barbara told us of another shop that carried articles made of this raw silk and other hand-woven materials, and is run by an Englishwoman who is a friend of hers. We bought a variety of things there from men's ties to luncheon sets. They were received so enthusiastically at home we were sorry we had not purchased more.

We did not experience these regrets, however, until we were in America. Darn suffered earlier. On one of these last crowded days in Athens I stopped in her room as I was leaving for my rounds of the day. I was not surprised to find her bending over the familiar notebook, but I was slightly taken aback when looking up from it she told me in dismay she had miscounted at Mykonos the number of friends for whom she was buying bags there. "I only bought seventeen," she said, "I should have taken twenty-two."

Each of us bought a number of things at the shop that is the headquarters of the Queen's Industry. It is directly across the street from the Grande Bretagne, and is something like the Woman's Exchange at home. At the Queen's instigation and under her personal supervision, women all over the country have been encouraged to produce in quantity their handicraft. These are assembled and marketed at the shop. Many of the articles have been made by patterns and designs set by the sophisticated, cosmopolitan women who run the industry. Therefore the articles have far greater style and chic than, undirected, would have resulted. For the traveler, however, there remains one obstacle to be overcome. A method of shipping has not as yet been introduced that will allow to be sent, articles too bulky or numerous to include in the hand luggage.

I purchased two rugs, one for each of my daughters. I thought them stunning. They were very coarse wool, long hair, one in natural color, the other dyed black. I could not carry them but when I asked to have them sent, I found no one knew how this might be done, though I visited the American Express, the travel agency and a bank to which I was sent. In the end I had to relinquish my purchases.

This is one of the few ways in which Greece has not as yet caught up with the inrush of tourists during the last few years. The country is better prepared for them this year than it was last. It will be even better equipped the following season. We saw government tourist hotels under construction in many of the parts of Greece we visited. The whole tourist pattern is being set up with extraordinary rapidity: information centers, tours by bus and by boat, cars and drivers for hire, all the needs of a traveler. The tourist rush had come on them suddenly with no warning of its size.

Geographers can chart the currents in bodies of water, but I doubt there is any scientist who can chart the course that next year's current of travel will follow. A few years ago it moved to Spain for no particular reason that anyone could either foresee or define; now with a mighty sweep it is turning to Greece. Greece is eager for this flood to come her way and preparing for it, but if there is a little leak here and there the traveler ought not to be impatient. The hospitality and warmth of the people more than compensate for an occasional lack of comfort or mechanical efficiency by which Americans have become spoiled.

Barbara spoke about this one evening during shoebag hour on the terrace. She is American by birth but has spent her married life in England. She is deliciously bi-loyal. If an Englishman criticizes an American she cuts him down with a tongue that is double-edged. If an American speaks slightingly of the British she effects a verbal uppercut. She herself speaks of both Americans and British affectionately and critically. That evening on the terrace she was examining American travelers with a British eye. "You are spoiled, you know," she began. When she is taking the Americans to task she calls them "you," when she is defending them to the British she refers to them as "we Americans."

"You carry umbrellas everywhere," she continued. "I don't mean a real umbrella; a Britisher always carries that. I mean an umbrella of protection. You're always putting it up against any inconvenience. 'I must have hot water,' you say. Up goes the umbrella. 'I have to have a room with a private bath.' The umbrella again. To a Britisher it's nonsense. You want everybody to be clean, provide the kind of food you're accustomed to at home, give you service on the jump, but allow you to pay for it in your own way and at your own time, and preferably in your own money. You are impatient with currency that is other than your own. Why can't everybody have nickels, dimes and quarters, is your attitude. When they haven't you put up your umbrella by holding out your hand with a handful of money in it and say, 'Take what's right, I can't make out this stuff. It's not real money anyway.' "

We protested this last accusation, all of us. Luz was the most articulate. "I don't think that is exclusively American," she insisted. "Yes, I've heard Americans do and say such a thing. But I've seen others, too. Those people are just boors in any language."

Barbara admitted this. "I think that was unfair," she conceded. "But I'm still right about the umbrellas." She laughed a little, and added, "Of course the reason I mind it is that I am an American and I happen to love Americans. That's why I want them to keep their umbrellas closed, or left at home."

Some time later, on our way out to dinner we paused at the hotel desk to leave our room keys. A man was leaning over the counter talking earnestly to the clerk.

"Have you no telephone operator," he was asking, "who can write down messages in English? I can't tell from these hieroglyphics who might have called me. Why can't your people be properly trained?" His accent was British, so were his clothes down to the furled umbrella, hooked by its handle over the traveler's arm.

"Those damn British," Barbara said, and moved on to the door.

At six o'clock on the afternoon of June 1 we left the King George for the last time. We had been in Greece a month, but we had seen so small a part of it. We had not, like some travelers, "done," four places in a day, but neither had we "done" any of the north. "We will come back," we promised aloud.

Three taxis in addition to Marino's car were required to carry us away. Our luggage totaled thirty-one pieces. Several of these, though bulging, were shining new. They had been purchased within the last eight hours to accommodate the overflow that had accumulated during the preceding thirty days.

The last person to see us off was Koula. Friends had called during the day, Marino had turned us over to porters at the dock and, shaking hands all around three or four times in rapid sequence, had driven off; but inside the entrance gate to the dock I saw Koula. She was being jostled by a rush of passengers on their way to board one of a number of boats anchored there. She was looking a little anxious as she peered in one direction and then another. When she caught sight of us her frown of anxiety disappeared and she ran forward smiling.

I had not told her the name of the boat we were taking because I had not bothered to remember it. Marino, I knew, would deliver us to the proper one. I do not know how Koula had located it and us. When I endeavored to find out she answered, "I asked."

She asked other things at our request. Without her help I think we could not have left Greece that night. Barbara was in some difficulty about her passport. The tickets of all of us required a signature we had not been told of before. We would not have learned this from the ticket collector at the gate. He merely waved us aside. Koula took us to a building a block away she learned of by asking the ticket collector what was wrong. Once there, she not only obtained the signatures but as interpreter straightened out Barbara's difficulty.

Luz, two hours earlier, while getting into her traveling clothes, had slipped on the tile floor of her bathroom and had a nasty fall. She was not up to walking rapidly. Koula obtained permission to take her ticket for its required signature.

I was the last to say good-by to her. I took both her hands in mine, "You will come to America," I promised her.

"Thank you, madame," she answered, "I will be ready."

I joined the others on the dock. "We can't find our boat," Darn announced, adding obscurely, "unless it's another one like the one to Chios."

At a dock near the one on which we stood, two large ships were anchored. A searchlight from a passing launch passed across their bows. I called out excitedly, "It's the *Queen Frederica*." The other was her rival, the *Olympia*.

As we looked wistfully across at what had been home a month ago I was aware of a man immediately below us who seemed to be endeavoring to attract our attention. He was standing in the stern of a large rowboat, holding with both hands the edge of the dock on which we stood. I called the attention of the others to him. "I think he's talking to us," I told them.

He was saying one thing over and over, and Darn suddenly gasped. "Why," she said, "that's the name of the boat we're going on."

I looked down with horror at his craft. "In that?" I asked.

The man, having caught our attention, pointed across the water beyond the end of the dock. We saw a boat, startlingly white in the dusk that had now dropped over the harbor, and in size somewhat smaller than the one I have seen taking excursionists around Manhattan Island. We did not need Koula to translate what was expected of us. With awful foreboding we knew we were to be rowed out to that little dainty on which we were to ride the seas for four days and nights. I thought the reason she had not come all the way in to the dock was she would sail away again untenanted. One look at her, especially alongside the *Queen Frederica,* and passengers would reclaim their baggage and make for the gate, changing their itinerary as they ran. I learned later it was economy and not shyness that kept her so far offshore. By not coming into the dock, her owners, the Yugoslavian Government, saved a harbor fee, or whatever that charge is called.

Sophy reached a hand down to the boatman's. "Well, let's go," she said, and jumped.

That decisive move on the part of our executive settled the matter for the rest of us. We had hung back, each with her own thoughts like mine, probably, of sweet home and loved ones we might never see again. We followed Sophy though I certainly did not jump. There was little conversation on the way out. Once Luz observed brightly that ships always appear smaller at a distance than they really are.

Darn answered ambiguously, "Not this one, or you wouldn't see it at all."

What a happy carefree jaunt that little row was compared with what awaited us at its end! Our boatman drew up alongside the glossy pet, and she was pretty. Looking up we saw two sailors at the rail on a deck above. We made no move to rise. We were waiting for them to lower a familiar flight of steps. That is not what those boys lowered. They tossed down over the side a rope ladder. A spindly little cross-barred contraption with scarcely enough bulk to make an audible sound as it slapped the side of the baby ship.

Other portions of my make-up have been labeled "stout"; but no one knowing me has ever applied that adjective to my heart. I can claim it now, and rightfully, because I climbed that ladder. It was when I was halfway up, and begging Providence to get me the rest of the way and then never allow me to stray so far from my native Indiana, that I thought of Leo Ganter. I saw myself outside the gypsy tent on the fairgrounds at Muncie and heard my voice assuring him he was destined to go to sea. I think that sudden realization of my mistake is what got me up the rest of the ladder. I felt I was fulfilling the destiny that had been marked for me, not Leo, and, therefore, I had better get on with it.

Darn during her upward passage wobbled a little, and moaned once or twice. Sophy was nimble, of course. Luz was sure but slow, only because her back hurt. Barbara, the last, came up something in the manner of a pirate. She carried her pocketbook by its handle between her teeth.

The minute we touched its deck we loved that little ship, first, of course, because we were so glad of anything solid beneath our feet, but after only a few minutes of exploration, because she was so clean and trim. Our cabins were small, but each of us had one to herself. Because Barbara carried the least luggage we piled our surplus in her stateroom. She complained, but Sophy told her not to put up an umbrella.

Our shoebag hour that evening was something more than a time of relaxation and pleasant talk at the end of the day. It had rather the quality of refreshment provided by St. Bernards to Alpine travelers. We partook of ours sitting side by side on a hard wooden bench backed against the inner wall of the deck. Sophy, as always, administered it. Barbara had told us not to wait for her, she wanted to change into more comfortable clothes than her traveling costume. We would not have waited in any case. Our need was greater for sustenance than for companionship.

Sophy, bartending, was mystified by a phenomenon that occurred each time she turned her back on the bench and went to the shoebag she had deposited on a chair a few feet away. She had poured out a drink for Barbara anent her coming but on subsequent trips for the rest of us observed, once, the glass was not there, again, it was partially empty. When on her third scrutiny she called our attention to it we saw a completely empty glass. As we looked at it with a slight sense of creepiness, a voice floated out a window behind us. "Come, come, my girl. No dallying. Fill it up, please." Barbara's arm stretched through the window. She picked up the glass and shook it impatiently.

This established the spot where all future shoebag hours on board were held. Those who could not crowd onto the bench sat inside on Barbara's bunk and reached through her window.

Dinner was delicious; when we had finished it we took a few turns around the deck so that Sophy might catch some fresh air before going to bed. On the promenade, we noticed with surprise and pleasure the kitchen was located there, occupying crosswise the center area, with a doorway onto the deck at either side, the door itself in two sections. We found later the upper half was almost always kept open. We were surprised by the sight because none of us on any other sea voyage had passed a kitchen on a promenade deck. We were pleased because this location enabled us to look in as we walked by, see how spotlessly clean the place was, and, later, sniff appreciatively the tantalizing aroma of what was on the stove for the next meal.

On our promenade we encountered a member of the crew who spoke enough English to convey to us that about one-thirty in the morning we would go through the Corinth Canal. After that news there was no question of our going to bed. We went instead to the deck above the promenade and found there in the stern several rows of benches one behind the other, like the seats in an old open trolley car. We returned temporarily to our respective cabins for extra coats and to put in at the bar an order for beer. Returning to the choice spot we had found we made ourselves comfortable, each at full length along a bench. The night was bright, no clouds and a full moon.

Strangely enough it *was* about one-thirty when we entered the canal. I am deeply grateful to the sailor. Without his message we might have been asleep and missed an experience I shall never forget. On either side of us the walls of the canal rose fearsomely, illuminated by, of all things, electric lights like street lamps, at intervals along the way. Darn wondered aloud how on earth the bulbs were changed. Here and there flowers and shrubs bloomed out of crevices in the rock. There was even a path distinguishable for some distance along the edge, and so close to our little ship it looked possible for a passenger to jump to it and move alongside us on the path; not I, certainly, but someone.

There was not a sound to be heard anywhere. We might have been riding through this eerie place on the back of a swan. At the end of our journey we found a ship waiting to enter the canal as soon as we would give place. Our vision had been so narrowed by the passage that the first sight of the ship waiting was a startling illusion that it was on land waiting to slip into the water, and we about to glide up out of it. Looking far, far up above our heads we could see the bridge on which we had stood when we saw the canal for the first time on our way to Cornith.

As unexpectedly as we had entered, we were out of that magnificently wrought passage that Nero had imagined.

Next morning at breakfast I thought Luz looked a little pale and seemed to move very slowly. I questioned her persistently, the others joining in. Our combined efforts finally drew out the reluctant admission she had not slept well because her muscles ached from the fall she had taken, and she found moving painful. She was persuaded to return to bed by our promises to call her at sight of anything remarkable on the horizon.

I went to my cabin and filled my hot-water bottle. Of all accessories to carry on a trip, this, in my opinion, is the indispensable. It soothes, it relaxes and restores to marching strength the weary sightseer. But that morning my comforter was a disappointment, not in itself but by its contents. The water from the tap in my cabin was less than lukewarm. I emptied the bottle and was close to accepting defeat when I was struck by an idea. Carrying the bottle I hurried out of my cabin and down the deck to the kitchen. The chef, a handsome creature with curling black mustache, was leaning over the lower half of the open door, his arms folded along its edge.

We smiled at each other and bowed a good morning. I held up my hot-water bottle, and like a magician, turned it upside down to show him there was nothing in it. Then on the deck I presented him with a moving enactment of a suffering creature in pain from head to foot, but who with the application of this hot-water bottle filled and pressed to the aching parts—I demonstrated these—would be so freed from pain as to be able to dance.

The chef was with me all the way, screwing up his face sympathetically at my friend's pain, echoing on his own frame the applications of the hot-water bottle, and executing a step of his own in corroboration of the cure, that together, we would bring about. He took the hot-water bottle from me, carried it to a tap and filled it. After he screwed on the cap, he put his hand against the outside and scowled. Disgustedly, he upturned and emptied it. He stood a moment, head lowered, obviously deep in thought. He suddenly raised his head, lifted the hot-water bottle in his hand and shook it exultantly high above his head. After that he turned around and carrying the bottle marched like a conqueror to the stove. There he paused a moment, turning his head to favor me with a wink. Then leaning forward he removed the lid of a large pot, took the handle of a ladle in the pot, and extending the bottle over it, filled it with boiling soup. He handed over the prize to me. I bore it wrapped in a towel to Luz. She drifted off to sleep, soothed both by the application of intense heat and the aroma of carrots, onion, beef and whatever else the chef had blended.

For months after that, each night when I filled it, my hot-water bottle sent out to me a faint whiff of soup. I was sad when it finally faded away.

While Luz slept the boat put in at Itea. Sophy, Barbara, Darn and and I promptly went ashore. Sophy and Barbara hired a car to drive them to Delphi. Looking up from the harbor, I could not quite see the hotel at which we had stayed, though standing on my balcony there I had seen this little harbor where our ship was docked. Darn and I by tacit understanding set out at once on one of our favorite pastimes, exploration on foot of a village.

We wandered up and down its streets. There is nothing that is required of the tourist to see, and so without any obligation to visit a ruin we wandered as we pleased. In one shop I saw and purchased door knockers I had been unable to find in Santorini, and these were the exact replicas of the ones on that far-off island. It was a reminder of the pervasive stamp the Turkish occupation had imprinted.

Darn was as triumphant as I, though her discovery and purchase were somewhat less picturesque than Turkish door knockers. Barbara had shouted umbrella at us when he had complained audibly going to bed and getting up that the water on the boat was loathsome, even for tooth brushing, let alone drinking. It was sulphurous, we agreed, and we disliked it.

Darn discovered, in Itea's general store, oranges, soda in bottles, and best of all, the clear, uncharged bottled drinking water that is in Greece what Evian is in France, and Fiuji in Italy. This is Lutrakio. To the happy astonishment of the proprietor Darn bought two dozen bottles of this and a dozen bottles of soda in addition to oranges, and olives. We acquired volunteers as well who carried our purchases and escorted us back to the ship. We deposited our purchases with the dining-room steward and came out on the dock again.

A ship alongside ours was loading bags of wool. I watched this for a long time and I might have been observing, I thought to myself, something that had happened a thousand years ago. A man performing the functions of an overseer squatted beside a primitive scale. His superiority in office to the other workers was marked because he wore a hat of straw with a wide brim, and shoes. The carriers were barefooted, with ragged trousers rolled above the knee, cotton blouse ragged, too, and bright-colored bandanna tight around the head. They brought the bags from one of a number of carts drawn by donkeys and lined up along the street by the dock. Each man stopped at the overseer, put his bag on the scales, the overseer noted it, made a straight mark on a large sheet spread out beside him of what looked more like parchment than paper, and then motioned the carrier onto the ship. The loading had begun when Darn and I first left the ship, and I had paused then to watch it. When we came on the dock the second time, after leaving our purchases below, there had evidently been an interval for lunch and in that period one of the carriers had somehow caught an octopus. He was delighted with his find, the others were openly envious. He had put it in a bucket of water but at sight of Darn and me held it up for us to see, at the same time with his free hand rubbing his stomach, simultaneously licking his chops, to show what a delicacy this was going to provide. He was pleased when I photographed him with his trophy.

Barbara and Sophy were back on board with not much time to spare before we sailed, though Barbara protested too much leeway had been gained by Sophy's forcing her to hurry, and turning British for the moment added, glowering, "Typically American, Sophy, to hurry. Such a pity."

We lunched on the boat. Darn and I were happy we had not in Itea found a taverna that would have tempted us to eat early there, because shortly after the beginning of the meal, we saw the dining-room steward passing round several of our bottles of Lutrakio to various tables. I secured his attention somewhat emphatically by leaving my seat and gathering up the bottles he had set down, explaining apologetically to such passengers as understood English, I was extremely sorry to seem so selfish but this was a private store and not refreshment provided by the ship's commissary. The headwaiter was surprised and grieved. He knew, he assured us in pantomime, this was our own purchase but it did not seem possible it could be just for ourselves. He was a Yugoslav.

We were due in Patras at three. We arrived at a quarter past two. From the *Guide Bleu* we found little of interest to see. We were irked, anyway, at being there because we had learned only that morning, and indirectly, the captain had no intention of putting in at Corfu, though this, advertised in pamphlets and by the travel agency, had been one of the main inducements for taking this trip. The whole body of passengers was indignant and relayed to the captain messages in this vein. His answer was the cargo was his first interest, passengers of no interest whatsoever. He had no cargo for Corfu, therefore, he did not propose to visit it. He did not care what publications or travel bureaus might say this ship would do. He was the captain, and sometimes he would put in at Corfu, other times not. There was no way of telling. Therefore we were at Patras where there is nothing to see.

Accordingly, we went swimming, at a pleasant beach a few miles out of town. The place was the selection of our taxi driver after consultation with a policeman, and we thoroughly approved their choice. There was the usual little taverna, tables and chairs set out under trees, a small building in the background. I suppose in wintertime customers are seated indoors, but at each taverna we visited the interior of the inn proper was without even tables and chairs; only the cooking was done there, and even in this department a lamb was always roasted on a spit outside the door. After our swim we sat at a table and drank Gazases.

A fisherman passed on the beach not far from our table. He carried a creel brimming with fish and obligingly paused within our view to make another cast. He carried in his hand what looked to be a length of line looped compactly for easy carrying, but as he flung it out over the water, it unfolded, to our astonishment, into a vast circular net with a diameter of perhaps six feet, or more. He drew this in slowly and extracted from it two good-sized fish that he added to his already well-filled basket. He shook out lesser marine life and folded up his net again much as a cowboy gathers in a lasso.

Luz, Sophy and I stalked him for a photograph, but at the moment when Luz's machine clicked healthily, Sophy discovered she had used up her film and my camera stuck for the first and only time on the trip. Luz, a creature of moderation, was so intoxicated by this triumph over those who had previously scoffed, she executed a few steps of an impromptu *pas seul* remarkably like a bacchanal. Simultaneously Barbara was moved to inquire if we might purchase some of his catch. Her idea was we might persuade the chef to cook them for our dinner. But between Luz's unexpected caprice and Barbara's stately approach, the young fisherman was evidently addled. He looked from one to the other, his eyes widening, and went off up the beach on the double.

The olives from Itea were our appetizers. We tasted those Greek delicacies for the last time as we sat on our bench for the shoebag hour, watching the sunset over the mountains of Greece. This was our farewell view of the country.

The sunrise we watched next morning was over Corfu, at least that is what we were told by the only passenger on the deck with us to see it. We chose to believe this was so, since this was the only view we would have of the place to which we had thought our boat was taking us.

When we returned to the deck after breakfast we looked out on the coast of Italy, flat here, a startling sight to us after a month in the mountains.

"Now," Sophy said, "we are sailing on the Adriatic."

I was the only one surprised by this statement, but when she offered to show me on the map how we had got there, I urged her not to bother.

"I believe what I am told," I explained; "I am profoundly distrustful of what anyone attempts to reveal to me by way of a map."

We stayed on the top deck almost all day. The views along the coast we were following distracted us most of the time from the discomfort of the trolley-car benches on which we had to sit. During the morning we learned the reason for this remarkable arrangement. A ship's officer, who was barely on speaking terms with the English language, conveyed to us that our ship was ordinarily an excursion boat, used on daytime trips. These benches accommodated a considerable crowd and gave an unobstructed view. The ship on which we should have been traveling according to our tickets was being "repressed," he said. Although it was a Yugoslavian boat we hoped

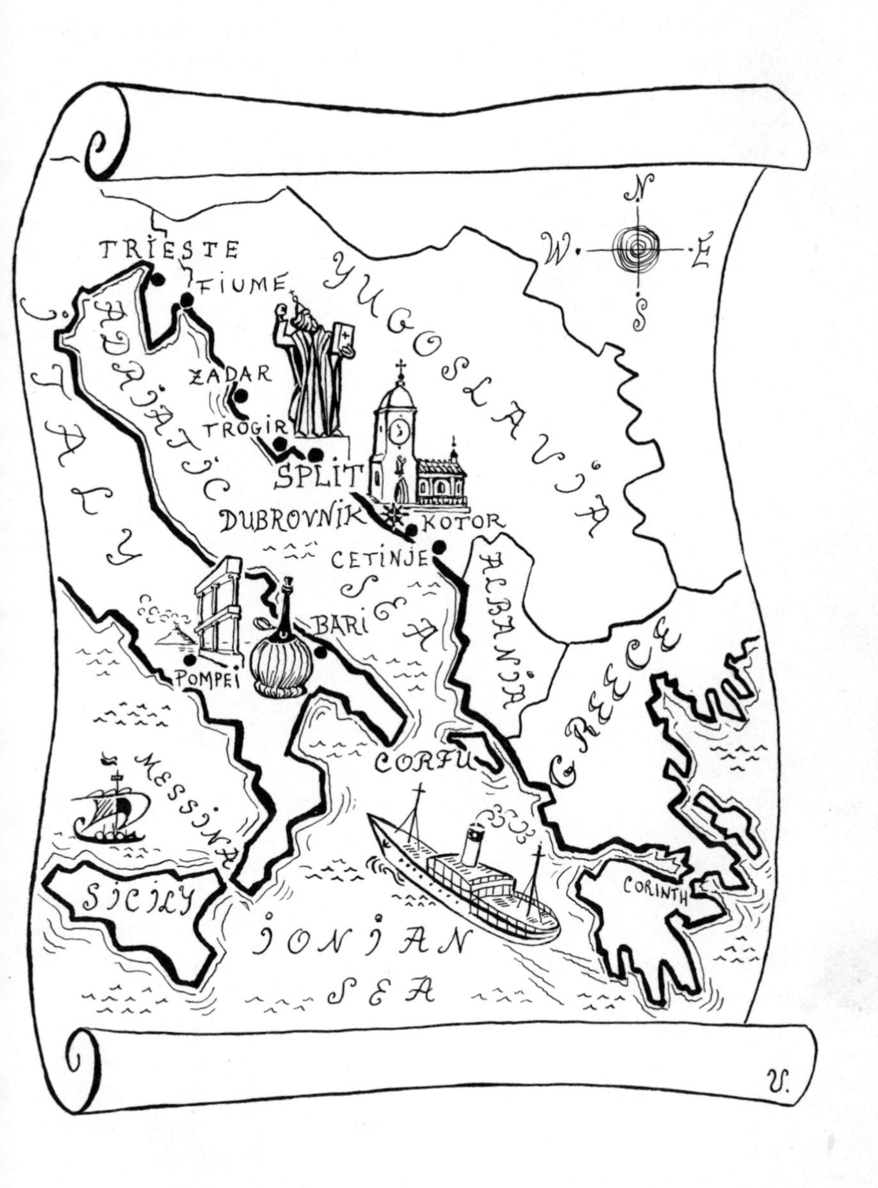
TRIESTE
FIUME
ADRIATIC
ITALY
ZADAR
TROGIR
SPLIT
DUBROVNIK
KOTOR
CETINJE
YUGOSLAVIA
N
W
E
S
SEA
BARI
POMPEI
ALBANIA
GREECE
CORFU
MESSINA
SICILY
CORINTH
IONIAN
SEA
V.

nothing more sinister than repairs was actually being imposed upon it. If his figures were more accurate than his other vocabulary, the vessel on which we were riding is 62 meters long and weighs 567 tons. No wonder, I said, it looked small in the harbor at Piraeus. It was still small on the Adriatic.

Chapter Eighteen

AT half past six that evening we docked at Bari in Italy. Our little band had decided to forgo dinner on board for a meal ashore. We did this, but dinner was a long time a-coming. We had not reckoned on the ceremony that attended a visit from customs officials. They came aboard at half past six. We were assembled in the lounge for the inspection of our papers. At a quarter to eight the customs officials had reached coffee and liqueurs, but not our papers. It was nine o'clock when the papers were restored to us and we were permitted to leave the ship.

We engaged a taxi immediately and with childlike confidence requested the driver to take us to the best restaurant. Since the Transatlancido is the only one we visited, I cannot say it is the best. I am reasonably certain, however, it is a greater distance from Bari than any other eating place in that area. It is, too, a delightful spot with excellent food. Because we were in Italy we had scampi, that delectable shrimp, and Italian wine with our meal. What rounded out for me an evening of happiness was the sight on our way back to the ship of a shoe shop that was open at eleven o'clock. I stopped the taxi, went in, bought two pairs. They are lovely.

On the morning of June 4, at a quarter past nine, we docked at Dubrovnik. There my troubles began that very nearly landed me in a Yugoslavian prison. We passed the first test satisfactorily, an examination of our papers made by officials who came on board immediately we had docked. This was no social function such as the Italians had made of their visit. These were grim men, who shook hands with the ship's officers without a smile and settled to work immediately at tables that had been placed in the lounge.

Sitting not far away, waiting my turn, I watched them for an hour or more. I did not see them look directly into the face of a passenger nor acknowledge with so much as a nod of the head, let alone a smile, the departure of one nor the arrival of his successor in the line. The only time they looked up at all was when it was necessary to compare the passport photograph with its subject.

These officials looked poor; their uniforms were shabby, fitting the wearers so badly they looked to have been made all of one size. I could not help thinking perhaps the uniforms were the only permanent fixtures of the job. The wearers might be replaced, but the uniforms remained. These men seemed to me, too, to be both uneducated and unintelligent. They read with obvious difficulty, moving a finger along under each word and forming every letter with their lips, almost audibly. As for their intelligence, several times I saw one of these officials summon a ship's officer and ask him something. Each time this happened I heard the officer repeat the same answer over and over before the questioner seemed able to grasp it. Without variation these men, and there were six of them, had broad cheekbones, low foreheads, small eyes, sparse straight hair, a little greasy, and very large hands with the thick knuckles that usually indicate a manual laborer.

Darn and Luz were the first of our coterie to be released. The examination of their papers was as cursory as a laborious spelling out and reading could effect. The reason for their relatively quick dismissal was a sad one for all our group. Dubrovnik would be the last place we would be together. Luz and Darn would spend only the day there and then continue on the same boat to Trieste, take a train there for Paris, and after a few days a boat for America. Barbara, Sophy and I were leaving this ship for a week's stay in Dubrovnik, then by another boat to Trieste, and by train and channel boat, England.

By the time Barbara, Sophy and I were off the boat, Luz and Darn were long since on their way to explore Dubrovnik. We would meet for lunch at the Hotel Argentina, where the three of us remaining had engaged rooms. Porters on the dock pushed in handcarts to the customs house the eighteen pieces of luggage that still remained after Darn's and Luz's had been separated. I do not advocate such encumbrance. That amount of luggage is a burden and a bore most of the time. On the other hand, of all the equipment I took with me, the only piece I did not use was a pair of long white gloves that were to have been my adornment when I was presented to the Queen, but we had not been presented. The invitation came after we had gone on our cruise on the *Semiramis*. Every other article in the eight bags attached to me had been out of the bag and in use more than once.

Our eighteen pieces were piled on a counter that is the trademark of a European customs house, and the inspection began. The customs officials looked like blood brothers of those we had just left on the ship. Among the several passengers who like us were stopping over in Dubrovnik, we were the first to pass and be dismissed from the boat. We were jubilant, entering the customs house to see the counter bare, save for our luggage. We were ahead of the crowd, we would be on our way when they had scarcely begun.

Three hours later we were still at the starting line and all the other passengers had long since passed us by. Sophy and Barbara could have gone with them. They had chosen to remain with me. I was a ship that looked to be sinking fast, and they were sticking with me. What threatened to drag me out of sight, perhaps forever, of all that I hold dear, was my Scrabble set; my beautiful traveling Scrabble set in a leather case with a handle by which to carry it. To the Yugoslavian low wits, it was a traveling code and since I carried such a thing I was an international spy.

The going had not been easy from the start. Every article in every bag had been removed, shaken and, where possible, turned inside out. Dresses take longer to shake than handkerchiefs, and gifts for the home folks that have been wrapped and tied take the longest of all. But we were making progress, not perceptible at a cursory glance but by a comparative scrutiny of what had been shaken with what was still unfolded. Then the Scrabble set came to the surface and was opened. In Greece I had pantomimed almost everything, but I had not had occasion to reproduce, in dumb show, a game of Scrabble. I did it in Dubrovnik and I gave the performance all I had in me of fervor and eloquence.

The result of this was my instant detention in the customs house.

From time to time over the hours an official I had not seen before arrived, and from the doorway looked me over slowly from head to foot, scowling but not saying anything. There was nothing he could say that I would understand and vice versa. Evidently each arrival was an official who had been summoned to this case. Of each visitor

I asked urgently for the American Consul, the American Express, or a piece of paper and a pencil. I had no answer from any one of them.

At the end of three hours my rescuer came. He was not an official, he was just a Lochinvar, aged some seventy-odd and come out of Dubrovnik by way of New York. He owned a market in the town, he told me later when I was free, and had come to the customs house to collect some produce he was expecting from across the border. Thanks be to God, he had once worked in New York. He learned from the assemblage of officials the case of the shut-in and asked permission to visit her. Thanks be to God, this was granted.

A heavenly choir will not sound sweeter to me than the cracked old voice of that angel of mercy saying to me, "You in trouble? Maybe I help. I speak English."

I could have flung my arms around the neck of that ragged, dirty old man, and planted a heartfelt buss on his unshaven cheek. Only because I was afraid this would make me in the eyes of the officials standing behind him an even more questionable character, I refrained.

Instead I said, "I thank you very much. I am in trouble," and explained the source of it.

When I had finished the old man did not throw back his head with gay laughter at such a bagatelle. Instead he shook it mournfully and answered, "That is much trouble. In Yugoslavia, no one play games. How I explain?"

I had no answer but I had a vivid picture of life in Yugoslavia.

The old man brooded a little, head down. He looked up suddenly, his eyes bright. He nodded once or twice. "Ah," he said, "old men here play dominoes in cafés."

The answer that came to my mind caused me to wince, but it was an answer that might open the door for me. "Tell them," I requested the old man and swallowed a little, finding it hard to say the words, "tell them that, in New York, old women," I beat my breast in sad identification, "play Scrabble."

It opened the door and I walked out, Scrabble set and all.

My dear companions rejoiced at the sight of me. They cooled a little when they learned how I had classified them in order to win my freedom.

The taxis we had seen on our arrival at the customs house had long since departed when we came out. They had carried off the passengers who had passed us by. We were the only travelers, and the only vehicle left for us was a seven-passenger open touring car of a model I have not seen in twenty-five years. The driver looked to be three times the age of the car. When I estimated his age aloud to Sophy, she answered acidly perhaps in that case I'd like to invite him up for an evening of Scrabble with the crones who played it.

A bewildering metamorphosis took place among the officials the instant we stepped outside the customs house. From grim, threatening dictators, they turned before our eyes into a group of grinning, prankish, rather boisterous schoolboys. They helped the porters pile the luggage on top and inside the ancient vehicle, assisting us in and then tucking pieces around us, shoving one another, laughing.

I have thought about that group many times. I could not forget it. I cannot explain to my satisfaction the extraordinary change we saw take place, but I think it had something to do with fear. Fear when they were on duty and an immediate release from it when they were not at work. Fear of whatever authority was over them lest that authority find they had been lacking in a performance of their duty. Fear that was sharpest when they must assume responsibility. This was why they had examined, inside and out, every article in every bag. When an old man, although he himself held no authority, said to them, "This is a harmless thing," he removed from them the burden of responsibility and that fear of authority. If he had been wrong they could still have escaped blame. They could have put it on someone else.

The automobile would not start. It was too old, of course, to have a self-starter, but the ancient cranked it again and again without success. He stepped aside to wipe with his sleeve his sweating forehead and the customs crew took this opportunity to hurl themselves with laughter and shouts at our carriage and push. With very little difficulty they set it in motion, and with exuberant enthusiasm, continued their play. We were facing the water and we very nearly went into it over the edge of the dock. Our escape, my second of the morning, was achieved by the old geezer, who, sprinting like a stripling, caught up with us, leapt into the driver's seat and wrenched the wheel that brought us on a careening curve away from the water and headed for the city with engine running. The officials and the porters waved and cheered us off, leaning against one another as they yelled with laughter at their prank.

Dubrovnik is not unlike Rhodes. They are both medieval cities, but by nature Dubrovnik is the more beautiful. The city is higher and looks down over a wider expanse of sea, mountains and rocks. The city proper within the walls is less magnificent.

I did not form these opinions on the trip from the dock to the hotel. I was neither in a physical position nor condition of mind to notice the scene we were passing. We passed through it with the speed of the wind because it was nature, not the engine that carried us. No engine so old as ours could have propelled us at a fraction of the rate at which we covered the miles. The road was downhill most of the way, and curved; the driver was afraid if his engine slowed down it would stop again. We did not pause for dogs, donkeys nor children, and the road was filled with them as we approached. It may have been strewn with them after we passed. I did not look back, nor did I look to either side. I stared ahead and thought of other places, Heaven mostly.

The Hotel Argentina provides simple rooms but comfortable, good food and a view from bedroom window and dining terrace that is reason enough for coming to Dubrovnik.

Luz and Darn arrived soon after we had registered. They wondered why they had not met us in the town. When I told them, they wondered we had met at all. It would not have occurred to them, Luz said, to have gone back to the customs house to look for us. Had we not been at the hotel they would have thought there was some misunderstanding and have gone on their way. Such a view into a possible future was so depressing Sophy immediately brought out her shoebag.

We lunched on the terrace of the Argentina under an arbor of jasmine in bloom. Below us a series of terraced gardens made stair steps to deep-blue water far below. Luz and Darn had come from the town by the waterway in a launch. They told us there was a bathing platform at the landing stage of the hotel and hundreds of steps from there up through the gardens to the terrace where we ate.

After lunch we parted, as the children say, "for keeps." Luz and

Darn went back to the ship. Sophy and I saw them off; Barbara tactfully went to her room to unpack. The four of us had had seven weeks of gay companionship and unforgettable sights shared. We reviewed some of those highlights during the last few minutes. We would review them again, we said, over and over, whenever we were together. We were miserably silent, Sophy and I, when we had waved them out of sight and turned back into the hotel.

No one can be miserable for long in Dubrovnik nor count this place the end of a trip. It is a trip in itself to a place unlike any other. Although in appearance a medieval town, actually it was settled in the seventh century A.D., by refugees from the Roman city, Epidaurus, invaded by the Avars, a horde allied to the Huns. In the Middle Ages it was a republic, governed by a body of individuals called rectors, each one in rotation serving a term as governor, occupying the palace, and separated during that period from his family. Its peak of prosperity was reached in the fifteenth century; then it declined until in 1814 it was given to Austria.

There is a story of that gift to Austria that was told to me three times in Dubrovnik. Sophy and Barbara heard it, too. That is the only verification I can give. I have not read it anywhere. The first one who told it to me was an old man, a native of Dubrovnik who had traveled in America, spoke English understandably and sat at a table adjoining mine at an outdoor café in the square where I was having tea one afternoon. The second person who told it, and this time Barbara and Sophy were with me, was a young woman guide in the palace, now a museum; the third was the proprietor of a shop that sold old jewelry.

This is the story. In the time when the rectors governed it, Dubrovnik boasted a distinguished aristocracy. They were a proud people, and this company of aristocrats was like the wall that surrounds the city, a closed circle, strong and untouchable. When Dubrovnik, or Ragusa, as it was then called, was handed over to Austria, the Emperor Francis paid a state visit to welcome this new acquisition into his benevolent protection. The citizens gathered in the great square to see the Emperor and hear him speak, the aristocrats separate from the citizenry, as befitted their position. There was no welcoming procession to greet the conqueror, there were not even banners hung from the walls. His Majesty was displeased. He expressed his displeasure in a speech that concluded in effect, "However ungracious and inhospitable your welcome has been today, the time will come when you," and he pointed to the band of aristocrats, "will be proud to say your sons are fighting for the great Austrian Empire."

There were no cheers when he finished, but there was an answering speech. It was short, made by the patriarch of the first family of the aristocrats. "Sire," he said, "in these families," he included the group of which he was the head, "there will be no sons."

Since that day there have been no children born to any members of those families; therefore, those families no longer exist.

The young woman who was an official guide in the museum and one of the three from whom I heard this story, referred to it at almost every object to which she directed our attention. "This," she would say, "is the sedan chair of the —— family. Of course that family does not exist any longer. This was a desk, a rug, whatever in the drawing room of the so-and-so family. This is a family, you understand, that had no descendants."

The charm of Dubrovnik is gentle. The gates to the city proper are closed at night; all the hotels and some residences are outside. There are no automobiles within the city at any time. Tiny streets open off broad squares and are so tiny and so steep they are like brooks rushing down a mountainside into the basin below. The city itself rises in uneven tiers to rampart walls at the very top. It is a steep climb up these flights of stairs; inhabitants of the houses on separate levels must develop the muscles of ballet dancers. From the top stratum the view over the Adriatic is superb, and down over the town, intimate and heartwarming. There is a convent where nuns, with turned-up robes and rubber aprons for protection, work in a vegetable garden. There are little garden plots where children play. There are flowers everywhere, on the walls, along the balconies, on window sills.

Darn and Luz were tantalized by what they saw in a day; we had not had our fill at the end of the week, although in addition to exploring on foot, very nearly every inch of the town, we had taken excursions outside it. We engaged a man to row us from our hotel to the nearby island of Lokrum, a beautiful, haunted place. Richard

Vasiliu

Coeur de Lion was shipwrecked here as he was returning from the Crusades and built a Benedictine monastery in gratitude for his rescue. On the site of this, King Maximilian built a palace in which he thought to live with his beautiful Empress, Carlotta. She died there instead, insane. Now there is a summer camp on the island close by the castle. It houses children from many nations. We heard their laughter as we wandered about the gardens of the castle. Sophy and Barbara swam off the rocks. Other people were swimming there, too, young couples, whole families. Even in Greece there is not such swimming as in Dubrovnik. There is scarcely a rock one passes on which there are not swimmers sunning themselves. They are strongly reminiscent of pictures I have seen of sealeries in Alaska.

Another afternoon we hired a motorboat for a trip that took us an hour and a half, and along all the way every prospect pleased us. Our destination was the island of Lopud, where there is a crescent-shaped harbor with fishing boats at anchor and nets drying on the quay.

We drove to Cavtat, about twenty-five kilometers out of Dubrovnik, a medieval town built on the site of that ancient Epidaurus from which the colonizers of Dubrovnik had fled.

Barbara and Sophy took an all-day excursion on a bus, leaving at 8 A.M. and returning at 8 P.M. They need not have left quite so early had anyone told them the bus would stop outside our hotel; it was not necessary to hurry on foot from the Argentina all the way across to the other side of the city.

This bus trip goes to Cetinje, the one-time capital of the one-time kingdom of Montenegro. The tour is via the ancient town of Kotor. It is a long trip and strenuous, with hairpin turns, they said, mountainous all the way, but beautiful and not to be missed. I passed the day happily in the town.

On Saturday, June 11, one week after our arrival, we left Dubrovnik at half past one. We had had a swim in the morning, a final walk around the town and a last lunch in our jasmine arbor. Barbara, who had been appalled in Athens at the amount of luggage with which the rest of us were encumbered, left Dubrovnik looking something like a Christmas tree, with packages strung about her person at very nearly every level.

The only thing about the boat from Dubrovnik better than the one that took us there from Piraeus was that it was attached to the dock and required no ladder climbing. Everything else about it was less satisfactory. To begin with it was an old coal-burner. Like an asthmatic it coughed day and night, not only audibly but visibly, exhaling a shower of black soot that rose from its funnel, and then, like the gentle rain from Heaven, fell over passengers on deck. The seating arrangement on this boat, too, was as extraordinary as the rows of benches on the other. This one had benches as well but instead of being placed in rows they ran the entire circle of the deck, with this curious focal point; the backs of the benches were against the rail so that, seated, the view was away from the sea directly into the bowels of the ship.

We did not need anything more to make us discomfited, but we had it. The purser who collected our tickets as we boarded this little jewel of the Adriatic read each one laboriously a number of times, and then looked up shaking his head in surprise and pity. The tickets he indicated graphically by violent thrusts at them, were for three cabins. This information did not surprise us; it was what we had ordered and paid for. He issued a news bulletin. Three *berths* were waiting for us, two in one cabin, one in another. Under the guidance of a steward we visited these cabins. Each included two bunks, one above the other, a washstand and a space between that could accommodate one passenger at a time.

"I will have words with the purser," I said.

Barbara chose to sit on a deck bench and watch the smokestack belch.

Sophy accompanied me to the lounge where the purser had set up office, but she remained in the doorway. I delivered a number of words to the purser, none that he understood. The gist got through to him, however, that we were not happy. He sent back a gist to me that our happiness was a matter of total indifference to him. I followed a pattern I had cut out long ago. I follow it at home and abroad with few alterations. Its general shape is the combatting of a situation I think can be bettered, then when I am convinced this is not going to be accomplished, an acceptance without whinnying. I plead, I suggest, I shout, then I shut up. I applied my pattern to the purser, all of it. When I left him I had shut up.

Sophy and I reported to Barbara. She received it graciously and had the further grace not to inject an I-told-you-so.

I engaged myself in oratory again. Shutting up is not easy for me, sustaining that condition even more difficult. It was ridiculous, I said, for either of them to take the odd bunk in a cabin with a total stranger. They were older friends with each other than I with either of them, therefore, by seniority, they should be roommates. Furthermore, I slept better than either of them. The only thing I wanted of a cabin was a place and an opportunity for sleep. Acquaintances might doubt this, but friends who have shared a room with me could verify that going to bed and getting up I did not talk. In the end I coaxed them over to my arrangement.

The steward who had shown us our cabins turned out to be friendly and able to speak English. Gathering up our excess baggage, and that was the greater part of it, he stowed it in a closet over which he had exclusive supervision and key. Before stowing our bags he dragged out from the closet three deck chairs he permitted us to rent from him, and set them up for us on the deck. They were old and frail. They collapsed unexpectedly but frequently and pinched our fingers each time we reassembled them. Nevertheless, they were more comfortable than the benches. We sat in them all afternoon under a steady rain of soot from the smokestack.

By the shoebag hour we had acquired the complexion of a coal heaver on duty. We went below to wash. On the threshold of my cabin I stopped in the doorway, not because of what I saw, but because of what I did not see. Every belonging of my unknown cabinmate that had been strewn about at the time of my other visit was gone. The room was clean and empty save for my overnight bag. In spite of that possession in the corner, I thought I must be in the wrong room. I backed out and looked at the number on the door. It was the one to which I had been assigned. I rang the bell for the steward and was still in the doorway when he arrived.

He grinned at the sight of me. "A little surprised, yes?" he said, and rubbed his hands with pleasure. "Just when boat sails," he continued, "lady that have this cabin runs on ship. She love Dubrovnik so much she will stay week. Take next boat. I help her. She jump off when boat is just going."

When I asked why on earth he hadn't told me this news he

answered as gleefully as a child he'd been keeping it for a surprise. I kept it for a surprise from my friends until we were on our way to bed. Barbara's comment was that as a reward of virtue it disgusted her, but as a stroke of luck, it pleased her very much.

Early next morning we put in at Split. Luz and Darn, pioneering for us, had written back we should by all means visit Trogir, a little town not far away. We decided to do this before exploring Split itself. I recommend this sequence. We selected a taxi conspicuously newer than the others assembled at the dock, and on the drive learned a good deal from the chauffeur. He spoke no English but a fair amount of German and some Italian, mementos of the war. I know no German, but Barbara and Sophy had spoken it in their childhood, found they remembered it sufficiently to understand the chauffeur, and translated for me, patronizingly.

The taxi had been a gift from an aunt of the driver who lived in Chicago. It represented what he would have inherited from her. The government would not have permitted him to receive money. The gift of the taxi was a way of setting him up in business. The purchase of a car in Yugoslavia entails payment of a tax that is the equivalent of the purchase price of the automobile. The driver was surprisingly communicative about other economic conditions. In the days before the government had taken them over, he said, the factories, and there were a number of them in that vicinity, had paid good wages. Now wages were so low and prices so high a pair of shoes cost a worker a month's salary.

We had discovered in Dubrovnik restaurants and hotel rooms were inexpensive, but all merchandise was costly and of inferior quality. Dubrovnik seemed prosperous because of tourists. The people of Trogir looked to be very poor, but the town is a gem. It was originally a fourth-century Greek settlement, but the beautiful cathedral is thirteenth century. At seven o'clock when we arrived, citizens were walking along the narrow streets. Some of these carried long loaves of bread, undoubtedly taking them home for breakfast, others were on their way to church and we followed these.

A First Communion was being held and the cathedral was jammed. We eased our way inside, a few steps at a time. We were no sooner across the threshold than we were noticed by three women not far away, who were standing on a bench. One of these stepped down, pushed her way through to us and beckoned us to follow. She led us to her friends, who moved over, reached down a hand and took us up beside them. Immediately we were placed—and it was a close fit—they pointed to a group of little children dressed in white, but only the color was fresh. The material of each little dress and suit looked so old as to be nearly threadbare, worn with many washings. These were the little communicants for whom the ceremony was being held. Except for the pitiful poverty of the congregation, it was a beautiful sight. The cathedral itself had no look of poverty, it has splendor of size and richness of *décor*. Candles lighted it, but out of their range the interior was dark, emphasizing the circle of white where the children knelt.

On our way out we passed an old woman in the portico. I had noticed her when we were trying to work our way in. She had a small boy by the hand, who looked to be about three, and was endeavoring to persuade him to enter the church with her. Before we had gone inside I had seen her bring him several times to the threshold, only to lose him, because the child, frightened, had broken away and run back to the outer steps. She would return to him, speak soothingly, and presently he would permit her to lead him forward once more. When we came out nothing had changed. The remarkable thing to me was that the grandmother, and I suppose that was her relationship, had not lost patience. She was still soothing, coaxing. I carried away a happy picture of tenderness. At first view those people do not seem to possess that quality.

We spent a considerable time at the doorway waiting until the crowd had dispersed so that we might examine with leisure and enjoyment the glorious Romanesque sculptured portal.

We were a long time, too, exploring the town itself because we found it so delightful. Nevertheless, it was only a little after ten when we returned to Split. The contrast was startling. Though we had seen a throng of people in Trogir they were village folk. Now we were in a bustling city. The streets were crowded, many shops were open, the sidewalk cafés filled. We went at once to the part of the city that is within the walls of the palace of Diocletian, I dragging behind because of frequent pauses to look in shop windows.

The first job I ever held was in the advertising department of a large department store. That experience made me so aware of merchandise the quality of it is one of the ways by which I measure the living standard in any town I visit. The standard is low in Split. The figures on price tags were appalling, the quality of the merchandise poor. Plastic handbags that at home would cost under ten dollars were priced here at the equivalent of twenty-five or thirty. Shoes that were clumsy in shape and heavy were the same price. Dresses, coats and hats, out of fashion by our counting, were of poor material but cost as much as I pay at home for far better.

The Palace of Diocletian is magnificent, though somewhat of a conglomeration of structures. It was built about 300 A.D. It occupies a considerable area and was surrounded by a high fortified wall. Streets run through the great gates in the center of each side so that the whole area occupies a little over four blocks. We walked almost all of this before we found the Mestrovic statue we were hunting, of heroic size in bronze of Bishop Grgur Ninski, commemorated because he had induced the Vatican to permit the substitution for Latin in the church services, of their own language in its ancient Slavic form. The strong figure with beautiful simplicity of line is well worth hunting. We were leaping back and forth among the centuries when, looking at the Mestrovic figure, we reminded one another it was from Split, and particularly from the Palace of Diocletian, that the Adam brothers had carried to England the designs on which they based the furniture they created.

Immediately we had left this area we leapt again, not through time but from aesthetics to food. We hunted and found not far away a little shop recommended on a postcard from our pioneers. In this shop, Darn had written, could be had one of the most delectable bits of pastry she and Luz had ever tasted. We endorse their appraisal. The pastry is a little like a doughnut yet why I should find such a similarity I cannot explain. The Split confection is larger than a doughnut, has no hole in the center, is as light as a puff, but it is dusted with sugar. One eats it piping hot. I do not know either why I say "it." Each of the three of us ate three. They are called *ponshkis*.

Our ship left Split a little after noon. Not long after dinner that evening the boat put in at Zadar and we went ashore. This town was fearfully bombed during the war. Large sections of it are still only hills of rubble and the dust of disintegration. It is dark and ominous. We moved quickly toward lights we could see beyond. This was in the rebuilt section of the town. All the streets here, though lighted, were deserted except one. Here a crowd of pedestrians so thick it overflowed the sidewalk on either side and completely filled the roadway between was promenading. This thoroughfare was so brightly lighted as to be almost dazzling. The tightly packed crowd moved slowly in two streams, one side into the middle of the road going in one direction; from the middle to the other side it moved the opposite way. We joined the procession for a little time, but when we left after perhaps half an hour we had learned neither its reason nor its destination. We found later it is simply the evening promenade.

We saw passengers from our ship in a shop across the road from where we were standing. We could see through the brightly lighted windows they were buying bottles of Maraschino. We had learned previously this is the principal product of the town and the town the principal source of that liqueur, but since none of the three of us like it we had been able to resist this once buying a souvenir. We would have visited the shop, however, in the hope of finding out what was going on outside, but we were unable to ford the stream of pedestrians. Instead we turned away and set out on an exploration of the deserted thoroughfares.

Within fifteen minutes we were lost and in something of a panic. We had planned on an allotment of fifteen minutes for a leisurely and devious return to the ship. We had been a little too devious and we ceased, on the instant of realization, to be leisurely. Barbara suggested we follow the shore. As a suggestion it was sound, as a means of returning to the ship, an erroneous idea. We found a shore but it was not a shore that held the dock to which our ship was tied, simply a coastline, empty of vessels. Behind us stretched a row of ruins of what had evidently at one time been resort hotels.

I took over.

Over the years of ignorance about maps I have learned to find my way by landmarks, sometimes trivial, sometimes conspicuous. The one at Zadar was conspicuous. I pointed to a spire, barely discernible in the sky.

"That's the steeple of the cathedral," I insisted. "I remember it. We know how we got to the cathedral. If we keep our eye on the steeple, we'll find its base and from there we'll remember the road to the ship."

We ran almost all the way. We found our boat by means of the cathedral. We boarded it as it was actually pulling away. No one had missed us.

After a boring day in Rijeka, that is the old Fiume, where we found nothing of any particular interest to see, we arrived on Tuesday in Trieste. We were about to leave the boat when I was stopped. Customs men had come on board, examined and passed quickly the papers of the passengers. An official who had stood beside the table where the men were working put his hand on my arm as I gathered up my passport and prepared to go. Barbara and Sophy had been ahead of me.

I called out to them, "Wait. Something's up."

They returned immediately.

Sophy muttered in my ear, "I bet it's that Scrabble set again. Why on earth didn't you leave it in Dubrovnik? You said you were going to."

My plaintive and apologetic answer was I hadn't been able to bring myself to carry out my threat because the set had been so expensive. Thank the Lord I have a thrifty nature. Thanks be to God that angry as I had been at my incarceration the day of our arrival in Dubrovnik, I had not been able to throw my set out the window into the sea. Had I done this I might still be in Yugoslavia, lost to sight, but I hope to a few memories dear.

What that special official wanted was a look at my Scrabble set. His instructions evidently had been to make sure I was taking it out of the country intact. Had I been without it, he and his superiors would have been convinced I had planted the code somewhere. Even had I been able to drag it up from the bottom of the sea where I had threatened to throw it, and I am no diver, I would still have had difficulty in explaining to the authorities how and why it had got there.

This official took out every letter from the set, turned it over and back, put it in its place, made sure there were no gaps in the set and no overflow. When he had satisfied himself on all these points, he marked a special stamp on my passport, and waved me permission to leave the ship and Yugoslavia.

For the first time since I had left America, I boarded a train. At Venice we changed to another. In Paris we had a stopover of a few hours that permitted us breakfast at the Café de la Paix, not an imaginative spot but convenient to the things we wanted to do, a little shopping and even a reunion with Darn. Luz, that morning, was being given an official welcome and an official tour of headquarters where American women in branches of our service were stationed. Darn reported, however, they had had wonderful days in Paris and were ready now to sail within two more. They were ready but they did not sail. A strike canceled all ship departures. They had to stay on and eventually fly back. They might have had the week with us in Dubrovnik, after all.

We were luckier than they. Continuing by train and then by boat from Calais, we landed in England on the very day its railway strike ended.

At seven o'clock that evening, Barbara had gone from the railway station to her own house, and Sophy and I were pushing the front doorbell of the Indian Embassy in London, where we were to be guests of the High Commissioner, Mme. Pandit.

The door opened, and on the other side, arms wide, Mme. Pandit welcomed us in.

Chapter Nineteen

THERE never was a more delightful companion nor more thoughtful hostess than ours. She had stayed with me in New York and Sophy had been her guest in India, but I had not before been under her roof. This was in itself a happy experience apart from the pleasure of her companionship. Less than a month before, we had been with a Greek family in their own setting; now we were in an Indian household at Kensington Palace Gardens, London.

Inside the house the range of people, interests and customs was as wide as the physical mileage between London and New Delhi. The staff included an Indian chef who began his service to Her Excellency when she was a bride, and has gone with her to every part of the world to which she has been assigned in service to her government. His superb cooking, consequently, was of the Indian or European school as the occasion demanded. The butler was British, his assistant, an Indian. The chambermaids were German, the secretaries Indian and British. There were two staff members whose titles indicated an area of service with which I was unfamiliar. These were "the messengers." Sophy and I were told they would give us our telephone messages, secure taxis, and see that we received our mail. I pictured nimble-footed little boys whose days were spent, for the most part, on the run. The messengers were portly, elderly and as British as boiled cabbage. They performed all the functions promised and in addition guarded the doors against curiosity seekers or other unwelcome guests, but I did not see them run.

The family proper included, while we were there, one of Her Excellency's three daughters, Tara, Tara's husband, Gotham Sahgal, and their two small, adorable children, four and six. The Sahgal family was on a holiday visit from India. Tara herself added mileage to this wide range. She had completed her formal education at

Wellesley, and before her marriage lived with her mother in a number of posts. To my mind, one of the most delightful and sensitive books of the year before had been her story of her childhood in India and girlhood in America, called *Prison and Chocolate Cake*.

We were talking at lunch one day, soon after Sophy's and my arrival, about her choice of such a thoroughly appropriate and yet provocative title. This, understandably, led to a conversation about food. We were, at the moment, eating an Indian meal. Her Excellency had asked me a day or two earlier if I had ever had a meal as it would be if I were in her own country. I had not had anything comparable, I told her, and so she had ordered it. It was in itself a token of her imaginative thoughtfulness.

The lunch was something to dream of and not the kind of dream, I assured her, invoked by a Welsh rarebit. It included a great deal of fruit and very little curry. When I mentioned this lack of what, at home, we picture as a staple of Indian diet, I saw Tara and her mother exchange a furtive smile. I begged them to divulge the secret. They were reluctant at first, but under persuasion, Her Excellency said,

"We didn't want to seem unappreciative, but if you insist, it's that in America a hostess with the kindest intention in the world almost invariably serves us a curry, and we do flinch a little. In the first place, we like Western food very much and want particularly to have the food of the country in which we are staying." She amplified, "You know, the way in France you order the *vin du pays*. But apart from that," she continued, "the curry you have we would scarcely recognize at home—powdered dust out of a bottle. We would not dream of using curry that is not freshly ground at the moment the dish with which it is to be used is being prepared. But," she interrupted herself with emphasis, "the very fact that you serve it is an example of a lovable American trait. In another country the food served would be its own, with pride, and the assumption that of course you will like it. The American is like a child, eager to please you, and at the same time have you know how happy he is you've come to see him."

"That's what we've been saying about the Greeks," I told her.

We talked about the food in Greece and this led us to a kind of game in which we endeavored to identify foods that were immediately associated in the mind with a particular country; roast beef, of course, in England, and marrow . . .

. . . Rice with the East, veal in France, and *haricots verts*, smorgasbord in Scandinavia.

We covered a good many countries before anyone mentioned America.

"It's hard to recognize," I said, "what things that are so familiar to you seem special to others. But," I continued ruminatively, "perhaps ham and eggs, possibly turkey." I thought a minute. "I have it," I added triumphantly, "pumpkin. Pumpkin pie in America at Thanksgiving and Christmas. Now there's something you probably wouldn't find anywhere else in the world."

The only guests at luncheon beside ourselves that day were three Indian men, their range of background almost as wide as Tara's and her mother's—education at Oxford and wide travel. At my announcement they burst into laughter. So did Her Excellency's family. The hostess herself put her hands over her face and rocked with mirth.

Sophy and I in astonishment looked from one to another of them and at each other, bewildered. Her Excellency lowered her hands, wiped her eyes a little and explained.

"My dear," she said to me, kindly, "I wouldn't for the world hurt your feelings by discounting the exclusive use of pumpkins by Americans, but you caught us off guard and I'm afraid I'll have to disillusion you. Pumpkin," she went on, and her shoulders shook a little, "is the cheapest food in India. Therefore, it is the basis of prison fare in India." She indicated her three guests with an affectionate circle of her hand. "We have had pumpkin in every form from soup to nuts, as you would say. I beg of you, give us curry in America, but for Heaven's sake spare us pumpkin."

London was very gay and so were Sophy and I. June was sunny, and what at home we would have called warm. On the day the thermometer nearly touched eighty, offices and some shops were closed, the employees sent home. "It is impossible to work," a newspaper said, "in such tropical heat, when one is not accustomed to it."

We saw friends and plays, sometimes with our hostess, sometimes with other friends or on our own. No matter how late we came in we always found Her Excellency awake and working. She would hear us however softly we tiptoed past her door on the second floor to reach our rooms on the third, and call us to join her in her upstairs sitting room for a last chat.

This is what I shall remember of them: a friend who was deeply and genuinely interested in what either Sophy or I had been doing. Had we had letters from our respective families? Was all well at home? (One of the letters I have had from Mme. Pandit was written on a plane as she was flying from India on an important and delicate mission. "Why haven't I heard from you about A?" it read. "Has she had her baby? I am worried. Please let me know at . . ." And she gave the address of the government head she was about to visit.) A friend quick to laugh and with a laughter as contagious as a child's, equally quick to show compassion, eager to share in any activity that looked to be fun or interesting with a total absence of self-importance, impatient of stupidity, slow and meditative when asked an opinion, easily exasperated by trivia, indignant at injustice, but within my view and hearing, incapable of sustaining deep anger. Laughter was always its detergent.

Visually I shall retain the picture of her as we left to go to bed. Turning at the doorway for a last good night, that postscript to a leavetaking one invariably sends back over the threshold, I would check it; probably she would not have heard had I sent it. She was at her work again. Bending over the low table in front of the couch on which she sat, lifting from it one of the papers with which its surface was piled, glasses on, folds of her sari tossed back over each shoulder for easier movement, she had returned to her job.

Next morning, before Sophy and I had breakfast, she would be on her way to her office, the working papers of the night before in a leather portfolio beside her on the seat of the car.

We went to the tennis matches at Wimbledon and the boat races at Henley, and though Sophy fumed like a boiling teakettle at putting on evening clothes in the middle of the afternoon, we went to Glyndebourne.

Glyndebourne is the country place of Mr. John Christie, where the annual Glyndebourne Festival Opera takes place. When the festival began in 1934 it was Mr. Christie's own, a personal communication with other lovers of opera, particularly of Mozart. It has continued with a break of only one season during the war, but now the burden of production is shared by the Glyndebourne Arts Trust, Limited.

The program, defining the present management, says, "The Trust was incorporated in 1954, and Mr. Christie thereupon arranged that the trustees should be granted a long lease of the opera house, private house and grounds of Glyndebourne, at a peppercorn rent. . . . Mr. Christie, as founder of the opera and head of the executive, will continue in executive control of the opera as in the past."

The purpose and principles of the Glyndebourne Opera are also set down in the program by Mr. Christie, who wrote, "Our purpose is to give the best possible performances, and we don't mind about Names." He reveals disarmingly, too, the scale on which the festival began. "A special train came into Lewes station on the second night in 1934 (*Cosi fan Tutte*) and seven people got into it to return to London. None of us was ruffled. The *Daily Telegraph* used these words in its criticism, 'Readers may be asked to make a note of our opinion that such a *Cosi fan Tutte* has never before been seen in our times.' " About the principles, he wrote, "One, the work must be better than normal. Two, the audience must take their part in showing their appreciation at the time. This is generally accepted as meaning they should take trouble about their clothes, they cannot come in late . . . they cannot smoke in the auditorium . . . and when the performance is over the audience, except in an emergency, should stay in their seats to say thank you to the artists."

This summer's season ran from the eighth of June to the twenty-sixth of July. Glyndebourne itself is fifty-four miles by road from London, by mileage an easy trip. We found the train consumed less time and, what was more important, less energy. By car there is traffic delay on the return, by train there is comfort all the way and a particular charm.

That is why, leaving a taxi to catch a 3:45 P.M. train, Sophy muttered an embarrassed resentment halfway across Victoria Station. "I feel such a fool," she said, "dressed like this in the middle of an afternoon. People must think we're mad. You mark my words, no one else will be got up this way. 'Crazy Americans,' that's what they'll say, 'showing off.' "

It was at this point in her scuttling progress, as I panted to keep up with her, she saw a considerable number of people converging from several points to the gate toward which we had been directed. Every individual was in evening clothes. We would indeed have felt ourselves fools, or show-off Americans, had we joined them dressed any other way.

A special carriage was reserved for the opera goers. Immediately the train had started, tea was served. The trip to Lewes takes one hour. Buses were waiting at the station. We drove through lovely green, rolling country, perhaps twenty minutes when our journey ended at Glyndebourne itself. There is time allowed before the performance begins to walk about the gardens, each of these set apart by hedges from its neighbor, and not one more beautiful than the rest. One could not have paid them such disrespect as to visit them in a tailored suit. Equally, the rustle of long dresses over the garden paths is a proper sound there.

We did not hear a Mozart opera. The bill that night was Rossini's *Le Comte Ory*, an opera in two acts. The performance was in the small, altogether charming theater that adjoins the house. Between the two acts there was an intermission long enough for dinner in one of two pavilions, where we could choose a cold buffet supper in one, or a more elaborate dinner in the other. After dinner there was time for another walk in the garden in what in England at eight o'clock or thereabouts is not quite twilight.

The performance itself was of an excellence Sophy and I agreed we had seldom heard. When it was over we stepped into one of the buses waiting at the very threshold, were delivered over at Lewes to the special train for us and before midnight were at home again.

Glyndebourne should be on every traveler's list of Things to Do and Places to See. The price of admission is two pounds. "The full details of timetables and special fares and facilities," the program reads, "may be obtained from the Glyndebourne London Box office, 23 Baker Street, London, W1. Telephone Welbeck 0572."

I think I have not dwelt entirely among the untrodden ways, but I know I had not trod the path to any embassy until I came to London this time, when I visited two, the Indian Embassy and our own. I visited Mme. Pandit in the conventional sense as the dictionary defines it, "to stay with as a guest for a more or less extended sojourn." (I wince a little at the phrase "more or less extended sojourn," remembering how extended ours was.) But the fault was not ours. The extension was demanded and executed by our hostess. Sophy and I had arrived intending to stay with Mme. Pandit one week, then we would move to a hotel. Accordingly, we made reservations. At the end of that week, and for five successive times Her Excellency, learning of the reservations, had them canceled.

My "visit" to the American Embassy was in the homely Hoosier sense a long cozy conversation, because Mrs. Aldrich, the wife of our Ambassador, injects the warmth implied in a Hoosier "visit." I cannot call her a close friend, but I was made conscious of this quality the first time I met her. I like to say aloud the incident because it is cause for pride that these attributes we tend to identify as characteristic of neighborliness in the small American town are attributes indigenous to the wife of our Ambassador.

I had gone one summer with my children to a small place in Maine where a friend of mine had offered me a house. She was the only person I knew in the community and on the day of our arrival had had to go away for a few hours and, therefore, was not on hand to meet us as she had planned. Our arrival was a nocturne in terms of gloom. The house was far bigger than we had anticipated. It had been built in a day when economy of space took no part in a blueprint. The maid I had brought with me walked from dining room to kitchen and returned immediately saying she would take the first train home. My twin daughters sat down in the living room regarding each other glumly and carried on a conversation ostensibly directed at each other, actually aimed at me.

The gist of it was, "It's a good thing we brought along our summer reading. That's about all we'll do. We'll certainly have plenty of time for it. I guess we could play tennis if we knew anybody to play with. I suppose there are boats if anybody would let you sail with them. But of course we don't know anybody and I don't suppose we will."

I have never before nor since exerted myself more in an attempt to spread lightness and cheer. I shot promises, hopes and jokes into the air. They fell to earth heavily at the feet of the twins, who stared moodily at the floor. As these efforts of mine were piling higher and higher underfoot, there was a knock at the door and simultaneously it was flung open to the accompaniment of a cheery "Hello, hello, anybody here?"

With this as an entrance cue, a woman came into the room followed and surrounded by a group of some four or five young people, and two or three dogs. Not waiting for an answer and pausing only to shake hands as the three of us rose dumbly to our feet, she continued.

"We're all so glad you've come; we've brought a little welcome." She waved to her group. "Girls, why don't you open some of that ginger ale or Coke, and where's the box of pretzels?"

Over the munching and giggling that followed within a minute or two, she continued talking. "We thought it would be fun to have a beach picnic tonight. We'll pick you up. Do you play tennis? Do you like to swim?" She addressed my young but did not wait for an answer. "If you haven't a boat you can always crew for one of us. We'd be delighted to have you. The races are Wednesdays and Saturdays, and there's tennis all the time."

I may have murmured something. I do not remember. I was looking at the faces of my girls, eager, eyes sparkling, cheeks flushed. They were already in noisy conversation with the young visitors.

My contemporary started for the door as unexpectedly as she'd entered, still talking. "We must get on to the post office before it closes. We'll be back around half past six for the picnic."

They all rushed out, the dogs leaping and barking. The noise continued after they had left, not perceptibly reduced in volume. My twins were performing an Indian dance around the floor of the living room, whooping at the same time, "We're going to sail, we're going to play tennis. Are we ever going to have fun!"

A minute or two later there was another entrance. This time the visitor had some difficulty making her presence noticed above the tumult. It was our friend, apologizing for and explaining her absence at our arrival. Reassuring her and quieting my Indians, I explained what had happened, and added, "Bless her heart, she's gathering us up for a picnic tonight, but I'm in a little cloud of confusion. I haven't the slightest idea who was here."

My friend laughed. "Don't you know?" she said. "How characteristic of her. I met her going down your driveway. That was Harriet Aldrich and her children."

It is a happy incident for all Americans that she is in England. She is an American Ambassador wherever she goes.

During our "visit" at tea, she asked what Sophy and I were doing while in England. I told her some of the things we had done and seen and added, "Now, we're going on a motor trip in the South of England, and after that on a boat we've chartered to go up the Thames."

As I said this the Ambassador joined us. He is a noteworthy and passionate sailor. The mention of a boat in his hearing brings him to an immediate stance not unlike a pointer's at a hint of partridge. Affable and kindly, he has at the same time no patience with irrelevancies when there are topics of interest to him in the air.

"What's this about a boat?" he asked, shaking hands with no other preface of conversation. "What kind of a boat? Where are you going on the Thames?"

"I don't know as yet," I told him, "but I'm finding out. It's just an idea I've had."

"Now see here," he answered, "we're very busy people at the Embassy. We have a lot of rather important things to do. We have no time nor people to spare for rescuing American women with ideas who get marooned or damage a boat on a bank of the Thames. I'd like to make that kind of a trip myself," he added.

But the motor trip came first.

Chapter Twenty

AT HALF past eight in the morning of the fifth of July, Sophy and I left the Indian Embassy in a car provided by Daimler Hire, driven by Alfred, also provided by D.H. We were on our way to the South of England. Kat,* the friend who could not go to Greece because she and her husband were going to England, had arrived in London. She would leave her husband for a few days to join us.

Sophy held in her hand an itinerary drawn up by Mr. Randall of Daimler Hire. Spread across her lap and piled beside her were maps and other guides; so many of these, the space they occupied wedged me into a far corner of the back seat. Sophy with her circulars was as happy as a child on Christmas Day poring over the contents of a stocking. She hummed contentedly "We're off to see the wizard, the wonderful wizard of Oz."

We had no specific destination but we had an objective. This, too, like the trip to Greece harked back to my childhood.

On a shelf in my family's library—I can see vividly in my memory the exact spot—was a set of two, perhaps three volumes, I am not sure of the number and I have now only a vague idea of their contents. At the time in which they meant so much to me I had even less idea. It was the title that was important. The title provided a game with which I put myself to sleep every night for a number of years. *Abbeys, Castles and Ancient Halls in England, Scotland and Wales* it read.

Abbey was a little girl, I thought, and she became my dearest friend. Every night in her company I visited one of her castles or ancient halls in England, Scotland or Wales. I can remember no ruder awakening than the moment when, years later, reading that title again, I saw Abbey perish before my grown-up eyes. I

* *So Near and Yet So Far.*

could not bring Abbey back, but in vivid memory of her I was on my way to some of the castles and ancient halls in England we had once shared. It would not have been possible to make this pilgrimage many years earlier; the actual owners of the castles and halls would not have welcomed, I think, a friend of Abbey's. But now many of these are open to visitors, and each year more estates are added to the list published by the British Travel and Holidays Association of "Historic Houses and Castles" available to the public. The tour has become very popular among the British themselves. "Doing the Dukes" they call it irreverently.

The literature on these places, together with the maps and other guides that were piled on and around Sophy, had been largely my accumulation. I had not gathered them with a lofty purpose of adding to my store of knowledge, though my knowledge of the part of the country we were about to visit was a mouse's store. My purpose, low and scheming, was to divert Sophy from driving the car. The two occupations that bring most acute pleasure to my old and valued friend, as I have observed her over the years, are driving a car and perusing maps and guidebooks.

She had been piqued, though resigned, at not driving a car in Greece, but had submitted to the indubitable obstacle of language there. Darn's equipment, splendid though it was, could not carry us over strange roads, with no oral directions from passersby, had we been able to force or cajole Sophy to ask them. There would be none of these difficulties in England; only one difficulty, but that as threatening to me as a Greek mountain; left side of the road driving. I admit, first, I am unreasonably nervous in a car, next, that with Sophy driving I am less of a floorboard pusher than with any other of my friends, and third, that drivers whose habitat is right-hand side of the road come to England every year and quickly accommodate themselves to the change.

But a few days before the start of this trip, an American sitting next to me at a party had told me he had driven a car every summer in England for ten years without difficulty or even threat of an accident; nevertheless, two days previously, on a narrow country lane, he had seen a car come unexpectedly from a concealed cross-road. Startled, he had clean forgot ten summers' experience, and reverting to his more fundamental instinct, swerved to the right.

Thanks to the other driver, an Englishman, there had been no accident. When the two owners had stopped their cars, the Britisher, smiling, had explained his skillful avoidance of disaster. "I saw your car was an American make. I thought you were, too, probably, and if you were as startled as I was you just might pull to the right, as you did."

"It might never happen again," the American said to me. "I doubt that it would. I'm not going to give myself a chance to find out. From now on I have a chauffeur."

I do not offer this as advice to other motorists. I submit it only as the explanation of why we had so many books and maps in the back seat, and a British chauffeur in the front.

We stopped first at Cobham Hall in Cobham, only twenty-seven miles from London. This was the seat of the Earl of Darnley. There are grizzly stories of the family. Eleanor, who died in 1443, practiced black magic and was accused of endeavoring to use it on the King, so that her husband, the Duke of Gloucester, might have the crown. Her commitment to prison included an ingenious detour. She was sentenced to perambulate the streets for three days, bareheaded with a burning taper in her hand. Then there was the tenth Lord Cobham, who was convicted of conspiring to place Arabella Stuart on the throne. He was reprieved and sent to the tower. Pardoned eventually, he had been reduced to such poverty he died, it is said, in the house of his laundress. Sir John Oldcastle was known as the good Lord Cobham. Nevertheless, in 1417, he was hung in chains upon a gallows and burned alive. The character, Falstaff, is thought to be a caricature of the good Lord Cobham.

Of the places we saw later, Cobham Hall is the only one that has not been at least pruned and neatened. It is sadly rundown, but there were literally fields, not garden beds, of lupin.

Cobham church is not far from the hall and is itself on the top of a bank at the very edge of a narrow road. It was built soon after the Magna Charta was signed in 1215 by one of the Crusader Lords of Cobham.

In order not to block the road, Alfred drew into the courtyard of an inn across the way. Sophy and I left the car and walked back, she leading the way. I should have reversed the order of our going. I know her magnetic response to an unconventional

CANTERBURY
SALISBURY
STONEHENGE
BATH
RYE
CHIDDINGFOLD
Vasiliu.

approach. As I scrambled and slid clutching at tufts, she led me up the steep bank through tall meadow grass, over a hummock of hay, around another to the door of the church. Waiting there a moment to catch my breath, I looked back and saw, a few yards to one side of the way by which we had come, a flight of steps from the road, and from that direct to the door a flower-bordered, gravel path to the place where I was standing.

We explored the interior, lingering over the beautiful old brasses. These are acknowledged to be among the finest in England. They are like a soft rug reflecting the light, in places the colors too, from the stained-glass windows. We lingered at the chancel where four tilting helmets hang, and following the guidebook, traced on one the Cobham crest, a Saracen's head wearing a gold wreath.

Before we left the village, we had a glass of beer at the inn, the Olde Leather Bottle. Gadshill, where Dickens lived, is a very short distance away. The inn, a sweet place with low ceilings and uneven floor levels, is crammed with souvenirs of its one-time neighbor. Alfred told us people from London like to drive out here to dine. I should like, another time, to spend a night or two there, using it as a base for wider excursions than we allowed ourselves, in the immediate countryside.

We drove only a few miles on before we stopped again, this time at Rochester, a lovely fourteenth-century Norman cathedral, and a Norman castle as well. We looked down from this on the Medway River. Alfred assured us that by tradition, once we had crossed this river, we would always belong in Kent. In the small portion of the world over which I have traveled I cannot count the number of places I have been told I must return to, or would belong to, once I had set foot there. It is the prevailing expression of local pride. If the superstition were to be fulfilled, I would be in almost perpetual flight, winging from place to place that "called me back." Happily, I have not been jerked about by such witchcraft, but I would find it hard to resist a tug toward the rolling, smiling countryside of Kent.

We drove through Aylesford. If I were inexorably drawn back to Kent I could live in that sweet village. Twenty-six miles beyond Rochester we reached Canterbury. Before the cathedral or the town itself we went to Chilham, one of the places to which Abbey may have taken me. Chilham is five miles out of town on the Canterbury-

Maidstone Road, and it is, I have written and underscored in my diary, "heavenly." There are three terraced gardens to wander through, each set off from another by brick walls softened to a dusty pink. Fig and peach trees are espaliered against these. In addition to the flower gardens there is a topiary, its fantasies shaped with beautiful precision. Its own little village is immediately outside the gates to the castle.

Before I could check myself I had said aloud that exasperating reversal the theater has brought to our point of view. "It's not real, of course. The villagers are about to enter from left and right for the opening chorus."

Down the hill and around the corner from the castle is the Woolpack and I, who nibble at home on cottage cheese, lettuce and Ry-Krisp, lunched there on steak-and-kidney pie. For that dish alone I would happily fulfill the Kentish prophecy.

In Canterbury we went immediately to our hotel. We had a very special errand that was not listed under either Things to Do nor Places to See. This was a person to see. The chance of completing this errand, we knew was very slim.

During the last war a British ship put into Philadelphia for extensive repairs. Sophy and I, each living there at that time, belonged to a group of volunteers that concerned itself with servicemen from overseas. Sophy's particular charge was the distribution of tickets to the Philadelphia Orchestra. With the arrival of this British ship two officers became regular applicants for seats. The two music lovers were Peter Drew, the captain, and Laird Cassidi, its doctor. They became friends of Sophy's, mine, and a third, Edna Welsh's. When they had gone, Edna of the three kept up a correspondence with them for a time, and then, as all too often happens, the line of communication was too slender, there were too few items of news to exchange that would be of mutual interest. The line frayed and finally broke.

In 1950, Sophy was in New Delhi, the guest of Mme. Pandit. At a garden party one afternoon at the house of the President, a fellow guest, an Indian, said to Sophy, "We have a number of British experts who are helping us in an advisory capacity. I am expecting one of them this afternoon. I think you will find him delightful. His name is Captain Peter Drew."

But Laird Cassidi had not been to India, nor other places in the intervening years to which any of the three of us had traveled. Edna, shortly before we left America, had put into my hand a slip of paper. "This was Laird's address," she said. "I found it the other day. I have no idea that he still lives there, but if you should by any chance happen to go to Canterbury" (we had not at that time anticipated going to England) "see if you can find where he is."

The porter of the Abbots Barton Hotel had scarcely left us in our rooms when I had the telephone book in my hands and was looking under the C's. I found the name and the very address Edna had given me. As the British say, "I rang up" immediately.

A maid answered. "No, madam, he's not here," she answered my query, and my heart sank. "He's away on his annual government service."

I thanked her and was about to hang up when she added, "Dr. Cassidi Senior is here, taking over the practice while the young doctor's away. He's out at the moment. Would you like to leave a message for him?"

I left a message that within a half hour brought Laird and his wife to our door. We had not, of course, met Mrs. Cassidi, though by way of Laird we felt we knew her well. She, as charming, delightful and congenial as we had known she would be, had long included us, she assured us, among her good friends. Both of them asked about our children and remembered their names, as well as the names of Edna's dogs and birds, of which she has a great many.

No matter how far we wandered over children and animals, we came back again and again to the lovely coincidence that we should be having tea together. Laird explained at least five times over, "I'm retired now. We live in Ireland. We haven't been back to Canterbury in a long time. I've grown lazy in my retirement, but when my son proposed I should take over, we couldn't resist the temptation to visit the old place. This is our last day. We go home tomorrow. Another day and we would have missed you after all these years!"

Then we were back once more into the time in the war years when he was in Philadelphia. We learned something of how that time had been for Mrs. Cassidi. There had been bad stretches for Laird from which those months in Philadelphia had been all too brief a respite. But the respite in Philadelphia was not a respite in Canterbury. That was the period of the worst bombing. We learned a little only by way of a story, because we were talking of British types.

During the bad times, she said, the Cassidi children were safely away. Alone in the house, she decided to stay there during the raids. This was a source of anxiety and exasperation to her air raid warden. He was a little man, she said, but when helmets were distributed, misfortune had placed upon his head one so many sizes too big for him that when, under stress, he forgot to keep his head at the particular angle required to hold it in place, the helmet would slide all the way down over his countenance. Since he was invariably talking when he was under the stress that provoked this, his voice would continue, though in a ghostly, hollow tone. Mrs. Cassidi had been the cause of several of these incidents because of her refusal to leave the house and her warden's insistence she must. Her conversion had been instantaneously accomplished, however, by a single threat delivered under the fallen helmet, with mournful echoes.

"We digs for two, but not for one."

When the Cassidis had gone, though it was late, we went ourselves at once to the cathedral. I wish every traveler might arrange his expedition so as to see the cathedral first at the time of day we first saw it, when the late-afternoon shadows are long, the light is soft, and pigeons in the close talk to one another sleepily. We were reverent pilgrims, come to one of the great cathedrals of the world, as we remembered we were in the place to which Chaucer's pilgrims had come. We hunted for, and found, the tombs of the Black Prince and of Henry IV, and the transept where Thomas à Becket was murdered, but we were made disgracefully mirthful by a guide in whose party we unexpectedly though briefly found ourselves.

The guide, female, was middle-aged, and in need like us of a strict adherence to cottage cheese and lettuce. She had a strong nose and a heavy foot. A pince-nez was attached to the former feature and further secured by a broad black ribbon around the neck; stout oxfords enveloped the latter. The area between was almost entirely covered by a straight mackintosh, so severe in line as not to permit a single fold. Crowning the entire structure was a straw hat with a wide brim adorned by a ribbon band and foolish little streamers down the back. We might have had sufficient restraint and dignity to remain longer in her train and benefit from her knowledge had she not within a moment of our finding ourselves in her immediate neighborhood, removed her pince-nez, wagged it coquettishly above her head in the direction of one of the great windows and said in a voice that was within a basso's range, "All those *dear, dear* little pieces of glass up there were taken away, one by one, and hidden oh, so carefully, during the war. But now . . ."

But now, we had gone by way of the nearest door.

Before we left Canterbury the next morning we had visited the cathedral again, and photographed with joy, among other things, enchanting old Tudor houses whose upper stories hang out over the River Stour. All their windows are lined with flower boxes. These were the houses in which the refugee Huguenot weavers once lived and worked.

From Canterbury we drove to Sandwich to spend an hour with one of Barbara's daughters, and see in her garden such madonna lilies as I had not known could grow.

Then we were on to Rye, where we stayed the night at the Mermaid in two rooms that were delightful, though they were under the eaves. (Mr. Randall of the Daimler Hire had sent a letter asking we be given particular consideration. This was, of course, why we were in the attic.) There was only one small area in either room in which one could stand upright; nevertheless, the view from the little dormer windows was the smiling landscape I love. The food in the restaurant was good, and the town itself, with its steep hills and cobblestoned streets, of such charm we walked it until the soles of our shoes threatened to give way.

All the way from Sandwich we had followed the coast, and we continued on it after Rye, passing through Brighton and other seaside spots whose names have become as familiar to Americans as I daresay Atlantic City is to the British. They are not unlike. A mile or two off the London-Portsmouth Road is the village of Chiddingfold, where we spent the night. It is a small place with no cathedral, castle or ancient hall to distinguish it, only an excellent inn, the Crown. It is not picturesque, but it is luxurious. We dined and slept well.

At Salisbury Kat joined us. We spent two nights there. We had stopped in Winchester on the way and spent a long time, because there is much to see in addition to the glorious cathedral. We had lunched at the Manor of God-Be-Got, a restaurant that opened around 1052. We had hunted, and found, the house in which Jane Austen had lived the last few months of her life, and died. It was not so much that we wanted to see the house in itself as that we wanted to go all the way with her, because we had driven through Chariton, in Hampshire, and stopped there to spend some time in her house. It is like the pieces of glass in the Canterbury Cathedral, a dear little place. It has been reclaimed from neglectful obscurity to a place that is charmingly filled with souvenirs of her, and is in itself a remarkable memorial. The restoration and accumulation of souvenirs was begun by a Londoner as a memorial to a son who was killed in the last war, but who during his lifetime had shared his father's love for Jane Austen.

In Salisbury we stayed with Kat at the Old George. It is old and it is adequate, but no more. The hotel to which a letter had been sent asking special consideration was unable to accommodate us at all. This was only one step beyond the attic rooms I had anticipated when I learned a letter had been sent. Without any letter heralding our approach, the Old George provided us with three of its best rooms. This did not surprise me either.

Kat, comes originally from Boston and is the wife of a banker; she expresses consistently both these conditionings. As a New Englander she flouts any manifestation of pixies, and as the wife of a banker she expects a specific return for an investment, whether that investment be of a monetary nature or in the form of a request for the best that is available. Accordingly she was inclined to be more fractious than pleased that, where the best had been requested, we were completely turned down, and where nothing had been asked, we were given the best. She is also not one to slacken her jaws on a perplexity once she has got it between her teeth. She spoke at some length about this paradox, but gave a spontaneous and heartfelt tribute to the beauty of Salisbury Cathedral when she admitted that, having seen it, she was not interested further in our hotel accommodations nor how we had got them.

The three of us hummed our motif about the wizard a number of times that day. It was an expression of deep contentment over the things we were seeing.

From Salisbury we drove to Warminster to see Longleat House, the property of the Marquess of Bath. We agreed this must be one of the most beautiful places in England. One of the numerous times this appraisal was given was in the garden. Kat said it aloud with something very close to awe. She was at the moment looking up at a row of delphiniums, taller than she, and of a blue so deep as to be close to violet. She added emphatically—Kat is usually emphatic —"I'd like to write a poem in answer to that nonsense about being in England in April. You wouldn't see such a sight as this. July is the month." She walked ahead of us down a garden path and turned so suddenly I immediately behind very nearly played an involuntary leapfrog. "How would you begin a poem like that?" she demanded.

Simultaneously and spontaneously, Sophy and I each took an arm and led her out of the garden. Wells Cathedral, we agreed over her head, would sober her to a prose level.

Wells did nothing of the kind. The cathedral is not overwhelming, it is exquisite. What with the bishop's castle, the moat around it, the bell-ringing swans in it that pull a bell rope at feeding time, all three of us were so intoxicated as to use extravagant language.

We spent a second night in Salisbury, a third in Bath, and the next day, on the eleventh, were home again in London, and what places we had seen! There is not one, on the published list of the historic houses I once thought Abbey owned, I would skip if I were to make the tour again. Only Bath itself I think I would not revisit. I am glad to have seen it but it is saddening, I think, to look at seedy grandeur.

Kat was restored to her husband in London. Sophy and I took to the water again.

Chapter Twenty-One

THE proposal of a boat trip up the Thames was mine. Sophy still talks about this wonderingly. She is unable to understand how I, who through all the waters of Greece had moaned for the corn-fields of Indiana and no water anywhere, should have promoted such an enterprise. I, in turn, find her bewilderment difficult to understand. As I pointed out to her when I proposed this outing, a river does not go uphill, much less over mountains. Furthermore, a river is not constructed at such a height it requires a ladder by which to reach or leave it. Finally, the constructions of the Thames itself is such, God be praised, that in most places either bank can be swum to from the middle in less than fifty strokes, which is my capacity.

The idea for the trip sprang full panoplied from my brow on a Sunday in Oxford when Sophy and I had gone to spend the day with her cousins, Dr. and Mrs. Lee. Dr. Lee is a distinguished don of Oxford University.* We had lunched with them in 1953, and on that day gone with them only to the university. This time our touring range was wider. We went to the Trout for tea, at one time an inn, now only a restaurant, I think. It is one of the pleasantest I have ever visited. We had tea on a terrace beside the river and later walked along the bank to one of the locks, where we watched boats waiting for the gates to open, and then moving through. That did it.

There were no sailboats but there was very nearly every other kind, from punts to motor launches. I saw people on these launches, idling in the sun, waiting for the gates to open. I could see through the windows on these craft a cabin where sometimes food was on a table, and up in the bow, clothes on hooks.

* *Forty Plus and Fancy Free.*

When I had looked at these things a few minutes I spoke. "Sophy," I said, and she tells me it was in a tone she has learned to dread because it invariably means I am toying with an idea. "Sophy," I repeated, "I don't believe all those boats are owned by the people who are on them. I've an idea you could rent one."

That was all I said at the time, but the next morning in London I was on the telephone with the British Travel Information Service. The young woman to whom I spoke seemed surprised by my request, and that surprised me. I should have thought this was something many travelers would want to do. Evidently I was mistaken. She would have to ring me back, she said, after she had gathered some information about boats for hire.

When she called back she was prepared with the names of several firms. I chose the one of W. Bates & Son in Chertsey. When I had ended my conversation with her I put in a call immediately to Chertsey. Presently, with no more popping sounds, cracklings, cut-offs and detours than the average call in England evokes, I was connected with the firm and after my first question put through to Mr. Bates.

I repeated it. "Would it be possible," I asked, "to hire a motor launch for a few days' cruise on the Thames?"

Mr. Bates assured me this was the very business in which he was engaged. Boats were hired by the week, he said. They went out on Saturday, and returned the following Saturday. For a shorter period, a special arrangement must be made. The boats comprise what he fancifully termed the Star Fleet, and vary in price according to size. Each piece of information I was given pleased me more than the preceding one. I reached such a peak of enthusiasm I cut short the recital.

"Mr. Bates," I said, "I would like to engage the *Bellatrix Star* for a week, beginning this Saturday, July 16."

He proceeded to a few details, contract to be sent and signed, the time of day when the boat would be available. These business minutiae attended to, I thought the conversation could be ended.

Thanking Mr. Bates and about to hang up the receiver, I added, "I need not tell you, I am sure, we want the man who runs the boat to be thoroughly dependable. I'm confident you would not send out anyone you did not consider competent."

Mr. Bates' answer was not the reassurance I had expected. "Oh, madam," he said, "we do not provide anyone to run the boat. You run it. But we give you an hour's tutoring lesson before you start."

I did not cancel our verbal contract. An idea once planted in my mind, I admit, becomes imbedded there.

I had trouble with Sophy, however, when I reported to her my morning's achievement and eased into the piece of news that had come at the end of my telephone conversation. Hearing it, Sophy threatened to bolt. I have seldom been more astonished, but I was able to bring her back into the traces into which I thought I had secured her.

"I'm sure it's just like driving a car," I told her soothingly. "I saw myself those boats have steering wheels. You'd rather drive a car than do almost anything else. You must admit that. And you have maps to read. Mr. Bates told me he provided them."

I had a further surprise for her, too, not of so much magnitude as Mr. Bates' final announcement, but one that had affected strongly by decision to take the boat, and it told on Sophy. "When you're on the water in England," I said, triumphantly, "you drive on the right-hand side."

Mme. Pandit was all for joining us if she could get away from her office. Accordingly, we telephoned Mr. Bates again to find out how we could communicate our whereabouts in case Her Excellency could come. We learned every lock keeper would telephone a message to the Bates office and they, in turn, would immediately relay it. Actually, Mme. Pandit was not able to get away, but we found this efficiency reassuring. If any emergency arose, if any unexpected news from home demanded our return, we could be told of it with not more than a two-hour lapse, the average length of time between locks.

On Saturday morning we drove to Chertsey in the same car from the Daimler Hire that had taken us on the motor trip the week before, but with another chauffeur. Alfred was engaged, Albert drove us. Albert revealed himself as a man with a hankering for a life at sea. He suggested shyly, but pointedly, he would have no trouble getting permission for a week off and was very handy with an engine.

"Ladies," he said, "don't enjoy messing with them," adding hopefully, "and there's bound to be a breakdown of one sort of another."

Sophy shuddered slightly but said nothing. I was the one who explained we really wanted the experience of running the boat ourselves. Another tremor passed over Sophy's frame. Furthermore the sleeping accommodations were not such as would make feasible including a man unless his association was of a family nature. Albert was resigned but wistful.

We bought provisions at the local store, ate a quick and early lunch at the inn. Its barmaid waitress inquired our plans and laughed uproariously when she heard them. "I'll stay a land sailor," she said, and patted Sophy's shoulder.

Sophy smiled wanly.

Albert loaded our bags and supplies on board the *Bellatrix Star* as she bobbed daintily at the basin dock. He was persuaded to leave the boat while we changed in the cabin from street clothes to shorts, sneakers and sweaters, but once we reappeared on deck, he leapt aboard with a mechanic who presented himself as our tutor and suggested we get under way.

He gave us considerably less than an hour's instructions. Looking back on it I think I was right to suggest at the outset he concentrate on Sophy, but I did not know then to what office this automatically allotted me. My reasons for not taking a turn at the wheel were, as I explained: if we were both asking questions we would both be confused. It would seem to me simpler for one to learn and then teach the other. That one ought to be Sophy since she would want to do the driving anyway.

Sophy nodded an agreement to this proposal. I had been made aware on the journey from London how uncommunicative, even taciturn, she had become. She did, however, ask a few questions of teacher. Not many, because he gave her little opportunity. He imparted to her his store of information at a pace I have only heard equalled by a cathedral guide making the last round of the day with his party before closing time.

"This is where the petrol goes," he rattled. "This is for water. Under the driver's seat is the gas tank. You turn it on there when you're ready to cook. Reverse is here. Accelerate like this. . . ." and so on, until listening and trying to understand, though I stood too far back to see the things at which he was pointing, I experienced a twinge of uneasiness. There seemed to be more bits of business involved in running a boat than I had imagined.

When we returned to the dock the mechanic and Albert leapt out. The mechanic tutor, however, held the boat for a moment and turned for the first time to me.

"Now, madam," he said, "you're the decky."

The term had not come into his previous instruction, and certainly I had not heard it anywhere else. "What the decky does is this," he continued. "As you're coming into a lock you take your place at the stern with the rope coiled in your hand. Your captain," he indicated Sophy, "she'll get the nod from the lock keeper which side he wants you to come in on. She'll pass that on to you. You'll take your place on whichever side she tells you, with the rope coiled in your hand. As you come in, heave it over a stanchion you will see there and hang onto it. That will moor the stern. Then she," pointing to Sophy again, "can leave off the wheel and moor her bow."

He released the boat, gave it a shove with his foot. "Good luck," he said, and waved.

Albert echoed, "Good luck," and also waved.

I waved. I could not think of anything to say.

The *Bellatrix Star* is thirty feet long. The Bates catalogue carries a picture of her and underneath the information that she has a raised saloon, forward fly bridge, aft cockpit with lounge sofa seat, a galley on the port side with stainless-steel sink, fresh-water pump, draining board with drawers and cupboards below, large Calor gas oven cooker with grill and boiling ring. Toilet opposite galley on starboard side with sliding door. A fore cabin fitted with two single bunks with foam-rubber mattresses, wardrobe at head of starboard bunk and dressing table fitted with drawer and cupboard shelves at head of port bunk. (Note: I did not find this. Perhaps I should have looked for it on hands and knees.)

The *Bellatrix Star* also has three lengths of rope, though the catalogue does not say so. I found two just where our tutor had said they would be, one at either side of the stern. I looked at them speculatively, running over in my mind what I had been told I was about to do with them. To the best of my recollection a rope had not passed through my hands since the days when I skipped one to the tune of "One, two, buckle my shoe."

I was interrupted in this rumination by my skipper. "My God," she said in a tone that was sharp and perceptibly higher than her usual range, "we're coming to a lock."

She was exactly right. We were approaching a lock whose gates were closed against us.

"What are you going to do?" I inquired, and it was anything but a rhetorical question.

"Turn around," she answered, "unless you can think of something better."

I had no other suggestion to offer. Accordingly, we turned around in the river. Happily for us and our purpose it was accommodatingly wide at that point. When we had circled once, the gates were still closed. Therefore, we circled again, and after that several more times, round and round in the middle of the river. Happily for us, too, our serpentine was the only river traffic at the moment. I remained in the stern. Presently I would perform my function as decky with one of my two ropes; at least that was what the tutor thought.

Each time our circle presented the stern and me toward the dock, I saw the tutor, with Albert beside him, both waving. I grew accustomed to this, so that when on the fifth or sixth circle, I saw them stiffen, their hands still high in the air as though they were playing still-pond-no-more-moving, I sensed all was not well ahead. My sensing was exactly right. I moved up beside Sophy and saw with her that each circle had brought us a little closer to the river bank than the one before. Now we were heading into it. At no great distance, scarcely any distance at all from it, she put the engine into reverse. Out of the corner of my eye I saw her do that, though my full gaze was hypnotically riveted like that of a novice bicyclist on the object we were about to hit.

To all appearances a boat in reverse behaves precisely as it does in forward speed. At least that was the behavior of the *Bellatrix*. We continued to advance as though Sophy had not touched the reverse lever. A fisherman sat on the bank at precisely the spot we would hit.

"That's British calm," I thought to myself. "I wonder if he'll move or wait for us to move him."

I managed another side glance at Sophy, perhaps with the idea of ascertaining whether she had found anything else to do. What I saw her do at that instant was so astounding I mistrusted my own vision. Sophy, the intrepid, the monument of strength in any crisis, was behaving like a Victorian heroine who would cry, helplessly, "Oh dear, oh dear, what shall I do?" She had taken her hands from the wheel and was shaking them agitatedly in the air.

She admits now she had never made such a gesture before in her life, but she insists, too, it was the best thing she could have done, because, she affirms, it brought the blood to her head and, by this stimulus, a recollection that the tutor had said, "At the moment of reversing you must also accelerate hard."

She accelerated hard. The *Bellatrix*, her nose not three inches from the bank, churned the water violently a minute, and reversed.

The fisherman on the bank had not moved by an inch his line nor any part of him.

As we nosed around toward the gates I was swung once more into view of the tutor and Albert. They had resumed waving.

Sophy has since admitted had the boat at that moment caught on fire, she would have been unable to quit it. "I couldn't even have stood up," she says. "My legs were quivering like telephone wires."

This admission has made me less censorious of what she did to me in the lock than I was at the time. Within five minutes of our escaping the bank preparatory to another turn on our merry-go-round, we saw the gates open slowly. Now we know there are posts along the approach to each lock to which one can moor while waiting for the lock to open. Other sailors, in this interim, do not make circles in the river.

As the gates opened boats came at us, even a river steamer. Nobody collided with anyone however. Sophy sidled dexterously out of their way. My confidence in her soared to new heights. The lock keeper beckoned my captain and she passed the word on to me. "Going in on the right," she said.

I stood up in the stern, grasped one end of the rope in my two hands, making a noose of it. No need, I thought, to tell Sophy there is not the slightest possibility of my getting this rope over anything whatever. She knows as well as I, if I held up my own foot in front of me I couldn't lasso it. We moved slowly through the gates; Sophy had cut the speed down as she had been instructed. We were in the lock itself. The walls on either side were high above our heads. Ranged along the top, I saw widely spaced a row of squat, low stanchions.

I threw the rope up into the air. Any aim on my part would have been silly, but the hand of the Lord must have caught it. Nothing I did could have placed the rope around a stanchion and returned the rope end down toward me. Stupefied at the sight, I nevertheless automatically reached out, grabbed the end in both hands, and I yelled. I shouted my triumph and my astonishment. "I've got it! I've got it!"

I should have made my announcement more quietly. I am ready to admit this. I have admitted it each time Sophy and I have rehearsed the incident. But when I pleaded I could not possibly have known what this would cause her to do, she has answered, she couldn't have known either. In her preoccupation with maneuvering the boat into the narrow channel she had not glanced up. She did not know we were in the range of stanchions, much less that I would take a fling at one of them. Therefore, my announcement at such a pitch was a surprise not only in volume but in news. This, she claims, is what caused her to perform the wrong half of the maneuver she had so recently, by the wringing of hands, remembered. She did not go into reverse, but she accelerated. And she accelerated me on the end of the rope right out of the boat and over the water. Not all the way out of the boat, however. The toes of one foot involuntarily hooked under a railing around the stern. Therefore, I stretched, but I did not swing.

"For God's sake, come back!" I yelled in volume double any vocal effort I have ever made in my life.

Sophy says she does not know how, with that bellow in her ears, she managed to find the reverse. She did find it, put it into effect, caught up the slack in me, though I was anything but slack. Before I could break apart, I was restored all of one piece to the haven of the *Bellatrix Star*.

The lock keeper told us he had never seen that happen before. Sophy assured him this was not our customary way of entering a lock, and she would endeavor not to use it again. She jumped from the bow to the steps that led from the water to the ground level above, and placed her own bow rope around another stanchion. I remained where I had dropped on the lounge seat in the stern and endeavored to pry the rope out of my hands.

As the water rose it brought us up to a level view of the place we were in, enabling us to see for the first time a lock keeper's domain.

It is a charming sight. His cottage is surrounded by a garden. It is not only a source of pride to each lock keeper, it is an obligation that goes with the job. There is an inspection at regular intervals of these properties, and each year a prize is awarded for the best and the most carefully tended.

Every lock keeper we encountered had a wife who assisted him in the opening and closing of the gates, though sometimes she yielded her place to one of the crowd of onlookers invariably gathered when the lock was filled. Sometimes the volunteer assistant was a small boy, sometimes a grown one, who understandably found it fun to turn on and off such giant spigots.

We came from the lock into a river crowded, that Saturday afternoon in July, with boats, swimmers and swans, all of them indifferent to our approach. This caused Sophy some nervous concern at first. However, she explained, acute anxiety is an emotion difficult to sustain. After the two crises through which we had passed, it was on the wane. Therefore, she steered through the traffic with relative unconcern.

Presently we both relaxed and allowed ourselves to appreciate a journey as close to a heavenly tour as this earth can provide. Green fields, wide-spreading trees along the banks, cows under them, sunlight on the river, now and then a beautiful garden that would not have been visible from a car. Furthermore, we said over and over to each other, a car could not be driven as slowly as we were gliding, giving us opportunity to see and savor each thing along our way.

We might have stopped at a number of places but moving as we were was such an enchantment we were reluctant to break it. Though daylight in England lasts in July until well after nine o'clock, the river authorities have found an effective way of preventing cruising at night. They order the locks closed at nine.

Around seven, we saw ahead of us two signposts. One of them identified as Bray the place we were approaching; the other advertised a Hotel de Paris. Simultaneously we remembered Kat on the motor trip had said she and her husband, with friends, had dined one evening at the Hotel de Paris on the river at Bray and found it an excellent restaurant and a delightful spot. The burden of decision was removed from us. We were no longer like picnickers saying, "Let's go a little further." We had been given a sign.

The hotel is on a little sidewater. Sophy made a beautiful turn into it, and immediately executed a fine roundabout upstream to the landing. A boy on duty there made the *Bellatrix* fast. Sophy requested him to secure reservations for us in the restaurant.

He returned in a few minutes with word there was no available table. This is a statement that invariably rouses me to contradiction.

"I'll go," I said.

In the cabin I changed from shorts to a costume I considered more appropriate for such an important meeting as an interview with a headwaiter. I strengthened my persuasion with something a little more tangible than words, and returned to the boat crowned with success and the promise of dinner at eight. Sophy had changed during my absence and had also ordered ice, soda and glasses to accompany the supplies she drew from her shoebag.

We had our drinks in our own lounge in the stern of our own boat. I doubt I shall ever again feel such kinship with royalty. We sat in detached splendor, as we considered our surroundings, looking out over the lawn that came down to the edge of the bank so close that, leaning over the side, we could place our glasses on it. Other guests, less privileged than we, sat at tables scattered about the lawn.

At eight o'clock we left our floating palace, were greeted by the headwaiter, and shown our table. The place was very gay, music played and people danced. We were, perhaps, an incongruous note in the picture. I doubt the hotel is accustomed to entertaining on a Saturday night two middle-aged women, but we enjoyed our surroundings as well as the food.

Returning to our dear *Bellatrix*, we had crème de menthe brought to us. Sipping it as we sat regally again in the stern, we watched the passing scene. When we had finished we set our glasses down on the lawn and, though it was still early, fastened down the curtains of our palace and went to bed. Taking one thing with another, we agreed it had been quite a day.

The last thing I heard as I drifted off to sleep were the sounds of the orchestra playing, and people laughing and talking at tables on the lawn, less than six feet away from my bunk. I do not know when they left nor when the music stopped. I slept like a child in a rocking cradle.

Chapter Twenty-Two

AT SEVEN o'clock the next morning, I had cooked breakfast, eaten it and was washing up. I had been on this cruise less than twenty-four hours but I had already learned two fundamental principles, though they had nothing to do with navigation. One: cruisers get up early, and two, whoever is not navigating does all the other jobs. As an office, decky is more inclusive than the word suggests. I was the cook, the mopper-upper and the bedmaker. The only part Sophy took in cooking was to lift herself a few inches from the captain's seat, at my request, allowing me to remove the cushion beneath her, expose the gas tank and turn on a supply for the stove; when the cooking was completed, by the same sequence, to turn it off again.

My captain voluntarily extended her area of activity beyond the bridge, however. In addition to leaping off the boat in order to moor the bow when we were in locks, she circled our deck morning and night, fastening the curtains down at bedtime and rolling them up in the morning. This was not so much evidence of a democratic spirit as a somewhat patronizing recognition of her decky's incompetence in these matters. She knew I could not leap from the boat. She had seen that my way of bridging a gap between dock and vessel was to make a bridge of myself, keeping my stern attached to one until my bow was firmly attached to something on the dock. She knew, too, that unless the boat were itself firmly attached to a dock, nothing on earth would induce me to go clamoring over the top of it, much less circle it. The passageway on either side between bow and stern—what I would call a runningboard, but goodness only knows what the nautical term is—was no wider than a ledge or a lip, and not a Ubangi lip either; a tight, narrow, mean lip. The only way to travel this was by setting one foot precisely in front of the other, with water, water everywhere, below. No, my captain knew I would have no dealings with such a promenade.

She made the circuit several times that morning in Bray, rolling up the curtains, opening windows, while I was cooking breakfast. When we had finished and I was standing over the dishpan she proposed to go even farther in every sense from the bridge.

"I don't believe in this kind of a place people get up very early," she said. "Nobody will see me if I sneak up to the kitchen with our garbage. I'll see if I can bribe somebody there to dispose of it and also let us have some ice."

Ice had been the umbrella we had raised at the very outset of the trip, and we did not choose to lower it. Looking over the *Bellatrix* before leaving, we had been surprised and dismayed to discover there was no icebox included in its equipment. Mr. Bates had been astonished we should want one. Such a thing had never been requested before. Nevertheless, he had recognized an American idiosyncrasy and had lent us his own thermos jug. "But," he had warned cheerfully as he put it in my hands, "I doubt you'll be able to get it filled."

The Hotel de Paris offered the first opportunity to disprove this. Dressed in shorts, carrying the garbage pail, Sophy set off across the lawn.

What followed is her story. I did not hear nor see any of it. Following the ancient pattern of class distinction I was where my status required me to be, below deck. Sophy's report to me later was this: she had crossed the lawn without encountering anyone and was sneaking around the corner of the terrace when a man's voice called out heartily, "Good morning." She whirled around to see, breakfasting a few yards away, an elderly couple. The gentleman repeated his salutation and added, "I've been watching you put your boat in order. She's a nice little craft and you seem to know your way about."

The lady, smiling, added to her husband's comment, "We've been envying your having such a nice boat here. You must be having a wonderful time."

From their accent Sophy recognized at once they were Americans. She told them she had chartered it with a friend for a week's cruise, and explained further, "Actually this is the first time I've run a motorboat. I really don't know a thing about it, but we *are* having a marvelous trip so far."

All this time, she said, she was holding the garbage pail behind her back and edging away. The American gentleman was persistent. He urged her to join them for a cup of coffee. She declined because, she said, she had just breakfasted, and furthermore we wanted to be on our way. With a curiosity I am told is characteristic of Americans, the man continued his questioning.

"You may not have handled a motorboat, but you've handled boats. Anybody who knows could recognize that from watching you this morning. What yacht club do you come from?"

The idea that any yacht club would claim greenhorns such as we was so preposterous, Sophy said, she took an involuntary step back that very nearly upset her into her own garbage. Recovering her balance with some difficulty, she immediately disclaimed association with any club.

The man, she emphasized to me, was not the least rude with his questioning, he was simply being friendly and disarmingly exposing the curiosity of a child.

"Club or not," he answered her disclaimer, "I can tell a sailor when I see one. You've been around boats."

Sophy could not deny this. "Well," she admitted, "I've done a bit of sailing."

"I knew it," he interrupted, triumphantly. "You couldn't fool me, and I can tell you're an American," he smiled engagingly, "just the way I'm sure you knew that we are."

Sophy admitted this.

Using this as good and sufficient reason for finding out more, he went about it. "I'm something of a sailor, too," he informed her, "as you probably guessed from my interest. Now where did you sail at home?"

As Sophy said later, she had no reason for trying to evade his question, except that she did want to get on with the garbage. By now, however, she had realized she could not leave without being rude until she had given all the information requested.

"I used to sail," she told him, "in a little place in Maine you probably never heard of. Northeast Harbor."

The man and wife, she said, looked at each other and their respective jaws dropped. "Never heard of it?" he answered. "I just happen to have been part of that Northeast Harbor fleet for fourteen years. Who on earth are you?"

She told him.

"Well, good Lord Almighty," was his answer. "I've raced your brother, season in and season out. Why I remember when your father . . . And I remember you when you were a kid."

On and on, she said, he continued down through the family with the same mounting excitement as he had shown curiosity. Suddenly he broke off and jumped up. "We'll be back in Northeast within the month," he said. "Wait until I tell them about seeing you." He slapped the table. "They'll never believe me. I tell you what I'm going to do. I'm going upstairs right now and get my camera, to take a picture of you and your boat. Will you let me do that? Stay right here. I won't be a moment."

Sophy was trapped. "Why yes, certainly," she said, and held out from behind her back the garbage pail, "if you'll just allow me first to get rid of the slops."

The snapshot taken and ice in our thermos, we took off. (Cast off is the nautical term I believe.)

The second day was even better than the first. The morning itself was warm to hot, but we were not so nervous as we had been at the start, even in the locks. I threw a rope only in one of them. At my first try, the rope went straight up into the air and straight down again into the water. I fished it out, threw it again. I had to work fast because the boat was moving beyond the stanchion that had been allotted to us. The second try caught the lock keeper in the face, and unfortunately that section of the rope was carrying a long trail of seaweed brought up from the water. He caught the rope as it hit him, so he was not hurt, only splattered. But the piece of seaweed, when we left, was still draped rakishly along one side of his face and over his ear. Unless his wife discovered it first, boaters following us may have considered this an odd sight.

After that lock, I did not try to throw again. The keeper, I discovered, was always at the gate we entered. I would stand with rope held above my head and, as we approached, call out wistfully, "May I give you this?"

There could not be kinder people than English lock keepers. No matter how wildly astray my rope went in the little toss required from my hands to the lock keeper's, the dear soul would retrieve and attach it with only words of encouragement to me.

MINA ST
Vasiliu

We were beginning to know, at least by sight, some of the other river travelers since the same group of us waited together in each lock. They were not stylish folk. Evidently by one of the mysterious dictates of "society," it is chic to punt on the Thames, to canoe or row, but not to run a motorboat. We were delighted with the group around us: homely, friendly folk.

In the locks we were all congenial. Some, like us, had chartered a boat for their summer holiday, as many as eight or ten sharing it; others were owners of their vessels. These infused an atmosphere of "a home away from home"—curtains at the windows, and sometimes, too, a bird in a cage. There were any numbers of dogs traveling, seasoned travelers, too. They could jump off a boat a great deal better than I, and knew just when to do this. They would leap ashore, scamper up the steps and run about.

The other boat captains were helpful as well as friendly to mine. Those who had moored ahead of us and were already standing on the wall would tell her to toss them her bow rope, and would attach it for her. If she came in a little too fast they would ward us off with their boathooks. Or again, if she had come in slightly askew, with the boathook they would ease her into line.

We passed Cliveden, that has a glorious approach from the river, and Maidenhead. I coveted a house at Cookham that carried a "For Sale" sign. At Shiplake we had run out of ice. We tried for more by cajolement and pay at the George and Dragon there, but these were the only proprietors or people in the whole cruise who were not co-operative. At the White Hart, however, in Sonning Eye, the proprietor is a dear man. We had stopped there because our engine was overheated and the captain thought it would be a good idea to "let her cool a little." As always, wherever we stopped we hunted for ice. This dear inn proprietor brought us two large blocks in his bare hands. As soon as we were under way I made iced tea for both of us.

By afternoon it was hot even by American standards. When I had washed up I was intolerably sleepy and lay down across one of the broad benches inside. The leather seat in the open stern, I had found, gave off uncomfortable evidence of the intensity of the sun's rays. Had I been outside, however, I might have heard a change in the sound of the water, but I fell asleep inside. Sophy heard nothing, either, but she gave a loud yell at what she saw, unexpectedly, and close in front of her.

I leapt to my feet. Sophy was turning the wheel, reversing and swearing. Directly ahead of us I saw a wide, deep and violent waterfall, but thanks to the crises of the day before, Sophy accelerated as she reversed. We backed away successfully, though we were perilously close, turned around, and came back safe to our proper channel. The lock keeper had seen us and scolded us mildly. We should have moored outside the gate, he said, and not been so impatient.

Neither of us found an answer to this. Impatience was the last attribute that could be appropriately attributed to us; we were river crawlers, particularly at an approach to a lock. If the gates were locked Sophy had to bring the boat as close as possible to a standstill beside one of the outer stanchions in order for me to get a rope around it. Also, we had discovered these waterfalls, and were highly nervous about them. Wherever there is a lock there is also a side channel. This is the "weir" one is always reading about in English novels. It looks like a quiet pond but at its far end there is a waterfall. This is an engineering development for the purpose of avoiding floods that at one time did wide damage. There is a sign that bears a pointing finger and the inscription "To the Locks." But the sign is not always easy to find; sometimes it is pinned to a tree that has almost entirely overgrown it. As decky, I was also lookout for these signs, but I had been asleep. Sophy, not seeing it, had not realized we were even approaching a lock. She had thought the weir was the main channel.

A group of little boys as well as the keeper watched our escape. The little boys were charmed by it. As soon as we were in the lock they began shouting questions. Why had we wanted to go there? Did we not know the way? However, they also asked us to hand up our ropes, and moored the *Bellatrix* for us.

Immediately on the other side of the lock we were in Pangbourne at about a quarter to seven. We tied up next a public boathouse. There was no room at its own dock, but the owner, helpful and friendly as we had found everyone along the way to be, except the proprietor of the George and Dragon, towed us a few yards beyond and moored us to a post in front of an abandoned house. If Mr. Charles Addams has not already seen that house and derived inspiration from it, he must travel there. Gargoyles leer from its roof, and beneath are broken and gaping windows. There are towers and towerlets, a sagging vestibule, broken steps from that, onto a paved terrace with most of its stones gone. As we looked it over in horrid fascination, we were interrupted by a deep sepulchral voice that came from somewhere in the direction of the house.

"Hello, there, hello, there," it said.

There was nothing particularly reassuring about discovering the voice belonged to a parrot. If there is anything more eerie than the sight of a fantastic house in ruins, it is created by the presence, on its dilapidated, crumbling steps, of a parrot in a cage. In my opinion, a man who came round the corner of that house a few moments later did not restore the scene to normalcy. He picked up the cage with the bird in it and seeing us staring from the stern of the *Bellatrix* called out, indicating the bird, "He asks me to bring him here on fine afternoons. He fancies a view of the river."

While Sophy shut up shop, or whatever one calls closing up a boat, I volunteered to walk to the village, find the inn and reserve places for dinner. Following a path I came out on a road. Around the bend, the road ran alongside a weir, though not the one from which we had so recently escaped. A low wall ran along this edge of the road.

I leaned on the top of the wall and looked down at the pond, still and dark in the late afternoon, with willows hanging so low some of the branches trailed in the water. As I stood packing into my memory this lovely spot, I felt a far-off memory emerging. It was not one I could identify, but it had something to do with my childhood. I argued with it. I had never seen a place like this before. Why should I sense something of my childhood nagging at me? But the more I looked, the stronger the nagging. I was discomfited when finally I walked away as one is when a memory will not come sufficiently into the open to be identified.

Presently I was in the village proper, and I found without difficulty the George Inn. I went in to "book" a table, as one says in England. The desk was empty. As I waited for a clerk I was sure would return, I turned idly with one hand a rotating display stack of postcards. I noticed as it passed a photograph of the weir I had recently been watching. I stopped the movement, withdrew from the rack the card, and read the inscription underneath. "Pangbourne, the home of Kenneth Grahame, author of *The Wind in the Willows*." *The Wind in the Willows* was a book I had so loved I once knew the whole of it almost by heart. This was why my childhood had nagged at me. I had been looking at the residences of Mr. Mole, even possibly Toad, of Toad Hall. As I remember, there is no specific picture of the weir in that book. I know positively I had never learned Kenneth Grahame lived and wrote in Pangbourne. I know most positively of all a communication other than a postcard told me I was in a familiar and loved place.

We slept on the boat. If any voice spoke from the deserted house during the night, we did not hear it.

In the morning while Sophy opened up, I walked back to the village, bought a newspaper from a shop that also sold bicycles, and provisions from the grocery store where the proprietor told me in considerable anatomical detail, with gestures, of an impending operation on his wife. As he described this he measured out for me sweet local butter, some cheese, also local, and put into two bags, one inside the other, because it was so hot, a loaf of bread just out of the oven.

The owner of the boathouse not only brought ice for us but took from us, for a very slight consideration, our garbage.

From Pangbourne to the Cleeve lock is a short run. The lock keeper's garden there had won prizes and deserved them. His wife did business on the side in lavender and krisps (potato chips) the one homegrown, the other homemade. We bought some of each. The lavender was threepence a bunch.

The sun was tempered by a cool breeze. The day was, like the little bear's porridge, just right.

From Cleeve to Benson is the longest reach between locks. In the middle of it, at half past eleven, our engine stopped. The only structure of any sort within sight was an imposing house of red brick, at some distance back from the river, but on a plumbline from the spot in which we were stuck. I suggested we try to pull the boat to the bank. From there I would hunt out the owner of the house and ask for assistance. Sophy considered this a sound undertaking but one that would be improved if I could ask for the owner by name. She consulted her guidebook and with no difficulty identified the establishment. It was the insane asylum. I withdrew my offer.

Had this happened the day before, Sunday, we would have been surrounded by other craft and swimmers as well. That morning the river was deserted. We had not shared the lock at Cleeve with other boats. Our neighbors of the day before were scattered; some of them we had passed before mooring at Pangbourne. They had dropped out, stopping for the night to make camp in a meadow, their boats tethered to trees by the bank.

With considerable difficulty we dropped anchor, deciding to wait until a boat came along as it must certainly come sometime during the day. We could send a message to the Cleeve or Benson lock keeper. At eleven forty-five no boat had come our way. We were not disturbed, the day was beautiful, so was the countryside. We sat lazily in the stern, and received callers. Two cows came leisurely down the bank and into the river. They stopped a short distance away, regarding us with a meditative cud chewing. A swan with two cygnets came closer. I went into the galley and brought back bread for them. The mother responded to my gift by endeavoring to get into the boat and attack me. I went inside immediately and closed the door to the afterdeck.

Sophy called out, "Don't be so silly," and followed me.

While we waited for the swan and her family to move on to business other than ours, Sophy, only to pass the time, pushed the starter button. The engine responded instantly. We pulled up anchor with as much difficulty as we had had putting it down and went on our way. Evidently we had overtaxed the engine and it had simply demanded a rest.

At half past twelve we were at the Benson lock. In the event the engine might be suffering from something more than overfatigue, Sophy asked the lock keeper if a mechanic were available. The best one on the river, he told us, lived in the nearby village, and he volunteered to telephone him. He returned with the message the mechanic would be with us in a few minutes.

He came two hours later. In the meantime we had tethered our boat just beyond the far gate of the lock, had our lunch of fresh bread, butter and cheese, and a bottle of beer, held long conversation with the lock keeper and his wife, met a delightful couple, and in all had a thoroughly enjoyable time. The lock keeper's wife, we learned, also operated a rowboat ferry across the weir that lay between the river and the village. She suggested we see the village but we were reluctant to leave the *Bellatrix* when the doctor was due, "in a few minutes." We would stop, we said, on our way back. We praised, enthusiastically and genuinely, the Benson lock garden. The keeper told us it was not at its best. He was waiting until Wednesday to do weeding and working, in order to have it at its best for the inspector. He was due on the weekend.

I do not know the name of the couple we met. The keeper addressed the husband as Mr. Reggie, and told us Mr. Reggie and his missus had come to this lock for several summers. They cruised up and down the river, he said, but always tied up at night at the spot "You see right there." He indicated with a broad thumb a craft tethered a few yards beyond ours. The boat was unoccupied, we thought, but a little while later Mr. and Mrs. Reggie hallooed for the ferry from the opposite side of the weir. Arriving on our side, they both whistled and called as they came along the path. A very elderly Dalmatian came out slowly from their boat to greet them. Mr. Reggie, a few minutes later, called on us.

Sophy and I were sitting on the roof looking, like Sister Anne, for someone coming who, we hoped, would be the mechanic. Mr. Reggie inquired if we were having trouble and we explained our predicament. Our caller was wearing shabby blue shorts and a faded flannel shirt with a kerchief knotted round the neck. He was unmistakably "a gent," probably a stylish one, yet he was cruising in a motor boat. Their Dalmatian, he told us, was seventeen years old and always accompanied them on their holiday cruises. He urged us to visit the village, assuring us its charm was the inducement that brought them to this spot every summer.

When the mechanic announced his arrival with a halloo from a boat across the weir, Mr. Reggie acted as ferryman, explaining as he picked up the oars this was by special permission of the lock keeper's wife, because he enjoyed it, and for the same reason he had special permission from the keeper himself to operate, occasionally, the gates.

The mechanic discovered the points of the engine needed sharpening. He mentioned, too, a few other things that required attention, not important, he assured us. I have only a vague idea of the names and functions of the things he was mentioning, but I have an even mistier conception of the points of navigation Mr. Reggie expounded while the mechanic worked.

Sophy insisted later they were of great help to her.

"A sentiment open to doubt," in my opinion; but I was, after all, only the decky.

After several repetitions of the word, I did understand that when Mr. Reggie said, "stahn" he was referring to what I am wont to call "the stern." No amount of repetition, I am afraid, would have conveyed to me what he meant by "the transom." The word, for all I know, may be something quite different by spelling; this is what it was by sound. It is the place where the decky ought to be when the boat is entering a lock.

Before we left he presented my captain with a copy of *The Thames Handbook of* '55, a volume issued by the Association of Thames Motorboat Clubs. It proved invaluable, with much information we had not had before.

Before we left, too, I invited the wife of the lock keeper to come on board. I had a feeling she wanted to look inside. I thought this was because she was curious to see what Americans would bring along on such a trip. To my astonishment, I discovered she had never seen the inside of any motorboat, though she was unable to estimate how many thousands had passed through their lock.

At three, with good-bys all around, the mechanic and Mr. Reggie shoved us off.

At four o'clock we were at Day's lock and stopped long enough to see the garden because our new handbook told us it had received third prize the preceding year. A soft rain began as we left. Sophy was occupied getting us out the gate; I told her not to stop on the other side; I could put up the canvas.

"It's only a matter of buttoning," I said.

It is also a matter of remembering the canvas goes down over an iron framework. The framework was in place. I jumped for the canvas rolled above it, and was forced to lie down a few minutes to recover from the impact of the top of my head against a bar of iron.

At half past four we were at Clifton lock. There, as I tossed the rope to the lock keeper I inadvertently and inexplicably passed my

Vasiliu

arm between two slats that comprise the back of a chair on our stern deck. It was not easy to disentangle it from the lock keeper and me.

My diary reads "Five twenty, Culham lock—a heller." I need no more than that to remind me of the heavy, wet, slippery chains that hung down the wall, instead of stanchions at the top. I had to seize one of these and hang on to it. It cut my hands and left rust and slime.

We docked for the night at Abingdon. A slim, blonde, youngish woman directed us to our mooring. Before we were tied up she had told us she hired out boats, also operated a ferry, one penny a ride, had taken seven hundred children back and forth on Sunday, has a life-saving certificate, having saved fifteen lives, her husband is an inspector at the motorcar factory, the work she does is a hobby that she wouldn't give up for worlds. "Energy," she explained, "that's what I've got." In the winter she serves at the bar of her aunt's hotel in Abingdon, has a sister in Montreal and plans to visit her next year.

We would not "for worlds" have interrupted her narrative, but she was interrupted by a call for the ferry.

We were moored in time to see a crew race between the pupils of a boys' school at Abingdon and their masters. A considerable crowd gathered on either bank and cheered enthusiastically. It was a mock race, we learned, providing "a high time" for everybody. The masters wore little boys' sailor suits, the pupils stovepipe hats. When the race was over we sat in the stern watching the crowd dispersing and villagers walking home along the path on the opposite bank. A flock of geese had taken possession of that area and challenged every passerby.

A pair of elderly ladies provided for us the high point of a late afternoon that had already given us considerable entertainment. These two invaders came through a turnstile onto the path occupied by the geese. They were angular women dressed entirely in black costumes that included a black sailor hat, a feminine version although not very, of what Englishmen call "a boater." Each carried a hand bag and, in addition, a large, bulging shopping bag. As they came through the turnstile they were talking. We could not hear what they said, but we could see their lips moving like the wings of a hummingbird. If they themselves saw the geese they could not have been aware the approach of the little flock boded ill. The attack when it came was not full on. The army circled the two innocents and made a sneaky rush from the rear, led by a wicked old gander. With neck outstretched and beak open, he cantered a few feet, then took off at exactly the right height from the ground to close his beak on the behind of his victim, the one of the elderly pair nearer to us.

She soared higher than the bird. The screech she sent out reached us clearly and must have traveled on into the village. When she touched ground again, she executed a series of twirls, like the pirouettes of a shot-putter, the carryall held between her outstretched hands precisely like such an athlete's implement. Her companion joined her in this remarkable maneuver. It proved successful. The geese retreated. The ladies lowered their implements, re-established with a firm pat their respective boaters, resumed their walk and, by the look of their lips and jaws, their talk.

Sophy pointed out this would be a good time for us to leave, before anyone else came along. Any subsequent arrival would provide a disappointing anticlimax in entertainment.

We dined excellently at the Crown and Thistle. The rain had stopped just before the boat race, the air was fresh, cool, and filled with a delicious smell of new-washed earth. We explored the village, the abbey, the old almshouses, called Christ's Hospital. We were in a far-off world as well as a far-off time, we agreed, until we came upon a sign that read, "London, 60 Miles." It was a rude shock. Sophy, by map, knew of course where we actually were, but had felt with me that on the river we were miles away from anywhere. We hurried back to it.

A wind came up in the early morning. It roused us about half past four, and neither of us slept again. The luxurious equipment of the *Bellatrix* stops before it reaches the cabin. The beds there—I use the word beds because that is what the catalogue calls them—are of the shape, size, thickness and inflexibility of an ironing board. When we crawled into them at night we were so sleepy, after a day in the open, we were unmindful of their construction. Waking in them made remaining in them intolerable. Accordingly, we were up at five.

Sophy went to the village for supplies this time, while I did a thorough housecleaning and a little light laundry. Our blonde hostess was up, too. She came down for a chat as we breakfasted before Sophy's departure. She told us the river at this point was just like a tin bucket, shallow on either side with a dip to fifteen feet in the center. That's what made it dangerous for swimmers, people stepping off the shallow edge into the bucket. But she was right there to pull them out. Children liked to hang on to the end of her ferry row-boat when she wasn't looking. Then when they'd get out over the bucket, they'd get scared and "leave go" and she'd have to jump out and rescue them. She always did, too, she admitted.

She pointed toward the center of the river. "In winter," she told us, solemnly, "at flood times, that bucket right there makes a whirly pool." She paused after this dramatic announcement. I took advantage of the pause to ask if she thought it possible for us to get ice. This was a poser, one that would baffle anybody else, she admitted, but she had a solution. She'd run up the road and see if she could get some from the fishmonger. His place ought to be open. She came back a few minutes later with a sizable chunk wrapped in newspaper. I took it gratefully and dropped it, paper and all, into our wide-mouthed thermos. We regretted leaving her, we said, but promised to stop on our way back.

That morning we saw cows chase a flock of ducks out of their meadow and into the river. I was sorry not to introduce those cows to the Abingdon geese.

Sophy, the day before, had begun to allow me to take a turn at the wheel, only between locks, of course, and when there was little or no traffic. My taking over allowed her a wider range of vision. She was as fascinated as I by the life on the river. We had brought books to read. Neither of us opened one. Even when I was below in the galley preparing a breakfast or lunch, or washing up, I found it impossible not to pop up several times to make sure I was not missing anything. A family of swans was a frequent sight. While they grabbed and seemed to enjoy every piece I dropped to them, they threatened me as soon as I stopped feeding. The children were badly brought up, I am afraid. It was not unusual to see a child nip its parent to make it move out of the way of a succulent morsel the child coveted. We saw blue heron too and foolish, nervous moorhens.

At ten o'clock that morning we were in the Sanford lock. This one, we read, is the deepest on the river. I enjoyed and I did not grow accustomed to the eerie sensation of rising in the locks, the water pushing us up with the speed of an elevator as though a giant hand were thrusting us impatiently up to ground level. We never tired of watching the life along the towpath that for mile after mile wandered along the river bank. People walked or cycled, children played along it.

Rounding a bend a little after eleven, we saw ahead of us a line of barges moored to the opposite bank. They were not like other barges; these were gaily, absurdly rococo, with curved balconies, not decks around them, ornate prows brightly painted. Neither of us had seen them before but simultaneously recognized the only things they could possibly be. "The Oxford barges," we said at one and the same time, and looking beyond them saw the spires of Oxford Town.

Chapter Twenty-Three

WE TIED up at the bank, using a tree as a mooring post.

Before leaving Chertsey at the start of our trip, we had telephoned Sophy's cousin, Mrs. Lee, in Oxford, asking if by any chance she could join us. After all, Sophy said, the idea of the cruise had been born at Oxford while we were with them. Her daughter Imogen, Mrs. Lee had said, was there from London to spend a few days with her parents. Mrs. Lee, thrown into a happy flutter by what she termed such an extraordinary invitation, had told us she could not let us know until we reached Oxford. She would talk it over with Imogen and Dr. Lee. Would Sophy telephone her there?

As soon as we were moored, Sophy went off up the towpath toward the town and a telephone. I read, took a walk along the towpath, and waited.

Some hours later, I saw to my delight three figures in the distance coming on the towpath toward me from Folly Bridge. I recognized Sophy and knew the other two must be Mrs. Lee and Imogen. They had come as we had hoped, and Sophy also brought cold ham, cheese, fresh fruit and a bottle of red wine.

My twins, on their first merry-go-round, were no more intoxicated with delight than Mrs. Lee on the first motorboat ride she had ever taken. She could not stay overnight she told us regretfully, she must be back with Dr. Lee by evening. But she loved eating on the boat, she said over and over, especially with a bottle of red wine as "such a dashing accompaniment." After lunch we pushed on as far as Osney Bridge. This was as far up the river as we could go on that tide, because the *Bellatrix* was too high to go under the bridge.

We turned back to Abingdon. Mrs. Lee had never before been on that stretch of the river, yet she knew the countryside with such loving intimacy she not only identified each detail, but spoke of its changed aspect seen from the river, as one would talk of an old friend in a new and becoming dress.

She left us at Abingdon. It was a short ride from there by bus to Oxford, she told us. Sophy and I flinched. The river was far from everywhere; it was its own world. We did not like to be disenchanted.

Our realization that the shoebag hour had arrived was both comforting and distracting. As Sophy set out on a table inside the stock from her receptacle, I boasted to Imogen of our success with ice. "Mr. Bates said we wouldn't be able to fill the thermos he gave us. It's never been empty. Right now there's a fresh supply. We got it this morning from the fishmonger."

I need not have identified the source. As I lifted the lid of the jug it proclaimed itself by a strong and pervasive smell of dead fish.

Sophy made rapidly for the door to the afterdeck; she has a weak stomach. Imogen jeered. With head averted as far as possible from my hands, I removed the ice, still in its newspaper wrapping, and threw it overboard. For the first and only time on our cruise, we took our drinks the British way, tepid.

Next morning Imogen had a swim off the boat before breakfast, though the day was chilly and overcast. By half past ten, however, the sun was out. Herons and moorhens fed along the banks as we passed; swan families besieged us. Imogen proved to be almost as familiar with the countryside as her mother had been. She identified what Sophy and I the day before had pointed out to each other as two crowns of trees on the hilltop.

"They're called Wittenham Clumps," she said. "They were planted in the eighteenth century and since then they've been a landmark for miles around."

At Clifton lock we had to wait outside for the gates to open and had some difficulty mooring there. I was surprised. Naïvely, I had thought the return trip would be even simpler than the outward passage. Unfortunately, I communicated this supposition to Sophy, explaining the logic behind it.

"Downstream is the equivalent of downhill. So instead of pushing I thought we'd be coasting," I suggested.

I was told emphatically my misconception. The *Bellatrix Star* was not coasting; it required, because of the current, expert handling, and, our captain assured me, was receiving it.

Our reception at Benson lock was in the nature of a welcome home from Mr. and Mrs. Reggie, the lock keeper and his wife. They abandoned themselves to such cordiality as to tell us their name.

"Mrs. Haines," the keeper said, and prodding with a stubby thumb the lady beside him, "the missus."

We shook hands all around.

After lunch on the boat we went to the village of Benson as we had promised we would do. Mr. Reggie rowed us across the weir. From there we walked along a path through a meadow in a kind of intoxication induced by the smell of new-mown hay, the sight of wildflowers all around us, and the sound of birds. At the end of the meadow we climbed over a stile, crossed a road, and found ourselves in the village of Benson.

I do not wish to learn how far Benson is from another place, nor how accessible to London. For me it is a sleepy, sunny, forgotten village. When we had walked through it we came to a sign that read, "One and three quarter miles to Ewelme." Imogen had once seen that place and urged us to it. Accordingly, we walked in the direction indicated. At the end of forty minutes we came to another sign that read, "One and a half miles to Ewelme." Far from making progress we were scarcely holding our own. While we were discussing the feasibility of continuing this unprogressive march, a car approached. Without an instant's hesitation Imogen strode to the middle of the road and flagged it.

After the unlikely things I had already done within a space of three months, I do not know why I should have been surprised to find myself hitchhiking. Nevertheless, this mode of travel was not one at my age I had thought of adopting. The elderly couple in the car showed some surprise themselves and even more reluctance to accept us. However, they did take us in and within a few minutes were chatting amicably. They were on a leisurely holiday trip, they told us, exploring old villages. On the day before they had driven through one that in retrospect had seemed so delightful they wanted to spend some time there. Unfortunately, they had not seen its name on their way through. Now they were retracing their steps in an endeavor to find it again.

When Imogen told them about the church we were going to see at Ewelme, they suggested they drive us all the way there in order to visit the place themselves. I think they were glad, by reason of the church, they had taken on the hitchhikers. They told us so repeatedly when we parted.

St. Mary's Church was built around 1430 when, as the guidebooks says, "Alice Chaucer was married to William de la Pole, First Duke of Suffolk, on the site of the older church, of which a major part of the fourteenth century western tower remains."

Alice Chaucer was the granddaughter of Geoffrey. The Chaucers are buried here. The church itself has been scarcely touched since the fifteenth-century builders completed it. The cloister is a lovely spot; a covered passage leads to it from a double doorway. A sign there requests visitors to go down the five-hundred-year-old steps with care, and quietly, because "the cloister is a private dwelling place." There are thirteen houses around it. They comprise the almshouse and include the muniment room and the master's lodging. The Ewelme School is said to be the oldest church school. Its foundation date was 1437.

Our pleasure in Ewelme led us to rehearse the happy coincidences by which we had arrived at it, from the breakdown of the engine, the stop at Benson lock, the promise made there to see the village, and the contribution from Imogen when we did. Imogen expressed her pleasure at our gratitude by immediately flagging another car. I found I enjoyed hitchhiking. I was sorry I had not taken it up earlier.

We were deposited at the stile. Mr. Reggie ferried us back across the weir and, with Mr. and Mrs. Haines, waved us off at about four o'clock.

That night we moored again by the eerie house in Pangbourne, dined at the George and spent the night there. We had thought we would like a change from the ironing boards. Though we did revel in the comforts of the beds, we did not enjoy, quixotically, other aspects of the change.

In the morning we were so aware of our closeness to London, we talked a little of ending the trip instead of winding our circuitous course along the river. Would it not be more sensible to recognize we had had enough? Let the boat be picked up and ourselves take a car back to London. Nevertheless, since we were in the village we visited the local store, bought some local corned beef, sweet butter and fresh loaves of bread. During the purchase I was happy to learn the operation on the wife of the proprietor had taken place and was accounted thoroughly successful.

On the boat we stowed the provisions, unrolled the canvas, as we discussed abandoning ship, weighing the possibility of staying at least through lunch. Suddenly, we knew nothing would induce us to leave our *Bellatrix* until the trip was completed. We were in the river world again. London was a far-off place to which we did not want to go.

At a quarter past two that afternoon we ran aground. I was disturbed while writing my diary by a queer, grinding noise, and a second later by the voice of the captain calling, "My God, get the boathook."

Imogen, an enthusiastic and far more competent decky than I, reached the boathook first. She skittered nimbly along the outer runningboard while I was endeavoring to climb over the roof. She wielded the implement vigorously and too effectively. With a Herculean shove, she released the *Bellatrix* and, at the same time, the boathook, and very nearly went in after it, unintentionally. Young people in a boat that came abreast of us retrieved our pole and restored it to us while I was restoring our guest by the heels.

At Reading we relinquished Imogen regretfully, but right side up. We urged her not to tell us how soon she would be back in London. We waved to her as she set out across a bridge toward the railway station, but we did not watch her out of sight.

As slowly as we had traveled up the river there were spots on the way down we vowed we had not seen before: a hedge perhaps ten feet high with openings cut at intervals to reveal an exquisite garden on the other side, yellow water lilies along a bank. We were commenting on the improbability these lovely things had come into existence since we had passed that way, when I called out sharply something was coming toward us we could not possibly have failed to notice on the up-river trip.

Sophy had been looking out the side at the yellow water lilies. At my exclamation she half rose from the driver's seat and shifted her attention to the direction in which I was pointing. She remained immobilized by astonishment in a half crouch. Coming toward us was a remarkable procession. Two launches abreast led it. Behind each of these was attached a string of boats carrying apiece some six or eight oarsmen. Each occupant held his oar upright within the boat and sat rigid as though at attention. The oarsmen in one string were dressed in scarlet livery, those in the other, in purple. The Royal Standard of scarlet flew at the stern of the last barge in each line. The colorful, incredible procession drew abreast of us while I took pictures furiously.

When it had gone, Sophy sank down into her accustomed position, looked at me and inquired what in Heaven's name we had just seen.

At Temple lock we learned what it was. A little boat with outboard motor carrying an elderly couple scuttled into the lock just after us. We had shared several locks during the day and had exchanged conversation. They called out to us simultaneously and a little breathlessly, as though it had been they and not their craft that had put on speed. The gist of their conversation and excitement was they had been so afraid they would not catch up with us they had pushed the little engine to the utmost. They did want to make sure we knew what luck we had had in what we had just seen. When we had assured them our ignorance and delight, they smiled happily at us and at each other and continued. Of all the days in the year, they said, we had been on the river at the time of the Swan Upping, the season of the year when the Queen's company of swan keepers and the Vintners' company mark each cygnet, one for the Queen, the next for the Vintners. This marking is called nicking. It is a nick made in the baby bird's beak. There is an old pub, the charming strangers told us, that carries the name The Swan With Two Necks. This is, they said, an ancient misspelling. It was meant to be The Swan With Two Nicks, commemorating, evidently, a bird that had been inadvertently marked both by the Queen's men and the Vintners'.

With so much to tell and so little time to tell it before the gates opened, they did not include the location of this old pub. I should like to find it one day.

We spent that night at Cookham. After dinner at the Ferry Hotel we walked along a lane that would bring us, the innkeeper said, to the village. A few yards beyond the inn we heard churchbells pealing in a fashion we thought we recognized by hearsay, but had never heard. We followed the sound through a churchyard, around the side of the church itself, and up a flight of stairs that led to the tower and the bells. We had come to a weekly practice of the bellringers. They welcomed us cordially and showed us this ancient art. The bellropes were wound in strips of scarlet and white. Around the wall of the room I saw charts and diagrams of "changes," about which I had first learned in Dorothy Sayers' book, *The Nine Tailors*. These members were young, but each one was a descendant of many generations of bellringers.

One of the team, young, muscular, very blond, told me during the war he had spent some time in Montana. He had liked America but was happy to be back in Cookham to take up again, as his hobby, his heritage of bellringing. When he had said good night in the churchyard to the rest of us, he mounted a motorbike. With a deafening roar of his engine he careened at fearful speed round the bend of the lane and was out of sight.

Saturday afternoon at a quarter to three we docked in Chertsey. As we left our dear *Bellatrix* and started up the dock, Sophy paused, turned round, and waved both hands in the air reminiscently at the opposite bank we had so nearly rammed one week before.

I hope I shall take that trip again, though I do not need to repeat it the better to remember it. Whatever other voyages I make there cannot be one that will hold in so short a period of time such rounded out, compact delight. It would be impossible to say, "I wish this or that had been otherwise." . . . "I loved such and such, but something or other else was tedious or unsatisfactory."

That week, like the air in Greece, was distilled to an essence of beauty and refreshment.

L'Envoi

ONE. On the seventh of April, Koula arrived in New York to live in my house.

TWO. Mrs. Papadakis, the erstwhile Miss Greece, presented Mr. Papadakis with a little Laconian.

THREE. Luz, at present on a trip in Norway, writes, "I am taking pictures like mad, but there is a slight defect in the finder."

From Darn's List of Helpful Hints

CONTENTS OF SOPHY'S MEDICINE KIT

Denatured alcohol
Iodine
Band-aids in various sizes
Large squares of gauze and a roll of adhesive tape, as well as a roll of bandage
Sulfathiasole ointment
Codeine tablets
B.F.I. powder, for any minor foot irritations
Spirits of ammonia
Milk of magnesia tablets
Aspirin
Paregoric
Kaopectate (invaluable when the traveler's bug attacks)
Phenobarbital tablets
Acromycin tablets, for an acute infection
An icebag
Plastic containers to diminish bulk and breakage.

CLOTHES AND ACCESSORIES

Cotton dresses with full skirts
Hat with a brim
Topsiders
Dark glasses
Warm topcoat
Coat hangers
Plenty of Kleenex
Bathing suit
Bathing shoes to wear in water (beaches are pebbled)
Hot-water bottle

EXCURSIONS*

Naples

Car to Pompeii and return—$12.00 & $2.00 tip

Guide—2500 lira for four. $4.25 plus $1.00 entrance fee, plus $1.00 tip—$6.25

Greece

Private car with chauffeur in and around Athens, tours to Daphni, Nauplia, Sunium. Trips to Kephissia. 4,500 drachmas, or $40 apiece for four for two weeks (14 days).

There are sailings every day from Piraeus to the Aegean Islands by way of ships of various sizes and quality. No schedules are available here but ships go to the more important islands several times weekly. These stay long enough in port to unload and load so they are readily available for tourists. The *Semiramis* is the only cruise ship.

TAE is the Greek airline which gives extensive local service. The flight from Athens to Crete—1 hour 10 minutes. The flight to Rhodes—1 hour 45 minutes. The flight to Mytilene—1 hour 20 minutes. The flight to Corfu—1 hour 35 minutes.

There are two types of train which go to Pirgos—thence local transportation the short distance to Olympia. There is the regular train and a so-called "Pocomotive" which means a two-car train. These go three times daily—the time required is 9½ hours. The pleasant highway for timid motorists is now open again.

There is a fine modern highway Athens to Salonika. By rail, time required 10½ to 13 hours. By air 1 hour 15 minutes—4 times a day in both directions.

Athens Bouliagmene Beach, near Lemos, for swimming—good sandy beach. Pleasant little taverna for drinks after swimming.

Sunium Tourist Pavilion—à la carte service.

Corinth Tourist Pavilion—excellent lunch, attractive surroundings.

Nauplia Bourzi Hotel—tiny island hotel. Cell-like comfortable rooms, each with balcony. Excellent food.

Amphitryon Hotel—on mainland, overlooking harbor and island of Bourzi. Comfortable, good food.

Mykonos Hotel Touriste Leto—small, clean, attractive. $10 for 2, including 3 meals.

* All excursions should be checked on arrival, even when reservations have been made before leaving the United States.

Crete Taverna Kharilaos—4 or 5 miles from dock. Excellent lunch. Swimming beach at Tobruk about 10 miles from harbor.

Rhodes Hotel des Roses—excellent, comfortable rooms overlooking the sea. Delicious food.

RESTAURANTS—ATHENS

Averof—2 Churchill St. Excellent Greek dinner with red wine (Castle Daniels) $3.00 apiece.

The Old Phoenix—10 Pindarou St. (Find it by the barrel sign hung at the entrance to a long whitewashed tunnel.) Lunch in the garden after selecting food in kitchen.

Vassili's—14 Jan Smuts St. Excellent wine. Dinner for 4 with 2 bottles and tip came to $6.00.

Flocka—Fashionable, excellent food.

Bukaresti Garden—Taverna in the Plaka. Dinner under the stars. Music and Greek dancing.

Costi—2 Korai St. (just off Churchill). Good food, simple.

Hotel Grande Bretagne—Venizelos Ave. and Constitution Square. Most fashionable and popular hotel in Athens.

Hotel King George—Constitution Square. Single room and bath, breakfast and one other meal at 167 drachmas—$5.55. Room per day unoccupied (while on side trips)—$3.30.

Be sure to order *dolmadis,* ground meat and rice, cooked in a grape leaf, served with lemon sauce.

SHOPS, TRAVEL AGENCIES, ETC.—ATHENS

Etea Organisation Tourisme, 8 Avenue Venizelos.

G. Stewart Richardson, 5 Stadium St. (same as Churchill St.). Inside courtyard, fourth door on left. Raw silk, raw cotton. Ties, table mats, wonderful.

I. Tzanetogleas, 15 Hermes St., in the passage 24. Shop for raw silk.

Martinos—Old Market Place, Monastirake. Old jewelry, antiques.

Pandrossos St. (Shoemaker St.), for shoes.

Antoine-Kammer, 11 Venizelos St. Hairdresser.

Marino Kyrifides, Saint Andrew 11, Nea Smyrni, Athens. Chauffeur.

Lily Litina, 60 Vatatzo St., Athens 7. Guide.

NOTE: On maps and elsewhere there is a baffling variety in the spelling of places mentioned in this book. For example, Bourzi is listed on some maps as Bourdzi, elsewhere Bourtse. Sunium is sometimes Sounium. There are many other instances.